Advance praise for

My Nebraska

"Roger Welsch, by far the greatest humorist to ever call
Dannebrog home, is indeed a Nebraska treasure. He is gifted; he
is very funny; Roger is our Will Rogers."

—*Charlie Thone, former governor of Nebraska*

"This new book by Roger Welsch is one that every red-blooded
Nebraskan should own—and, if time and blood pressure permit,
should read. Welsch is indeed Captain Nebraska, with or without
a cape. He is the state's consummate storyteller, and *My Nebraska*,
which chronicles the perceptions and attitudes and subtle biases
of an irascible but lovable geezer, is no doubt his penultimate
achievement."

—*William Kloefkorn, Nebraska State Poet*

"As a Nebraskan by Choice and former Governor of Nebraska, I
too share Roger Welsch's appreciation of this state. While Roger
and I may not have the same perspective on 'some things,' we
are totally in agreement when it comes to the beauty of the state
and its people. His view is unique and refreshing."

—*Kay Orr, former governor of Nebraska*

"Read this book and no one gets hurt."

—*Bob Kerrey, former Nebraska governor and senator
and current president of the New School University in New York City*

My Nebraska

The Good, the Bad, and the Husker

Roger Welsch

With Original Sketches of
Nebraska Scenic Sites by the Author

The
Globe
Pequot
Press

GUILFORD, CONNECTICUT

Copyright 2006 by Roger Welsch

Design by Casey Shain

Verses from "The Red Wind Comes!" by John Neihardt, from his collection *The Poet's Town, 1908–1912,* are reprinted with permission courtesy of The John Neihardt Trust and the University of Nebraska Press.

Library of Congress Cataloging-in-Publication Data

Welsch, Roger L.
   My Nebraska : the good, the bad, and the husker : with original sketches of Nebraska scenic sites / by the author, Roger Welsch.—1st ed.
      p. cm.
   ISBN: 978-0-7627-4250-9
   1. Nebraska—Description and travel. 2. Nebraska—Social life and customs. 3. Nebraska—History, Local. 4. Historic sites—Nebraska. 5. Landscape—Nebraska. I. Title.
   F666.W45 2006
   978.2—dc22

                                                                    2006017863

Manufactured in the United States of America
First Edition/Second Printing

For my Linda

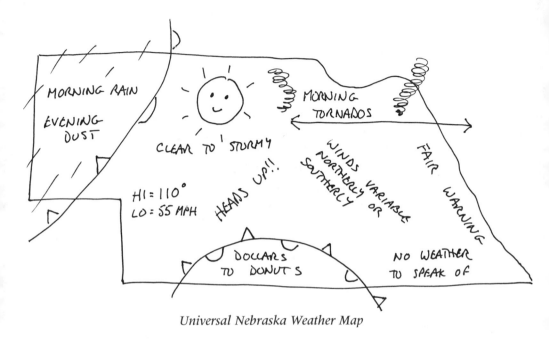

Universal Nebraska Weather Map

Contents

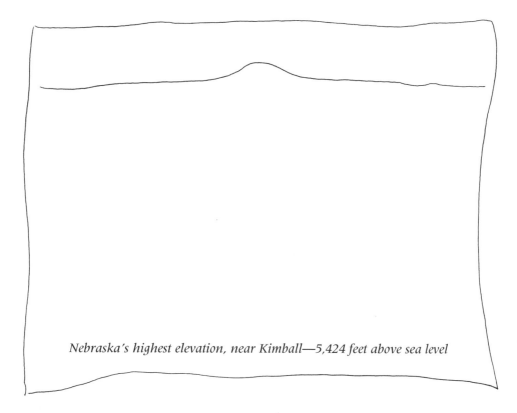

Nebraska's highest elevation, near Kimball—5,424 feet above sea level

C H A P T E R   O N E

Whose Nebraska Are We Talking About? Who Are You Kidding with This *My* Nebraska Stuff, Welsch?

I can imagine some folks thinking it takes a lot of gall for someone to call Nebraska "his," as if he has some special claim on it. Especially Nebraskans, who tend to be a feisty bunch when the topic of Nebraska comes up. Even when nothing ill is being said about this "hulking giant," as one snarly critic called it, we tend to get defensive. But one of the things I have learned over a long life is that there is no one absolute reality. We like to think that we see what is, that seeing is believing, that reality is reality and the truth is so obvious it might just as well rear up and slap you alongside the head with a two-by-four.

1

Well, obviously that's not the case. The Supreme Court disagrees about what the meaning of just a few pages of vellum called the Constitution is saying, and they've been working at that problem for well more than 200 years now. The most brilliant scientists in the world dispute even the most basic assumptions, and we don't need to go very far in our examination of religion—where we should be able to find the clearest "truth" there is, after all—to realize that wherever two shall gather, as the phrase goes, the one thing you can count on is that those two aren't going to agree about much of anything, including religion.

What You See Is Not What You Get

What I'm talking about is, believe it or not, an even deeper division than things like religion and politics. I'm talking about not how we interpret what we see—no one doubts what the *words* are on things like the Constitution or a page of any particular holy book; they just disagree what those words mean—but what we see in our individual minds when we look at Nebraska. I have learned from a lifelong association with other cultures, such as the Omaha, Pawnee, and Lakota Tribes, that there are cases where not only do we put different interpretations on what we see, but our eyes actually see different things when we look at something.

I have been married twice and have three daughters, so I can tell you for a fact that men and women see things differently. Europeans and Asians look at our geography and see one thing; we look at the selfsame vista and see something completely different. The Omaha and Lakota looked at what we call the Plains 200 years ago and saw something diametrically opposed to what the pioneers saw while looking at the very same scenery. And the pioneers saw something completely different in Nebraska and the Plains than their great-grandchildren see here today.

It's not simply that the landscape has changed—and heaven knows, it has, and in spades! But our *eyes* have changed. The neurons and synapses through which the images pass interpret what we see in a very different way. The pioneers came in large part from northern and central Europe: Germany, Czechoslovakia, Norway, Sweden, Denmark, Poland. Their understanding of a "farm," insofar as they even had such a notion, was six to ten acres. The average farm in Germany even today is less than twenty acres, probably rocky, heavily wooded, steeply sloped, perhaps water-sodden, and almost assuredly owned by someone else. European fields to this day are measured by the square yard (okay, meter) rather than by something as vast as an acre. Some ranches in the Nebraska Sandhills today are measured in sections—square miles!—sometimes a dozen, sometimes twenty, sometimes as many as a hundred, which makes them as big as some of the European duchies our forebears came from. There are parts of eastern Nebraska where you can find fieldstones abandoned here by retreating Pleistocene glaciers, and there are even some rock outcroppings along the eastern and southern boundaries of the state and in isolated pockets like *Rock*ville, but they scarcely deserve mention. (I have always been amazed that once you cross the artificial political boundaries from Nebraska into South Dakota or Kansas, you almost instantly start seeing rocks, strewn around fields, exposed in road cuts and ditches, installed as elements of building construction, or even used as fence posts.)

As for trees, our dedication to them as embodied in our state-born national holiday of Arbor Day is a matter of our desire to have more of them. We wanted to become the Tree Planter State long before we were the Cornhuskers. There weren't many trees here when the pioneers came, buffalo and fire pretty much eliminating survival beyond the seedling stage for any trees other than those protected on river islands or in narrow wetlands between waterways. And it wasn't long before there were far fewer trees, because they were sought out and cut down for log houses and then soddie rafters, railroad ties, and firewood. All his life the European farmer had cursed his stony, tree-bound fields scarcely 100 yards long. His pattern was to walk two steps as he plowed or hayed, pick up and throw a rock toward the fence line, take another couple of steps, cut the root fouling the plow lay with a hand ax, take another couple of steps . . . Now, however, he could write back to the folks he'd left behind in the homeland that here in this place called Nebraska, he could set his plow in the soil at the edge of his north eighty and plow in an arrow-straight line for a quarter mile without ever stopping for a root or a rock. His glee is hard to imagine. No modern farmer worries about roots or rocks, or plowing a straight line, or, for that matter, about plowing at all!

And Nebraska is flat. To be sure, it's not as flat as it appears out the window of a passenger airplane flying 6 miles up and almost at the speed of sound. Or even from the window of an air-conditioned SUV moving at a tenth the speed of sound on the interstate only yards from the Platte (French for "flat"!) River. But for the Swede, Czech, or Norwegian accustomed to plowing while balancing his entire weight on one foot, the absence of topographic definition on the Plains was something he could have fantasized only in his wildest agricultural dreams. Never stopping once in his horizon-bound ripping of the ground for a root or a rock, marching ahead on dead-level ground, taking strides that would have been impossible in the Old Country . . .

As if that weren't enough, this land was not on loan or rent to him from someone else who owned it and lived high on his sweat. No, this was *his* land. Or would be just as soon as he "proved up"—that is, proved himself equal to the demands of this new and harsh landscape and outlasted its ferocity, demonstrating to the satisfaction of the government or the railroad or the banker that he was, by God, tougher than Nebraska. (Thus, one of my several suggestions for a new Nebraska state motto: "The Hell I Can't.")

Rock around the Clock

An important factor in the pioneer's understanding of the Great Plains was the speed and distance at which he saw it. On the Oregon and Mormon Trails, those crossing Nebraska saw it at the rate of a couple of miles an hour, covering in a day a little less than vehicles on Interstate 80 now go in under fifteen minutes. Today we have the notion that Chimney Rock must have been roughly the height of the State Capitol, the way the Oregon Trailers go on and on about it in their journals and reports. But if you look at the tops of other prominences in the same area, all cut from the same tableland Chimney Rock was carved from, you'll see that they are all about the same height. The real difference in what Sweet Betsy from Pike saw from her wagon train on the Oregon Trail, and what you see from your family car doing maybe 80 miles an hour in exactly the same place but more than a century and a half later, is that one morning the wagon train topped a hill 30 or 40 miles east of Chimney Rock and saw it as a bump on the horizon, and that night when they stopped to make camp there it still was, pretty much in the same place but just a tad larger. And the next night it was still there, but larger. And the next night, they still saw it, now more imposing, in part because the air was then crystal clear and it was the first vertical thing they had seen since they left the last tree outside Independence, Missouri, two months earlier. That night, when they camped almost at Chimney Rock's foot, they were amazed at it. And at the campsite the next night, from which they could now see Scotts Bluff dead ahead to the west, behind them to the east there it still was—Chimney Rock.

Today from the windshields of our automobiles, Chimney Rock appears and disappears in less than an hour's time. A century and a half ago it dominated a person's eyesight and mind for almost a week. While we're imagining, think about what the sod buster saw as he walked behind a horse-drawn plow at the pace of about a mile an hour, his eyes only 5 feet from the newly opened soil beneath him, compared with what the modern farmer sees in exactly the same field from the cab of a tractor or even a combine 10 or 12 feet above the surface of the ground, moving at the speed of maybe 7 miles an hour—a day's journey on the Oregon Trail.

Square and Straight

Of course the landscape has changed, too. I don't suppose there's that much difference between the green of corn and beans and that of native grasses except that the ubiquity of irrigation means that things are greener these days than they were 150 years ago. But curiously the big difference between then and now is not so much "what" but "how"; that is, the rigidly straight lines in which the crops are planted. On the naked, wild Plains there wasn't much to be seen by way of straight lines and right angles; today not just crops but also roads, houses, posts and poles, streets and parks are all laid out in an almost fanatical rectilinearity unmatched nearly anywhere else in the world, and most assuredly not in the eastern parts of the United States and in Europe from where the Plains crossers and later the homesteaders and settlers had come.

While the pioneers found rare verticality in Chimney Rock, today we see at least something more by way of height . . . although I shouldn't perhaps make too much of this. (I once called a friend in Dannebrog when our bank failed and asked how folks there in town were taking the bad news. He said that the really tough part was that since there was only one two-story building in town, everyone was trying to kill himself or herself by jumping off the curb.) Okay, so there aren't a *lot* of tall structures on today's Plains, but there are grain elevators, telephone poles and towers, broadcasting antennas, and now and then even a tall building.

Pioneers often died of something they called "wind sickness," often as not at their own hands. Coming from the arbored woodlands of the East or the mountains, fjords, and tall spruce forests of Europe, the new Nebraskans weren't quite ready for the vast openness of the Plains. It was, in fact, psychologically crushing. The sky was an unbearable burden that pressed them right down into the ground. Today, even in Nebraska, we work in cubicles, windowless offices, air-conditioned and heated buildings with artificial light, cramped and crowded, fighting traffic while we are surrounded on every side by other people, pressing, pressing, pressing in on us. Not so on the pioneer Plains. Settlers from Germany, Sweden, or Czechoslovakia were accustomed to hearing the church bells from the neighboring town, or maybe even seeing its church steeple from the center of their own little town. The neighboring farmer's house might lie no more than a couple of hundred feet away, the words of scolding spouses or crying children easily heard from his own doorway.

The population density of most of Nebraska has dropped since the earliest days of settlement, and most assuredly since the Native inhabitants hunted unbothered by what my Hochunk brother Louie LaRose calls "the boat people." But even in the earliest years, when you could expect four farms per section and therefore twelve to thirty people per square mile even in rural areas, the isolation the newcomers encountered on the Plains was unaccustomed and unexpected. The total lack of roads and the severity of weather exacerbated the loneliness. A woman (men more often risked the rigors of travel and the demands of commercial trade than their wives) might go many months without seeing another human being or hearing another female voice outside her own household in this new land.

All of these factors meant enormous adjustments for the pioneers, of course, and also that we have a difficult—if not impossible—task in trying to see this landscape as they did. Today we come home from work and want to enjoy the outdoors, so we cook and eat our supper on the patio. Weekends we want to forget the constriction of the office, so we camp out in the park. At retirement we move to the country so we can finally enjoy some privacy. My mother moved from a Lincoln apartment to a new location out here in rural Nebraska and for the first time in several decades saw the sun rise and set, enjoyed rainbows and storms, had a vista beyond her neighbor's windows. For her the openness of Nebraska's naked Plains was a welcome change.

The pioneers, on the other hand, took every opportunity to gather together with neighbors and even with their own families. The quiet, cool, windless darkness of the tiny soddie or log house was a welcome respite. You can imagine why I despair when I see today's Nebraskans peering into a museum replica of a sod house interior and clicking their tongues in sympathy for the poor pioneers who had to suffer in that small space! Far from being a hardship, the close shelter of their frontier hovels was a comfort.

You Are What You Eat . . . or Won't Eat

What the white man saw in the Plains, and for that matter what the white man still sees here, is not by a long shot what the Native Indian saw and to this day sees. For the white man, this is a landscape to be conquered, won, tamed, subdued . . . For the Indian it was and is a gentle mother, generous and providing, loving and embracing, to be honored and enjoyed. Pioneer families starved while just over the hill the residents of an Indian village harvested nature's bounty, filled their soup bowls and winter caches, and as always followed their culture's tradition of hospitality by offering their new white neighbors not only food from their own stores but even information about where more food could be found than they could possibly gather and put away in their small houses.

Moreover, when frontiersmen tasted food offered them by Indians or when they gathered the "Indian foods" themselves for survival during times of severe famine (or, as was too often the case, when newcomers stole victuals from Indian caches without an invitation), they recorded again and again that the food was really quite good: wild turnips, groundnuts, dried and smoked bison meat. Nonetheless the settlers survived on disgustingly rancid, maggot-infested pork, moldy flour, and rock-hard crackers because, as they admitted themselves, they were not about to be reduced to the savagery of eating that damned Indian food and thus admitting that they had not indeed conquered the land and its original inhabitants but were instead surrendering to them. *Better to starve than to turn Injun* was the snarled invective hurled at the notion of a meal of chokecherry soup and pemmican.

Often while driving across Nebraska, I think about what this same landscape must have been like for a band of Omaha youth crossing the state on their way to the flint mines of northeastern Wyoming. Or Lakota warriors venturing toward the Pawnee villages along the "ladder of rivers"—the parallel Loup Rivers. They had no maps. There were no landmarks, or at least none to the modern white man's eyes. But just as the Omaha, Ponca, Pawnee, and Lakota knew the subtle landmarks of topography that told them precisely where they were on the gigantic open landscape, they also knew precisely where to find small patches of oak trees—and their acorns—at harvesttime, the best places for wild plums or sandcherries in summer, the thickest beds of groundnuts, the best sources of wild rice, the juiciest wild grapes, the best arrowhead roots . . . and the right time of the year to find them. For the Indian this "trackless wilderness devoid of water and wood," as early explorers described it, was like a well-stocked serve-yourself supermarket.

Who Exactly Is the Enemy?

Nor can the Indian understand to this day why one would need to—or want to—conquer one's mother. Even the modern, sophisticated, well-educated white Nebraskan is almost certain to be ignorant of Native holy sites, as sacred to tribal custom, theology, and tradition as Golgotha would be to a Christian or Masada to a Jew. Blithely the white man builds roads and houses on sacred sites, slams posts for billboards into sacred ground, plows grave sites, and scrapes away the covering of holy soil without so much as a nod, let alone an apology. Every year awards are given to Nebraska farm families who have been on their land for a full hundred years, yet I know of no similar recognition of Omaha families that still live on land that has been in their family's care for four or five centuries. In fact, if you listen, you will hear white newcomers (like my own family, where I am only the second generation born in this hemisphere) talking as if it is the Indians who are the interlopers and newcomers.

Indians have a different perspective on time—in my opinion, one a lot closer to making sense than mainstream white America's understanding. But I've written all about that elsewhere. In terms of their tenure on this land, Indian tribes don't think in terms of a century. Or even centuries. Some tribes dispute any notion that we are all immigrants to this continent because even Native peoples came here originally across the land bridge from Asia. No, they feel that they have always been here. Some tribes can show you the hole in the ground out of which human beings originally came to reside on this earth . . . and in more cases than not, those original people were members of *that* particular tribe.

The white man may not know it, but his tenure also has two ends to it: the frontier at the front edge and, well, something else at the conclusion. Again, Indians may not see it quite that way. In his book *Coyote Warrior*, Paul VanDevelder reports that at a meeting where some high-powered engineers, politicians, and other officials were seeking a way to warn generations thousands of years down the line about the dangers posed by nuclear waste storage areas, it was a Yakima Indian who observed (probably correctly), "Don't worry, we'll tell them." And in her monograph *Lakota Naming: A Modern-Day Hunka Ceremony*, Marla Powers notes that "some [Lakota] old-timers still believe that the White man is a passing phenomenon. . . ." Obviously, these people see the Plains and the white man's tenancy here in very different terms from how most Nebraskans with names like *Petersen, Hockelschmecker, Lklowicz,* or *Smith* do.

So it is that this book is about *my* Nebraska. We all see a different reality, and I believe those differences are even greater, even more dramatic, even more important when it comes to this place we call home, the heart of America's Great Plains, Nebraska. *My* Nebraska. The Nebraska I see through these eyes and filtered through this mind. I want to tell you about the Nebraska I know and love. The chances are good to excellent that it is not the same place you know and love. Or the place you find boring, desolate, or even repugnant. Heaven knows, plenty of people feel that way.

The Bad, the Worse, and the Ugly

As much as I love Nebraska, I know there is a generous supply of people who don't. Long ago I started a file of what I consider to be the most interesting slurs about Nebraska, from both within and without the state's boundaries, from purposeful expressions of contempt to inadvertent insults by well-meaning boobs.

There are the jokes:

"What is the best thing to come out of Nebraska? Interstate 80."

"Custer gathered the last of his men together as the battle of the Little Bighorn approached its inevitable climax and said to them, 'Men, I have bad news and I have good news. The bad news is there's no way in hell any of us are going to come out of this mess alive. On the other hand, the good news is . . . we don't have to go back through Nebraska!' "

And that cynical view of this place is nothing new. The jokes have been here from the beginning. At a gathering of citizens around the time of the Civil War, members of the audience were invited to cheer for their respective states. The Nebraskans in attendance, it was later reported, shouted "Hurrah for Hell!"

An old-timer once remarked to me that living in Nebraska has a lot in common with being hanged: "The initial jolt is fairly sudden but after you hang there awhile, you kinda get used to it."

In the field of folklore, we speak of the "Es-Ex Factor," the important differences with things like jokes or insults when spoken within a cultural group (the *eso*teric part of the formula) and those directed at that group from outside (the *exo*teric half of the factor). It's one thing for me, a 100 percent German-Russian from the Volga Valley, to refer to myself and my people as "rooshens"; it is quite another when the term is used by an outsider, especially when it is meant not in jest but as an insult. That's the way it is with commentary about Nebraska. The license plates on my car say CAPTNEB—I can joke about this place I love and am so identified with. But when the slurs come from a Coloradan or Iowan, or especially from Texas . . . well, then they're fighting words!

Don't get me wrong—I appreciate passion and firm opinions. I've been known to have a few of those myself. I'm a romantic, not a scientist. Objectivity is drastically overrated, in my opinion, in part because there isn't much of it around despite the high praise lavished on it. It's pretty hard for any human being to look at something and arrive at a cold, objective opinion about it. Maybe it's even impossible. I have my opinions about Nebraska (you may agree with some of them, and I'm willing to bet that you will for damned sure disagree with some) and I am old, educated, and experienced enough to know that other people have their own, often (if not usually) differing opinions. And I have my opinions about their opinions: They are sometimes strange, sometimes wrong, and often downright stupid.

Tell Me When to Laugh

For example, in the early 1970s I bristled when the eponymously named Doug Looney wrote in an article in *Sports Illustrated:*

> . . . when God went to work creating Nebraska, he thought: "Okay, I keep giving other areas of this country mountains, beaches, stuff like that. Everywhere I look, beauty. I need a change." What resulted is a landscape of wall-to-wall dust. It's the perfect environment if you're a vacuum sweeper.

Similarly and at about the same time, Bill Gray (!) wrote in the *Detroit News:*

> My back-from-the-West-vacation column this time is going to take on an . . . area of the country that I'm certain will cause nary a ripple of controversy: Nebraska. Now, nobody can get hot about an anti-Nebraska column because nobody, including—I suspect—the people who live there can even state a legitimate case for the state. And I, like the rest of America, could easily forget about this hulking geographical giant except that every time I drive to and from Colorado on I–80 I have to contend with Nebraska's 450 miles of wheat, corn, and cows sprawled over some of the dullest, flattest, brownest land on either side of the Mississippi. *[This sorry drudge has obviously never looked to either side as he was crossing his own eastern Colorado! Is there any place bleaker this side of Mars? —RW]* . . . One day as I spent a month trudging through Nebraska I found myself fantasizing about an airlift that would pick up Nebraska and move it north somewhere in Canada. Colorado and Iowa would then be pushed together in the airlift's second phase.

Mr. Sunshine goes on like this for another couple of thousand banal words and then concludes:

You can complain about Detroit and all its problems with strong jus-
tification. No one, not even Mayor Coleman Young, says this
lifestyle's perfect. [!!!] But after trudging through Nebraska I've got
to admit that at least my city can be counted among the living and
breathing. The beat goes on in Detroit. It has stopped in Nebraska.

I wonder when the last time was that Mr. Gray ate a slab of
prime rib with a chunk of crisp, buttered French bread made from
cows fed and wheat grown on "snow-covered mountain peaks." The
man is obviously an idiot. Remember, now—Gray is writing about
Detroit! De-damned-troit, for God's sake! Paterson, New Jersey, is the
Shining City on the Hill compared with *Detroit.*

Did I bristle the first time I saw this crap? Man, did I ever! Then
I began not only to realize that this ignorant clod had likely never
been in Nebraska, but also to wonder if he'd ever been in Detroit!
I've been in Detroit. And yeah, if you don't watch what part of the
city you happen to stumble into, the beat will indeed go on. Until
you have surrendered your billfold, your shoes, and maybe your life.
My first reaction was to snarl back in a letter to his newspaper, but
then I got to thinking: *You can't teach anyone this stupid anything new.*
And then I thought, *Well, maybe if he actually did see Nebraska, he would
change his mind.* But you know, does Nebraska really need him?

Ignorance Can Be Bliss If We All Cooperate

And then, courtesy of clods like Looney and Gray (do the Great
Naming Gods have a sense of humor or what?), I began to develop
one of my basic principles of life: The worst thing you can do to people
is point out where they are wrong, especially where they are *really*
wrong. The Christian thing to do is to nod politely and agree. Or
maybe even reinforce their ignorant prejudices by affirming them. "Oh
man, Looney, you don't know how bad it is. You've only skimmed the
surface. For entertainment on Saturdays around here we go over to
Red's barbershop and watch a couple of haircuts. Or maybe over to the
switching station to listen to the transformers buzz. But the dust ain't
so bad, actually. Sometimes it's all we have to eat, after all."

"Gosh, Dick, there isn't a Nebraskan alive who wouldn't sell his sister to have one of those high-rise caves you have in Detroit. And farmers who are stuck way out in the wilderness, having to walk out into their fields every day, spend a good part of their winters dreaming of a job in a Detroit automobile factory, maybe turning tight the top bolt on the rear left door top hinge on green Ford Tauruses all day long. And then driving two hours through traffic back to that postage-stamp property. Yep, you guys in Motor City really have it made. I hope when you get back home, you remember how lucky you are, and that your city is still breathing. But hopefully not inhaling too deep. That would only agitate your emphysema, after all."

And as If Detroit Weren't Bad Enough . . .

It has become almost the vogue to insult Nebraska. Fredrick V. Grunfeld's article "La Mancha" in *Horizon* describes that area of Spain as "a vast, parched plain . . . a rather vague region. . . . No one ever goes there just to see it; La Mancha is the Nebraska of Spain." And more recently an unofficial circle started collecting slurs against the state (and region!), from a columnist for the *Texarkana Gazette:*

> One of the great mysteries of Nebraska is why, no matter where you find yourself situated within its borders, it still takes at least 8 hours to get out of the state. This is true no matter which direction you are headed or at what speed. This is why, for the sake of brevity, there has been serious discussion in intellectual circles about lopping off the western half of the state. Too many people can't understand the reason for it, and suggest doing so would be a boon for the travel industry and result in reduced airfares on shorter coast-to-coast flights. In truth, discarding 40,000 square miles of Nebraska isn't too much to ask of a nation that has practically everything.

There's more. The author of this trash-talk was graced by those Naming Gods with the unbelievably appropriate moniker of . . . Les Minor. I swear I am telling you the truth here, no kidding. I mean, you can't make this kind of thing up.

And I ask you, do any of you recall inviting Mr. Less Insignificant to come to Nebraska? I sure don't. But I think we can all understand his impatience with the burdens of the hours it takes to cross 400 miles of Nebraska on I–80, can't we? I mean, of course it's not like the *800* miles of scenic wonder on the interstate system from Hell Paso to Tex-arcane! I can only imagine that living in Texas . . . so far as it can be called living . . . finally got to Mr. Minor.

I have been to Texas on numerous occasions, crossed it both ways, spent time on the side roads and small towns, and I have had some wonderful times there. New Braunfels, Fredrickstadt, Boerne, San Antonio, barbecue joints where the finest cooking in the world was served on old newspapers, and . . . well, but I've seen the worst that Texas has to offer, too, and I have never seen anything like that in Nebraska, ever, anywhere.

Most of the people who spout such venom about Nebraska can't even locate the state on a map, or draw its outline, or even pronounce the word. In my own life I have heard Nebraska identified as the capital of Arizona! I found it rather charming when I once had a package sent from Quebec to my parents in Lincoln and found, on my return, that the bundle had been addressed to "New Brasque." I like that: "New Brasque." Just imagine, if you can, the variations I have seen and heard on *Dannebrog*: Dannenberg, Dangerbrong, Damnearburg (that's a gooder!), Darnaborg, and, my personal favorite, DannebRog.

While we're on the subject, I suppose we might consider Nebraska place-names. One sure way to folks who are new to Nebraska or who spend too much time in Lincoln or Omaha is how they pronounce some of our place-names. Unadilla is a good test item. Or Kearney, Chadron, Ogallala (if not the pronunciation, then the spelling thereof), Keya Paha (a Lincoln television weatherman who is from small-town Nebraska, has lived here all his life, and has seen a lot of the state nonetheless never has gotten this one right), and Beatrice are always a challenge for the newcomer. County names are favorites of mine; the suggestion that we put county names on our license plates is always thwarted by the ladies of Hooker County. Which, by the way, like Sherman, Howard, Custer, McPherson, Grant, and several other Nebraska counties, is named for a military general. Many of these men achieved their fame in the Civil War—which Nebraskans tended to take personally even though we were well west of the battlegrounds of that horror—or the Indian wars, whose military leaders might well have been prosecuted for atrocities in a civilized nation. I am especially fond of Broken Bow, named for an Indian relic discovered at the town's founding site, where the high school sports teams call themselves the Custer County Indians. Get it? Custer? Indians? You have to admit, someone has a nice sense of irony. Or maybe none at all.

Here's a brain-teaser for you: What three Nebraska counties are named for animals? You will find the answer at the very end of the book, so read the whole thing. Yes, there will be a test.

Hard to Tell, but Since They're Friends . . .

To my mind, the saddest slurs against my beloved Nebr-Nebr Land are those that come from well-meaning booster boobs who try to put a good face on things and in the process wind up only showcasing the very things they are trying to conceal or ignore. The worst offender in this category is the Travel and Tourism Division of Nebraska's Department of Economic Development. It hasn't always been that way, I should make clear, nor is it always the case even now. Occasionally a bright light comes forth like the irrepressible Mary Ethel Emanuel—it should be spelled *Ethyl,* considering her endless, explosive energy—or the director of the agency a few years back, Peg Briggs.

Peg's story is a real lesson, and as usual one that has been totally ignored by everyone who counts. Except me. I knew Peg for many years as the secretary-receptionist for the English Department at a college where I was teaching, Nebraska Wesleyan in Lincoln. As is always the case with secretaries, she pretty much ran things, saving the sorry butts of countless clueless English professors, deans, and department chairs. The secretaries at the University of Nebraska

English and Anthropology Departments where I later taught were the same—the real organizers, leaders, workers, and shepherds, goading along a crowd of hapless dolts in their charge . . . and getting paid a fraction of what the professors were getting and of what they deserved. Even though the professors themselves have traditionally also been underappreciated in comparison with drones like administrators and athletic coaches.

Anyway, the next time I found Peg she was performing the same tasks for the political hack bumbling around in the big corner office of the Travel and Tourism Division. As usual, she was doing all the work while the Big Cheese in the expensive silk suit and imported necktie took credit for her work. Then someone did something so brilliant I can only presume it was an accident. Good stuff like this almost never happens on purpose. The Big Cheese was moved upstairs to yet another position he was inadequate to handle and someone . . . I can't believe it to this day . . . someone put Peg in charge of the entire agency. And in half a dozen years she transformed the operation into a sleek, efficient, honest, trusted, powerful economic force in the state. Of course when the next governor took office, he replaced Peg with yet another political hack and everything went to hell again. Whew . . . at last things are back to normal.

Discover the Difference

Anyway, back to what I was telling you. Traditionally these booster boobs crank out idiotic, slick, blatantly dishonest propaganda that they think will lure tourists and investors to some bleak area of the continent where no one actually wants to go, with the result that anyone dumb enough to fall for this stuff gets to the place described as paradise, finds out what it really is, and goes away thoroughly angry with the unconscionable dishonesty of the hucksters who led them there. Which is to say, Nebraska.

My favorite advertisement from the pre-Peg DED was a slick page that appeared in countless popular magazines around the country. In the background you see a wooded canyon through which slashes a bubbling whitewater river. I suspect the photo is of our Niobrara, a truly gorgeous wild river at the northwesternmost edge of the state. There are smaller inset photos of an elk herd shoulder-deep in grass, thousands of birds crossing a crimson sun, and cowboys headed out on a cattle drive. The text embedded in all this reads "NEBRASKA . . . Discover crystal streams winding through pine-studded canyons. White sand beaches. Dense forests. And outdoor recreation all year 'round. . . ."

Well, okay. There *are* crystal streams and pine-studded canyons in Nebraska. There *are* white sand beaches and dense-ish forests even. And if you don't mind withering heat, raging prairie fires, arctic blizzards, hailstones the size of grapefruit, and tornadoes dancing through your campsite, sure . . . you can camp year 'round. Perhaps the clincher, the thing I came to love intensely about this ad campaign, the one redeeming phrase in it, the punch line that required either a wonderful, wonderful sense of irony or a cruel talent for sarcasm, followed all the above. I tingle with joy as I look again at my tattered copy of this advertisement from the *National Geographic* magazine . . . I brace myself for the immense pleasure of forming the words in my mouth again . . . *"Discover the Difference!"*

No one could complain about that. Not even if you came here expecting crystal streams, pine-studded canyons, and white sand beaches only to find that there are one or two crystal streams at the very boundaries of the state, packed bank-to-bank with drunk and reveling canoers, not to mention that you have to apply for a permit and a number just to get into the quota of floaters allowed on the river that day, while the rest of the state's rivers *are* the "white-sand beaches," having been sucked dry by irrigators so that every piece of living nature that needs the river water has withered and died. No, no complaints please about the only "dense forests" being within a quarter mile of the Missouri River, almost more Iowa than Nebraska, while elsewhere farmers are knocking down the windbreak trees their grandfathers planted in response to the Dust Bowl so they can bring in a few more bushels of surplus corn that scarcely brings in enough profit to pay for the fuel to harvest it. No, you have no complaints coming, because there it is, in plain English, as honest as Nebraska itself—*Discover the Difference!*

Yikes.

Byootiful Nebraskee

Okay, to be sure, some of the excessive enthusiasm and clouded vision of what we have here at the very heart of the Great Plains is not really hucksterism but rather sincere emotion. I know many a man who proudly looks on the worst farm, the ugliest wife, the dumbest children, and the meanest cur in the world and professes that no man could be more fortunate on this earth than he is, surrounded with one of God's gifts after another—farm, wife, kids, dog. And he could pass a polygraph test to that effect. He isn't lying, mostly—he's just seeing things from his own perspective.

I believe that to be the case with our state song, composed by Jim Fras in 1967, sung by countless enslaved school choirs and endured by endless audiences since. A sample:

> *Beautiful Nebraska, peaceful prairie land,*
> *Laced with many rivers and the hills of sand;*
> *Dark green valleys cradled in the earth,*
> *Rain and sunshine bring abundant birth.*

My most tender memory of this prairie paean was a time when I had just spoken to a gathering of state officials, legislators, administrators, and other grand poobahs at an elegant dinner in the governor's mansion. I spoke of the pioneers, sang some frontier folk songs, told some tall tales . . . the kind of thing I made a living at for forty years. After my performance, my old friend Frank Marsh, then our secretary of state and a real enthusiast for our state song, approached me genially and pulling me close told me that if ever there were an occasion when it would be most appropriate to lead gathered Nebraskans in a cheery round of our state song, this had to be it. He urged me passionately, insistently. He wanted to praise this land we all love so much . . . you know, "Beautiful Nebraska, peaceful prairie land . . . rain and sunshine bring abundant birth . . . All these wonders by our Master's hand . . . ," and all that.

Well, Frank's idea might have been a good idea at another time, although my own disposition simply isn't strong enough to stand the strain of the most general and blatant ironies of the song. But on this night, when I–80 had been shut down because of severe drifting and killing cold, when all schools including the university had already been closed for the next day (and as it turned out the next several days), as law enforcement officials present urged us to close our meeting early and then travel as quickly as we could safely move to secure shelters to weather this killer storm with its subzero temperatures, gale-force winds, freezing sleet, and blinding fury, somehow I simply could not rise to the occasion. Well, yes, Frank, God rest your gentle soul, I do love this state, at least as much as you do. But even wearing the rosy glasses of love, I can't in good conscience and straight face warble:

> *Beautiful Nebraska, as you look around,*
> *you will find a rainbow reaching to the ground;*
> *All these wonders by the Master's hand;*
> *Beautiful Nebraska land.*

Small wonder that a parody verse set to the same tune has sprung up in the state and is probably sung about as often as the official words and, I wager, with a lot more enthusiasm and a clearer conscience:

> *Beautiful Nebraska, peaceful prairie land.*
> *Misery and suffering abound on every hand;*
> *Blizzards, snakes, and lizards,*
> *Tornadoes, hail, and sand!*
> *Beautiful Nebraska land!*

The chamber-of-commerce vision of this Plains Eden is nothing new. I think the Bible even says that nothing under the sun is new, and what the Bible says is often right, far more often in fact than the people who make a habit of referring to it for truth without knowing what they are talking about. A book titled *The Sod House,* written by Cass G. Barnes and published in 1930, says (no kidding), "Considering climate, rainfall, soil, and freedom from hot winds and cyclones, no state was dealt with more generously by nature than Nebraska. . . ." Huh? What? Did he maybe mean New Hampshire? Then Barnes pooh-poohs the prevailing nonsense that west of Kearney, the land "was considered fit for cattle grazing only." Hmmm . . . wonder where folks would have gotten an idea like that. Maybe from the general reality that the land west of Kearney is fit for cattle grazing only? My bet is that Mr. Barnes had plenty of time and reason to reconsider his words during the decade that followed the publication of his book!

Nebraska as It Is?

One of my favorite books of all time is John Burch's *Nebraska As It Is,* a boomer book published in 1878 and designed to lure more settlers out onto the Great Plains. Try to contain your glee while I share with you just a sample of Burch's effusive praise for the benefits of the Nebraska Good Life:

> The Nebraska summer is a long and genial warm season with delightful, breezy days and cool refreshing nights. The hottest days of July and August are tempered by the almost constant southerly and southwest winds. The high tone and stimulus of the atmosphere of this region are proverbial. A clear case of sunstroke in Nebraska is yet to be recorded.

Folks, I am not making this up. I am writing this directly from Burch's book. Now, pull yourselves together and quit that silly giggling. Here's more. Brace yourself:

> The cool still nights are a restful and refreshing pleasure to be experienced in but few regions of the world. The Nebraska winter, as compared to the rigorous, snowy, frost-bound winter of New England, New York, and Wisconsin, is a very mild and pleasant season. Nine-tenths of the cold season is made up of bright, dry, mild weather. The snowfall is light and rarely lies upon the ground more than a week. February and March give an occasional severe storm

of short duration. The best commentary upon the winter of this country is the grazing of cattle and sheep upon the ranges in the west half of the State, the year round, their only shelter from the storm being the native groves, gulches, and ravines.

As I chuckle my way through Burch's euphoric text for the hundredth time, I can't help thinking at this point yet again of Wright Morris's wonderful narrative in his *The Works of Love* about a similarly overly rosy description his grandfather sent to his grandmother as he tried to lure the Civil War widow from Ohio to come join him and live here on the brutal pioneer Plains. In wonderfully florid prose he tells her of his appreciation for the beauty he sees in her photograph . . . although Morris tells us she was in reality "plain . . . very plain." He tells her of his own restrained and cultured hope she will see something in him, too. But he doesn't have a lot to say to his prospective bride about his situation somewhere outside where Central City now lies. As Morris so beautifully phrases it, "There was hardly room, in letters such as this, to speak of grasshopper plagues like swirling clouds in the sky, or of the wooden shapes of cattle frozen stiffly upright out on the range. No, it was hardly the place. . . ."

More of Burch's soaring gushery:

> The soft blue haze, subdued mellow sunshine and gorgeous red sunsets of autumn in Nebraska make that season a benediction. The cold winds are the only unpleasant feature of the cold season, but the settler easily gets accustomed to these and they are known to be most effective CONSERVATORS OF HEALTH. They sweep away any possible malarial influence and leave the climate with every needed condition to normal health. The rare, invigorating, life-inspiring atmosphere gives remarkable brilliancy to the climate and leaves its impress on every form of life. A strong electric influence pervades everything that is not absolutely non-conducting. Men and animals move with quick, elastic step and even the vegetable kingdom expresses the presence of these vitalizing forces in a wonderful degree.

Well, yes. Maybe. Sort of. If you squint a little. Or a lot.

Inventing History

There are several common ways to manipulate history to make it
more palatable, or more profitable. On one hand, you can manufacture "attractions" where they have never existed or have no business
existing. There are museums, for example, that draw in money at the
gate with reenactments of historical events that never happened.
Another word for this would be *fakery,* but that would be unkind. A
museum near us offers Civil War reenactments; never mind that there
was no Civil War action in Nebraska. What's worse, the inevitable,
annual result of this "educational" process is that people—especially
and explicitly children—come away bubbling about how wonderful it
all was. As one little boy enthused a couple of years ago after watching a bunch of fat old duffers shoot blanks at each other, fall dead, and
then get up laughing to demonstrate camaraderie by having a tailgate
picnic, "It sure must have been fun. I wish I'd been alive during the
Civil War." Yeah, kid, that Civil War frolic was nothing but laughs.

The hideous "Arch" construction (actually more of a railroad
trestle design) obstructing I–80 just east of Kearney fictionalizes,
scrubs, and lightens up history and geography for the few people who
go to the trouble of stopping at it, generally showing them shallow
and painfully artificial replicas of what they could have seen if they
had gone just as far off the highway in another direction and taken
the time and trouble to visit the actual thing. That is, you can stop at
the Arch, pay too much to get in, and see images of where the
Oregon and Mormon Trails crossed the Plains, or you could drive a
few miles to the north and south and see the actual trails themselves.
I suppose that such artificiality says more about America than it says
about the Arch, but to me this is a painful slap in the face. It is saying, in essence, *What we have to offer by way of reality just isn't up to snuff.
Believe me, you'd be bored. So instead, we'll fix it up, slap some paint on it,
fancy it up a bit, improve the story, buff out the rough spots, and let you see
what we want you to believe . . . not to mention what you want to believe . . .
instead of that messy, troublesome, actually true historical stuff. Besides, it's too
hot and there might be spiders out there.* This approach exposes a painful

embarrassment, a tacit confession that what we have isn't good enough. So we have to fake something to hold your attention.

This is an important factor for me in regard to this book because I'm not going to do that. That's not what I do, and there are reasons for that beyond the fact that I can be abrasive and annoying, traits that my wife, Linda, calls to my attention with regularity. I have no such embarrassment about Nebraska. I think there is more than enough here to keep anyone with an active and inquisitive mind and just a bit of energy occupied, if not fascinated. No, it's not all lined up along the interstate highway and packaged in such a way as to make it easy to see in three minutes and digest in two. To my mind that makes it all the more interesting. I intend to tell you the truth in this book, not some sort of stuccoed false facade, a Potemkin replica designed to feed your ignorance rather than your curiosity.

I've done well with this approach. Twenty or so years ago, I picked up a book about Lincoln by three local schoolteachers. I lived in Lincoln most of my life, I have always liked Lincoln—and certainly Nebraska—so I am always curious about new approaches to understanding them and knowing more about them. Well, the more I read into this book, the madder I got. This was not the Lincoln I knew. This was a kind a chamber-of-commerce, goody-goody, whitewashed version of a city I had always thought of as pretty darned interesting. No kidding, this book suggested in the chapter "Places to Eat" the several McDonald's sites around town. While I was still reeling from that obscenity, I got to the section on "Things to Do in Lincoln" and found . . . again, I am being as serious as I can be under the circumstances . . . "Places to Jog." Sweet Jesus.

Still fuming, I sat down at my word processor and pounded out a small volume titled *Inside Lincoln,* self-published it, hand-carried it to bookstores, and sold it at little more than the cost of paper and binding just to head off the nonsense of the schoolteachers' book. In my book I told about the mysteries of Lincoln, the unlikely and bizarre facts, the really stupid and corrupt politicians and other criminals, the scandals and lunacies, and the things the chamber of commerce hopes no one ever finds out about. I revealed the locations of old whorehouses, debunked historical fantasies, and exploded sanctimonious myths. I told about unlikely places to get good food and pricked just about every proper and self-righteous prig I could find any dirt on. People gobbled it up. I couldn't update, print, and bind new editions fast enough to keep up with the demand. I sold a mess of those books out of my garage, made a nice pile of money, and went though several more editions because the demand only grew over the next few years. If I had the energy and time, I'd still be cranking that thing out, I imagine.

Now, I didn't tell you that story just to amuse you or to demonstrate that Linda's opinions of me are usually right (although they usually are). What I think I learned and proved with that little exercise in indignation is that while people like information, and there is some demand for print pabulum, what true Americans and, God knows, true Nebraskans really like is spicy, even slightly scandalous truth. In fact, if your intention is to endear yourself to the Nebraska audience, you may not even want to stop with the most obvious unvarnished truth. Dig deep. You know, down to the juicy stuff.

The attraction we have to the seamier side of life may be universal. We all point with far more enthusiasm (if only tentative pride) to the scandals, scoundrels, and horse thieves in our family trees than we do the pillars of the community, virtuous but boring yeoman farmers, and dutiful wives. Who would you rather have as an ancestor, the Reverend Wilbur Hammerfarkel, first minister of the Hallelujah Evangelical Lutheran Church of Plainview, Nebraska? Or . . . Jesse James? Now, don't lie to me! We all know the truth on this one!

So don't expect a book of boosterism here. Yes, I love Nebraska, but I love her for what she is, not what she should be, or would be, or what others might prefer. You may love other things about the state than I do, and some of what I say about the place may really set your blood to boiling. That's okay. I don't really care. The title of the book, if you will take the time and trouble to check yet once again, is *My Nebraska*, not *Your Nebraska*. Not *Our Nebraska*. *MY Nebraska*.

Personally, I think we should take a lesson from the pioneers: not the boosters who were trying to get suckers to come out here to settle but the actual homesteaders who plowed the ground and built the soddies. They figured out pretty quickly that if they strutted and boasted about how wonderful things are out here on the Plains, it wouldn't be long before someone asked them why, if things were so cushy in Nebraska, they were living in a mud hut and weren't stinking rich. So the standard pioneer approach was to go in the other direction: Instead of extolling Nebraska's virtues, the custom became endemic and hyperbolic bad-mouthing. "It's not the end of the earth . . . but we can see it from here." "We'd try to have a family but the way our crops have gone, we figure we'd be lucky to get our seed back." "When I die, I hope I go to hell . . . because I could use the improvement after living all my life in Nebraska." "Dying in Nebraska is redundant." Et cetera, et cetera, et cetera.

"Living in Nebraska," they would say, "is so horrible, no normal human being can possibly make it out here." And after a dramatic pause they might add, "Me? Oh, I'm doing fine." I'm not sure they weren't right: The Plains have constituted a kind of petri dish for accelerated natural selection, a refining of the gene pool that quickly culled out the puny, timid, insufficient genes and developed to a fine edge those of us who remain. As a result, now we hardly ever boast or brag.

Too Much of a Good Thing . . . In This Case, Honesty

The thing is, early and even contemporary observers who aren't trying to peddle as 200-bushel-an-acre farmland ground that won't even support two-cow-calf-per-acre pasture saw this place pretty much for what it is. It's fashionable these days to ridicule those who called this region "badlands" or "the Great American Desert," but you know, when you come from Norway or Germany or Czechoslovakia or Poland and figure a dry year is only 40 or even 60 inches of rain, the 20 to 24 inches we get here at our place probably pretty well fit their understanding of what a desert is.

James Fenimore Cooper had a pretty good idea of the Plains, I think. In his writings he reveals that even in the early nineteenth century, even having never been here, even writing in prose drenched with goofy romanticism, somewhere, somehow he had a real grasp of the conditions explorers were finding here. In his *The Prairie* he nails this specific central Nebraska area precisely, right down to exact landmarks. He had been talking with someone who actually had been here, I am sure. He wrote:

> The second description of these natural meadows lies west of the Mississippi at a distance of a few hundred miles from that river, and is called the Great Prairies. They resemble the steppes of Tartary more than any other known portion of the world, being in fact a vast country incapable of sustaining a dense population in the absence of the two great necessaries [of wood and water]. Rivers abound, it is true; but this region is nearly destitute of brooks and the smaller watercourses, which tend so much to comfort and fertility.

I'll have more to say about Nebraska's geography, rivers, flora, and so forth, later on in these pages, but for the moment let's grant Cooper in all honesty that he was pretty much right about the American Great Plains. Not until the windmill was devised, as well as other sources of fuel and ways to transport it here into the Hinterlands, was the place capable of sustaining a dense population, and I can see some legitimate argument about the finer distinctions of that fact even today. Dense population? I don't know what you call *dense*, but two people per square mile, even with fuel and water, strikes me as being on the puny side, if not downright anorexic. Water? At this very moment I am having daily conversations with my beloved Linda, trying to convince her that a wet year is going to be coming along soon so she won't have to watch all her trees and flowers wither and die in the summer sun yet again.

Tough Love

Wright Morris is one of my favorite Nebraska writers, partially because he grew up over in Central City, just down Ormsby Road from my place, but also because I really love the way he writes. The first time I read his book *The Works of Love*, I was so stunned by the first thirteen pages that I instantly bought a dozen copies and sent them out to friends around the country. Almost at once I began to get phone calls and letters inquiring about my health . . . actually, about my mental stability . . . because they had read *past* the first thirteen pages to the part about depression, misery, and suicide. Hell, I was just excited about what he had written about Nebraska!

In fact, one of the reasons I sit here at this very moment where I do is the opening line of that book by Morris—"West of the 98th Meridian, where it sometimes rains, and it sometimes doesn't. . . ." The 98th Meridian runs smack down the center of Central City, just a block away from Morris's childhood home, right down the center stripe of State Highway 14, and just a touch east of where I now live.

Again, later in these pages I'm going to rant and rave on and on about things like weather, rain, seasons, water, trees, lunatics home-grown, imported, exiled, and forbidden, but what really knocked me out about Morris's opening narrative—in which he tells us about his ancestors' coming to this region—was the closing paragraph of his first chapter: Nowhere have I seen a better explanation of the impact this landscape has had on me, or on Cather and Sandoz, or on Dick Cavett or Johnny Carson, certainly on Wright Morris, and perhaps even on you. Morris tells how his grandmother (Caroline Clayton in this fictionalized form) came to Nebraska to marry his grandfather, identified in the pages of this book as Adam Brady, and then in conclusion reveals the true Nebraskan's tortured love–hate inner conflict about the state in the thoughts of his father, Will:

> This desolate place, this rim of the world, had been God's country to Adam Brady, but to his wife, Caroline Clayton, a god-forsaken hole. Perhaps only Will Brady could combine these two points of view. He could leave it, that is, but he would never get over it.

My God, rarely is truth so well put. If that's not Nebraska, I'll kiss your ass. We might leave it, but we sure as billyhell are not likely to get over it.

Popper Party Poopers and Others

I have already confessed a nagging uneasiness about my righteous indignation at Nebraska's detractors. While some are clearly far outside any reasonable limits of sanity (complaining about Nebraska from the septic tanks of Texas or Detroit comes to mind), even as I howl my fury at the lunacy I have to admit that, well, yes, it's not as if the whiners are *completely* off base. I don't like to weaken my own position by being reasonable—that would be downright un-American—but I'm not sure I can forever conceal my doubt. Nowhere is that harder than it is when I consider the idiocy of Drs. Frank and Deborah Popper of Rutgers University, originators of the so-called Buffalo Commons scheme.

These two blazing intellectual lights from the East Coast (insofar as you can, try to imagine me saying that with a contemptuous sneer) theorized in 1987 that seein's as how there's nothing out here on the Plains anyway—there weren't many people to begin with and increasingly there are large areas with even fewer—and considering the fact that nothing of value comes from this region . . . what the hell, why not just turn it back over to the buffalo? Their reasoning was based, as academic research often is, on previous work. Fredrick Jackson said that the frontier ended when there were more than six people per square mile; huge areas of Nebraska, the Dakotas, and Kansas have fewer than *two* people per square mile, so it must be obvious that they are the detritus of a failed frontier. I mean, jeez, Fredrick damned *Jackson* said it, and since he must have gotten the figure straight from God, it must be right, so there you are. Much of Kansas has fewer people now than it did in 1890, and a large portion of Nebraska is in the same situation even more recently, since 1904. So what could possibly be the sense in letting people stay there moldering away in the wilderness, the Popper Poopers asked?

Well, duuuuuuh . . . There are also huge parts of Paterson and Camden, New Jersey, following the seasonal rioting there, that have fewer people than they did fifty years ago, so I guess it follows: This

area should be abandoned and redesignated as the Free Fire
Commons, where New Jersey's particular and peculiar species of
wildlife can frolic and romp to its heart's content. Or maybe we could
enlarge the area to even larger wastelands and call it the Old Jersey
Crack and Industrial Waste Commons.

What do I have against New Jersey? Not a thing. I even like
parts of New Jersey, such as the beautiful Pine Barrens area. My
friend Bill Geist lives in New Jersey and it hasn't ruined him. My bet
is that there are a lot of nice people in New Jersey. The thing is, I am
trying to use the sort of solid reasoning exercised so blithely by the
Poppers. You see, they are based in New Jersey, and, seeing nothing
there that needs their attention, they have generously turned their
gifted eyes to helping us folks out here in the Middle of Nowhere.
Moreover, they are *urban* friggin' planners and detecting nothing that
might need their genius in the cities, they have instead decided to
correct the misguided lives of those of us out here in rural America.

No, I have nothing against New Jersey. In fact, as a rural Plains
folklorist I feel I have precisely the same credentials to redesign other
people's lives and other geographic regions as the Poppers do, so I can
also see converting the hurricane-raked, reptile-infested (and I am
not just talking politics here, mind you) swamps of Florida into the
Alligator Commons. In my opinion that makes one hell of a lot more
sense than this talk about a *Buffalo* Commons. Besides, if we are
going to start returning regions to their rightful owners, wouldn't the
Lakota, Pawnee, Omaha, and Mandan Tribes be somewhere toward
the head of the line where deeds are being written over?

I wonder where the Poppers think that beef came from that they
enjoyed at supper last night? A chemical processing plant in Newark?
I don't see a lot of problems that would be solved by dragging ranchers off their cattle lands on the western Plains, but I can sure imagine
life being easier for America if huge areas of New Jersey and Florida
were walled off and turned over to the denizens of the night.

Okay. Whew. I'm glad I got that rant off my chest. I've been
throwing this verbal equivalent of septic tank contents into a file for

twenty years now, just waiting for this chance to vent my fury. And since this is my chance, I'm exercising flat-out fulmination. I feel a lot better now. Sort of.

The thing is, some of the Popper scenario is happening, whether people like me like it or not. People are already leaving the least populated parts of our state and moving to the eastern edge and along the I–80 corridor . . . actually, the Platte River Corridor. And the buffalo are moving in, courtesy of a lot of small bison herd keepers like our friends the Harder family just upriver from us, some government bison raisers such as the herd at Fort Niobrara southeast of Valentine, and even tribal holdings like the Hochunk herd south of Sioux City. And special thanks to at least one enormous human factor: Ted Turner. Turner is buying up gigantic parcels of land in the Nebraska Sandhills, hundreds of thousands of acres at a time, and converting them into . . . well, into . . . uh . . . into a . . . okay, I'll say it . . . into a *Buffalo Commons*.

And I find myself begrudgingly applauding the man and his vision. There are some who object to the fact that by buying up land as he is, Turner is raising property values in the Sandhills and thereby raising taxes, but hey, if he's raising property values, he's also paying huge amounts of taxes and in the process he's making people who own land there very much richer than they already are. It's hard to take seriously complaints that you have to pay higher taxes because you are getting so much richer, don't you think?

I like the idea of fences falling and rightful "owners" coming back, of the land being given a chance to heal and regain its natural equilibrium. Besides, Linda and I eat a lot of buffalo meat and find it unexpectedly savory. (In fact, Linda has wondered aloud if maybe her predilection for buffalo meat might not be because in a previous life she was captured by a cruel savage and taken from her gentle and civilized home into a heathen wilderness to live a life of brutal desperation. "Sort of like now," she adds.)

I worried about what Turner had in mind for all this ground . . . I love the Sandhills way too much to see them despoiled. But reliable sources tell me that his plan is as benign and benevolent as it could possibly be; that he is going to deed it to The Nature Conservancy, where it will still be taxable ground, left undeveloped (and believe me, I say that in the most positive, indeed gleeful way possible), and populated again hopefully forever by Brother Buffalo.

And there it is: I despise outsiders like the Poppers arrogantly and hypocritically suggesting that they know best what to do with the region I love so much and the people who live on it. Even though they may be right. It's that Es-Ex Factor thing again. It's okay for those of us on the inside to make such decisions and take such actions, but somehow it just isn't quite as acceptable when it comes from some smart-aleck rural planners from Rutgers University in New Jersey.

As for the well-meaning boobs who try to say nice things about Nebraska and in the process make us look like idiots, well, there's not much to be done there. And when it comes to those who simply hate the very idea of Nebraska, the more the state and region become what these people hate—open, unpeopled, honest, rich and productive—the more they will hate it, and the more those of us who love it will love it. Besides, do we really want the Nebraska haters to change their minds and come here? Why do we care what they think? In most cases—like the blithering idiots I've quoted above—they come from locales that are laughably inferior to Nebraska, so if they prefer that, let 'em.

Fellow Nebrophiles

Now we're getting to the good stuff, the people whom I consider genuine Nebraskans, people who really love this place for what it is. There are plenty of us; you know who you are. It's not that we know all that much more than everyone else; we're just more curious than the others. We not only like what we see but are eager to know more. Nebraska still surprises us, and pleases us. I have spent my life traveling Nebraska's roads, meeting Nebraskans, spending time loitering in small towns and their school gyms, cafes, churches, and fire halls. I don't waste my precious travel time competing with idiots on the interstate; no, I am perfectly content to take what my friend Bill Least Heat Moon called his "blue highways"—state roads, county roads, gravel and dirt, sometimes with numbers, sometimes not. I'm the slow guy who is gawking at the status of the milo, the passing flock of birds, or the water in the ditches as you pass him up. I'm in no hurry because I already am where I'm going . . . on this road, right here and now.

My old and now sadly departed friend Albert Fahlbusch in Scottsbluff (Katz ihr Loch, as my father inevitably tacked on to the official place-name) once gave me the perfect philosophical capsule to explain his and my own feelings. Albert was our state's one National Heritage Award winner, simultaneously the Stradivarius and the Yehudi Menuhin of his instrument, the hammered dulcimer, making the best dulcimers there are and playing them best, too. I was once in his shop talking with him about his talent and I noted that I had run into a lot of *Hackbrett* (German for "hammered dulcimer") players the last few years—in Michigan, in Lincoln, even in Denver, not all that far from Scottsbluff, after all. "You know, Albert, sometime you should drop on down to Denver and meet some of those players down there," I suggested.

Albert thought about that a moment and then said quietly and honestly and truthfully, "Roger, why would I want to go anywhere? I'm *in* Scottsbluff." Of course. Why would anyone here want to be anywhere else when we're already in Nebraska? Why, rolling down this wonderful Nebraska gravel road at 45 miles an hour on a beautiful autumn day with the milo just reaching that incredibly beautiful rust color that exists nowhere else in such vastness except maybe on Mars, would I conceivably want to be anywhere else? So . . . what's the hurry? Don't bother to honk. I know I'm going slow. Just go on around and get to wherever it is that *you* would rather be.

There aren't many surprises to be found on I–80. At least not pleasant ones. To that degree the writers I've cited above pissing and whining about how boring Nebraska is have it right. If you had an invitation to spend a day sitting in the dressing room of ten or twenty supermodels while they change in and out of their clothes, sometimes naked, sometimes richly adorned, always moving, bending, stretching, taking off, pulling on, I imagine you could spend that day with your chair turned to the wall staring at a light switch and legitimately conclude by evening that there really was nothing much going on, nothing to be seen, nothing interesting to speak of. And that would also make you an idiot. Crossing Nebraska on I–80 is like that.

And lordy, what you'd be missing sitting there staring at that light switch! My CBS News crew—Izzy Bleckman, Danny Gianneschi, Bud Lamoureaux—and I were once traveling from story site to story site and as usual running behind schedule. Logic would tell you that the quickest way to get somewhere is that legendary straight line, and that would be the smart road to take. Luckily we did exactly that on this occasion. Instead of sticking to the big "fast" highway, we stopped at a now defunct service station on Highway 2, just southeast of Dunning, and asked the greasy but helpful attendant if maybe there wasn't a quicker, shorter way to Arnold than Highway 2, even one that we didn't see on the map, not a highway but a plain old *road*. He assured us there was, and pointed just down the road at a turnoff—an unnumbered, roughly paved county road. "That one goes right straight south to Arnold," he said helpfully, not bothering to tell us the surprises we were in for.

Now, for one thing, you have to remember that I was traveling in this van jammed with luggage and equipment with three good friends who are anything but Nebraskans. Two were from Chicago, one from New York. So coming to Nebraska was always something of an adventure for them, and for me, because I love sharing this state and what I love about it with any outsiders. This time, however, the surprise was going to be on me. First there was the splendid, naked, empty, grand landscape of Nebraska's Sandhills ranch country and its endless sky. Then we encountered a leathery-skinned husband-and-wife team driving a herd of cattle from one pasture to another . . .

down the road. No, I don't mean *along* the road, or *across* the road, I
mean *on* the road. We were in something of a hurry—after all, we
had taken this back road as a shortcut—but this was such a wonder
for my Big City buddies, even I reveled in the wild westernness of it.
One of the drovers rode back to us to explain why they were holding
us up and we wound up talking with her for a good half hour, just
enjoying her attitude, as open and frank as the landscape. Note: She
didn't apologize. She explained. What she had to do, she assumed—
correctly—was certain to be at least as important as what we might
be doing, and so no apology was in order. Those cattle had to be
moved, and she and her crew were moving them. She didn't figure
any further explanation was needed.

Once past the herd we drove on south toward Arnold and
Callaway. And suddenly a sight opened up before us that virtually
stopped us dead. Izzy, the cameraman and driver, pulled our vehicle
to the narrow shoulder of the road and said something wonderfully
appropriate like "Holy shit! Would you look at that!" We had come
onto a vista the like of which I had never before seen in Nebraska
except maybe from the top of Scotts Bluff or somewhere on the Pine
Ridge far to the northwest. But here we were, not an hour from my
own farm at Dannebrog, looking out from an almost mountainside
road over a rugged scarp with a wide valley and off into the distance,
as far as our eyes could reach. The beauty of the scene that unfolded
around us was staggering. We crept slowly ahead, hoping no one
came up behind us too fast. We finally found a pull-off where we
could park and appreciate the panorama. My friends all turned to
me—"What the hell is *this?*" they sputtered. "Why haven't you told
us about this before! Why didn't we come here years ago!"

"Well, uh . . . ," I sputtered through my own amazement,
"Because, I, well, because I had no idea this existed! I've never been
here before in my life!"

"And you call yourself 'Captain Nebraska'!" Bud said. "You
know, Rog, we have to do a story on this road. Kuralt said we should
do stories about unlikely beauty in unlikely places, and if there was

ever such a thing, this is it." So we did a story on that numberless county road north of Arnold, because for damned sure if Charles Kuralt said it, it had to be the right thing to do.

Charles Kuralt, the noted and beloved CBS News correspondent, was one of many unlikely and famous people who loved Nebraska not in spite of their lifelong exposure to the rest of the wonders of the world but because of it. Kuralt came through this state again and again, not simply because it lies on the road to almost everywhere else but because he *liked* it. In fact, he liked it a lot. He often said that one of the most beautiful highways in America is Highway 2 from Grand Island to Alliance, slashing directly across the Nebraska Sandhills. (I'll deal specifically with both the Sandhills and Highway 2 below, although I might argue with Kuralt a bit because I think maybe Highway 92 is even more spectacular.) He loved our eateries, from what he considered the best Chinese fare in America in Lincoln to the best steaks in Grand Island and Boelus. (We can skip his opinion of our coffee out of courtesy to Kuralt, coffee, and the tender ears of any children present.)

Never Get Over It

Thus we can perhaps find some comfort and even revenge for the carping of the insignificant zeros cited above like Looney, Minor, and Gray in the balancing fact that real luminaries have found this landscape exciting, challenging, and even endearing. It is understandable, I suppose, that native sons like Dick Cavett and Johnny Carson, who have left Nebraska for browner pastures, still nourish enormous affection for the state. Cavett frequently comes back to his home and roams Nebraska aimlessly, especially the Sandhills, simply soaking up a landscape he loves, so different from the Long Island and Manhattan contexts where he finds himself more often these days. But how do we explain why someone like Saul Steinberg, one of the most recognized illustrators of *The New Yorker* magazine, had an affection for our Sandhills and, according to reports, came here often to enjoy them?

In case the name *Saul Steinberg* doesn't ring a bell, he's the one who drew angular and eccentric cartoons, not so much funny as evocative. One of his most famous drawings, a *New Yorker* cover immortalized in a poster that now graces tens of thousands of walls around America but especially in Nebraska—including our upstairs hall—is *The New Yorker's View of America,* with an exaggeratedly large Long Island, trickling off into insignificant regions and landscapes to the west across the Hudson River . . . among them a prominent NEBRASKA in the middle of absolutely nowhere and nothing.

I imagine that if I'd had the chance to ask Steinberg what the attraction was that Nebraska had for him, the consummate New Yorker, he might have had trouble arriving at an answer. It's not that easy. One of America's foremost literary figures today, certainly one of our most prominent essayists, novelists, and screenwriters, is Jim Harrison, author of classics *Dalva* and *Legends of the Fall.* And Jim Harrison loves Nebraska. I am honored to consider Jim a good friend, and I'm almost afraid to ask him why he comes here when he can go pretty much anywhere in the world he cares to, why he seems to revel in our admittedly humble hospitality, cuisine, and intellectual company when he spends his time otherwise in the company of literary and artistic giants in Paris, or Livingston, Montana, or San Francisco, eating foods known only by their French names and drinking wines reserved in cellars by sommeliers only for the tables of guests with tastes worthy of them. Harrison seems content enough in the company of other aging and easily besotted bulls like my friends John Carter, Beef Torrey, or Bill Quigley, eating greasy burgers in Dannebrog or wolfing down prime beef in Lincoln. Harrison likes Nebraska, its people, and its landscape, and makes a point of at least mentioning them in his work.

There are tens of thousands, like Kuralt, Steinberg, and Harrison but with names you wouldn't recognize, who have also come to love Nebraska and consider the place at least a second home, if not a first. I don't know how many people have come even to my little village of Dannebrog, intending to visit, maybe spend a day, perhaps have some of Harriett's fabled fried chicken (only on Wednesdays), maybe take in the annual Danish Festival (first weekend of June)—or maybe they just had a front bearing go out and wound up enjoying the day stranded even more than they would have if they had made it to their high school reunion in Sioux Falls. And coming back. Sometimes again and again. Sometimes often enough that we get to know their names . . . Kathleen, Errol, Al. Sometimes those who come here to visit wind up settling in permanently. And that's just this little village I call home. I'm betting that every little burg across the state from Rulo to Harrison, Haigler to Wynot, hosts the same kind of honorary citizens, not lucky enough to live here but still fortunate to have discovered the place and found a Nebraska niche where they can be comfortable.

So those of us who do love Nebraska and the Plains are not alone, and I'm not at all sure we should care about those who don't. I certainly don't. This book is for those of you who do. And if you don't, I can only wonder why you have bothered to read this far.

So Who's This "Me"?

My license plate and e-mail address declare my allegiance and love— CAPTNEB . . . "Captain Nebraska, fighting non-Plains regionalisms wherever they may raise their ugly heads." I have to be careful not to get too carried away, I know. I once remarked that all I needed in my role as Nebraskaland's caped crusader was the cape, and the next thing I knew a finely tailored red cape saying CAPTAIN NEBRASKA was hanging in my closet.

I guess that kind of arrogance alone deserves some explanation, not to mention the gall of titling this book *My Nebraska*. I was born and raised in Lincoln, a 100 percent German Russian lad in a home of very modest income. My father was a laborer and eventually a Class A stationary steam engineer at the Goodyear factory; my mother was a housewife, which in those days was considered a noble occupation, and occasionally a part-time domesticate. I attended grade school with such notables as Charles Starkweather and high school with Dick Cavett and Sandy Dennis. I spent four undistinguished years studying languages at the University of Nebraska, in part in what became a pattern of indignant reaction in my life after a high school teacher told me, quite justifiably I should note, that she would not admit me to a third year of German studies because I was "one of those people who are not endowed with the gift of tongues." I took some pleasure in returning to her classroom five years later to tell her I was now doing fairly well. In my German classes. But also in my Latin, Icelandic, Old Norse, French, and Hebrew classes.

I was a terrible student in high school and at the university. The only way I survived was by the good fortune that our home in Lincoln just happened to be directly across the street from Dr. William Pfeiler's home, and he was the chair of the university's German Department. He took mercy on my parents and me and nursed me along despite my lassitude. I found other kind hearts in professors like Robert Knoll in English and Paul Schach in German; their patience and tolerance must have been enormous. I'll admit it: I was a dumb, lazy lout. But I had found some intellectual fire in two places: first, in a curious cross-interest that arose in my idle time and in my studies, and second, in my part-time job shelving books at our city library.

My mother was not happy with me when I spent $12 of my meager savings on a guitar. I had been a colossal failure as a trumpet player. For three years in junior high school and another three in high school, I held something of a lock on the last chair in the band marching section, after all, and now here I was a couple years later spending money on a *guitar*. But some things were happening in my life, from the work songs of Harry Belafonte that were popular at the time and which I very much enjoyed to a course I took in German Romanticism, the period when the Grimm Brothers were collecting their folktales and Rousseau and Heine were finding charm and art in the songs and sayings of the common people.

The operative key to my mental machinery, as it turned out, is "the common people." While my people were all German, the Germans I had studied for all those years in university classes sure

weren't the same kind of German. My people didn't compose sym-
phonies, write classical dramas, or paint oils that were hung in galleries; they sang street songs at three-day weddings in the lower-class
area of Lincoln, put together lyrics that appeared in Lincoln's German
newspaper *Die Welt-Post,* and pieced quilts that won prizes at the
county fair. But here, now, in this thing called folklore, I found the
art of my people. And hey, it was for all the world like the kinds of
songs Harry Belafonte was singing . . . except in German! And *never*
about loading bananas!

I have always been an obsessive. I got into real trouble when I
was working at the city library because Miss Eschnauer, my work
supervisor, would find that my locker in the basement was jammed
full of books that should have been on the shelves and available for
the patrons. But, well, you know, I'd be shelving books, and I'd see
something I thought looked really interesting, so I would take it to
my locker and then home, as many as I could carry at a time. I would
get off onto one author, or one topic, and then I'd read every single
thing I could find by that person or about that topic. As a result,
while I was being a terrible student in school, I was one hell of a
scholar in my own bedroom.

And one of the things I found most fascinating was curiously one
of the things I found least interesting in class . . . history. More specifically, Nebraska history. Somehow, the drudges who taught history in
high school, mostly coaches who also begrudgingly dealt with a history class or two, and then the stuffy professors at the university, managed to make what I now knew was the most interesting thing in the
world into a plodding, boring grind. So now things seemed to be coming together for me, in a totally unexpected and probably not even
recognizable way. History . . . folklore . . . Nebraska . . . hmmm . . .

If you are getting the idea that I rarely had any idea what the
hell I was doing with my life, you are absolutely right. But even
stranger, as I was drifting along oarless in the torrent of life, I seemed
to be saved from disaster and moved precisely where I should be
going again and again by some invisible force. (Later I came to iden-

tify this Great Mysterious, as it is known to the Lakota and Omaha, in the metaphor of Coyote the Trickster—because just as surely as there is such a force, there is a wonderful and ironic sense of humor in play that other theological paradigms seem to have consistently, and lamentably, missed. But all that is for another book, maybe with a title like *My God*.)

An additional factor in what became me was that Doc Pfeiler put me to work in his department. It wasn't much, just supervising language laboratories for other undergraduates. But I found, for one thing, that I really enjoyed it. Moreover, I was good at it. Furthermore, while I had little internal motivation to study and learn, I sure didn't want to be humiliated in my lab sessions when asked questions about German by other students. So I studied hard for the first time in my life. And then I wound up as a graduate instructor teaching German and in 1958 was standing before my first class. I discovered then that I was not only good at teaching, I was damned good at teaching.

So I wound up being a German teacher. There followed a tumult of strokes of good fortune there simply is not room for here: a one-year teaching job at a beautiful little school, Dana College, in Blair, Nebraska, that expanded eventually to four years. By pure chance I met Vic Lane, a folk music enthusiast and German teacher too, who eventually put enormous faith in me, my work, and my teaching and hired me for his languages department at Nebraska Wesleyan University. I fell in with an eccentric (actually, to be honest, a total nut case) folksinger and folklore professor at the University of Colorado, John Greenway. He sent me off to the Folklore Institute at Indiana University. I worked there in the library and again wound up checking out more books than the patrons, including a mimeographed copy of some WPA Federal Writers' Project papers titled "Nebraska Folklore," made up of material collected by fieldworkers during the 1930s. As a result, I was immersed up to my eyeballs—actually, way over my head—in Nebraska folklore, putting the Federal Writers' Project materials in a manuscript that then appeared as my first book, *A Treasury of*

Nebraska Pioneer Folkore, in 1966. And my new obsession became writing and publishing.

I continued in this direction through the arrival of children, the pain of a betrayed marriage, financial struggle, and the confusion that is simply, I now realize, a part of life. And yet for all that, the asset side of my life ledger continued to outbalance the debit side—so dramatically, in fact, that at times it became laughable. (Good ol' Coyote . . . he's always there.) With a good fortune fall beyond any possibility of pure chance, I got a job at the University of Nebraska, where I could focus on teaching nothing but folklore and Plains literature.

With extraordinary serendipity I was hired by the Smithsonian to do fieldwork in German folklore, and then by the National Endowment for the Arts. Friends appeared from nowhere to direct my interests and life as if by design—colleagues like Jay Anderson, Barre Toelken, Bob Byington, Bert Wilson, on and on and on. Sometimes it was students who became the teachers: Lynne Ireland, John Carter, Kay Young, Ann Billesbach . . . Despite my most determined resolution to never again expose myself unnecessarily to the pain of opening my heart, I found Linda Hotovy, and was instantly in love with one of the most precious gifts Coyote ever threw my way, a treasure I prize to this very day, now more than twenty-five years later. I don't want to get mushy here, but I have to acknowledge the incredible good fortune I have enjoyed in this life. After all, it has been in large part nothing more than poor luck that led me to my love for Nebraska, that has allowed me to indulge that passion, and that has given me ways to understand the peculiarities of my attraction for this place so many others find not particularly attractive.

There's not room in this one book to list it all. How the hell did I wind up from among all the people who adored Kuralt being taken under his tutelage and given the incredible opportunity of saying to the entire nation what I thought, what I loved, what I was passionate about, in almost 200 "Postcard from Nebraska" essays I wrote and hosted on camera for his CBS News award-winning *Sunday Morning* show? How, by sheer accident, did I wind up getting the absolutely perfect and precious bit of ground I have here at the edge of Dannebrog and the Nebraska Sandhills at precisely the right point in my life? By what incredible good fortune was I adopted as a brother by Alfred Gilpin Jr. and brought into intimate contact with the Omaha people I now call my own? Why have the people I admire most in this world like Mick Maun and Dick Day come to be my friends . . . or even more preposterously, like Louie LaRose and Chuck Trimble, come to be my relatives? Not least of all, how did I avoid paying the consequences I most assuredly had coming for all the thoroughly stupid things I did throughout the years? I cannot for the life of me imagine. Coyote, I guess. It's the only explanation that makes sense.

Dar Roger, Dar Hat Iver Di Rache Uf

But the point here is not my own story or the good fortune that has graced it, but how it explains my feelings about My Nebraska. A less obvious product of my lifestyle has been my opportunity during a good part of my years to travel the world, the country, and best and most of all, My Nebraska. I was not just a sedentary desk- and classroom-bound professor; through my work with the National Endowments, the Smithsonian, various museum and educational consultancies and appointments, and especially a lifetime of speaking engagements, I spent many days on the road, and more precisely on the back roads. I spoke at teachers' conferences, customer appreciation banquets, centennial celebrations, agricultural implement shows, meetings, conferences, conventions . . . you name it, I was in attendance, always at the head table, always ready and able to say what I wanted to say about Nebraska. Nebraska history, Nebraska folklore, Nebraskans . . . ready to hear more stories, it was all grist for my mill, and I ground away at it with all my might.

I was once in my university office sorting through student evaluations of my classes the previous semester. A couple of student-friends were there with me, so when I came across a form on which the student had written "Being in this class was more like being in an audience than in a class," I could ask my friends what they thought it meant. Was that an insult, or a compliment, or . . . or what? It was Dan Newton who gave me the best opinion, and one that I have treasured ever since. He said, "Well, Rog, actually, being in your classes isn't exactly like being in a class *or* an audience. It's more like being in a congregation."

Point well taken. I am not just talking about something I know about, or even just something I care about. When I talk about Nebraska and Nebraska folklore, I deliver fire-and-brimstone gospel about the passion of my life, something I want to share simply because I find it consuming but also because I think it's something everyone should find consuming—especially Nebraskans or anyone who aspires to be a Nebraskan.

That's what this book is about, too. It is meant for Nebraskans. I don't know how much of what you read here is going to be useful to you, but then it's not about facts and information. What I want to do is (1) express my own passion about what Dick Gray called "this hulking giant" and (2) hope that in at least some small degree some of that passion rubs off on you or reinforces a passion you might have been just a trifle embarrassed by up to now.

Besides, my mother was once mightily offended when one of my elderly German aunts from Lincoln's North Bottoms made the comment about me, *"Dar Roger, dar hat iver di Rache uf!"* (That Roger, he always has his big trap open!) When she told me that, her teeth clenched in indignation, I laughed and said, "Well, Mom, you have to admit, she's not all that wrong, if you think about it. Dar Roger . . . he does always have his big Rache uf!" And this just goes to show you that if I don't corner you into listening to one of my fiery sermons, I'm going to get you in print. Every time.

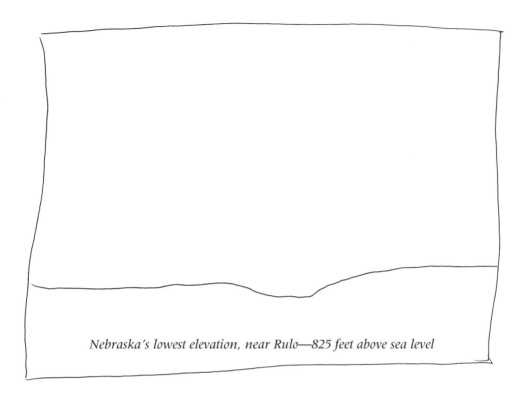

Nebraska's lowest elevation, near Rulo—825 feet above sea level

CHAPTER TWO

What Is Nebraska?

Now that I have covered to a fare-thee-well the *first* word of this book's title, *My,* I turn my attention to the second: *Nebraska.* (I know what you're thinking: *It's about time!*) Nebraska is not an easy thing to define. Only one of her boundaries is natural, the Missouri River, and you can understand how that came to be, because that most powerful and mighty of North American waterways wouldn't be easy to ignore or deny. It held up the press of the frontier for a long time on its eastern banks and even today is something of a barrier to transportation and travel, although those of us who whiz across it in automobiles on an interstate bridge may scarcely notice it, one heck of a departure from the Indians and frontiersmen who not all that long ago stood on the bank at the river's edge, looking across that incredible expanse of boiling, roiling water. Tell you what: By way of an assignment for our next class (there is still something of the professor in me, I guess), the next time you are in Sioux City, or Blair, or Omaha, or Nebraska City, make your way down to the edge of the Missouri River. It's not all that hard to do if you put even a modest effort into it. One of my favorite places to do this is right out the door of my favorite hotel in this world, the Marina Inn in South Sioux City. (Be sure you get a room on the river side so you can look out across the water all night long and think about Lewis and Clark coming up that very same water, or steamboats struggling, snagging, and sinking . . . right there. The only thing bad about the elegant Marina Inn, in my opinion, is that sooner or later you have to turn out the lights and go to sleep. I can imagine sitting up all night watching the river.)

Anyway, there wasn't much choice but to make the Missouri River Nebraska's easternmost boundary. But then beyond the Wide Missoori, as the song goes, there aren't many landmarks to use as political boundaries. So in order to divvy up the land into manageable chunks, politicians in Washington, DC, simply drew some lines on pieces of paper and hoped to God they hadn't done something really, really stupid. In fact, Nebraskans are invariably amused to see early maps of the state. Some depictions of the Nebraska Territory engulf Wyoming, the Dakotas, Kansas, and even Montana! My favorite is an 1862 Johnson and Ward map of "Nebraska, Dakota, Colorado, & Kansas" in my own personal Nebraska map collection that shows a Nebraska of roughly its present boundaries, clearly recognizable, except for an obscenely long panhandle, which extends unbroken all the way across Wyoming and right to Utah. I love that one, and I think we should put some major efforts into restoring the state to that configuration. The thing is, some people in the Nebraska Panhandle complain that they don't get their proper share of attention from the state capital in Lincoln or the population and economic center in Omaha, so they petition now and again to secede from this state and append themselves to Wyoming, putting them much closer to their new capital of Laramie. Well, if we simply extended the state all the way across Wyoming to Utah, communities like Scottsbluff, Gering, Kimball, and Henry would be smack in the *middle* of the state. I don't see how anyone could complain about that.

But seriously, folks, it's pretty hard to tell when you cross the state line into South Dakota, Wyoming, Kansas, or Colorado. (Don't let the different colors of the states on some maps confuse you about that, as they did me in my childhood. I can't tell you how disappointed I was when we first crossed into Wyoming and there was no distinguishable change in the color. This was one of the first indications I had that official information is not always reliable information.)

Which is to say, that area that is called Nebraska is pretty much an arbitrary entity that might just as well have been defined by some guy holding a pen against a piece of paper with his eyes closed. Or perhaps more accurately, some guy with a T-square. I have always been grateful that at least we are not one of the hopelessly unimaginative "rectangle" states: Wyoming, Kansas, the Dakotas, and Colorado. Even though Nebraska defies nature with boundaries following no particular phenomenon (other than the Missouri River) existing in nature, and all the boundaries other than the Missouri are relentlessly rectilinear, we at least aren't simply an extension of the other states. Nebraska's political boundaries manage to form jarring disjunctures with the boundaries of other states, our lines never quite matching up with those of others. There is that shrugged shoulder to the east, the defiant Panhandle to the west, forming a silhouette that clearly distinguishes Nebraska from every other state in the Union. If there is an official geometric term for Nebraska's distinctive profile, I don't know what it is.

Defining Defining

I have long been interested in the nature of defining . . . words, regions, states, ideas. It's not an easily understood process, and while definitions are meant to explain what exists, all too often people who

don't know better come somehow to understand that it is the definitions that set the rules, not the realities the definitions are meant to
describe. Some benighted souls think of the dictionary, therefore, as
being a kind of rule book, when it is in reality a catalog of stabs at
giving some kind of idea of what a word can or might mean, or once
meant. A word definition tries to draw lines around a bunch of the
most common ideas implied by the word; it is not an official decree of
what that word shall mean. Nebraska is defined by lines drawn on
paper by someone or another, or more likely a committee, with no
idea whatsoever what was inside or outside those lines, or if the lines
had anything whatsoever to do with what was on one side or the
other. That is to say, Nebraska's boundaries (again, other than the
Missouri) have nothing to do with anything.

While that complication may be discouraging for those who prefer certainty, believe me, it could be worse (which, by the way, is yet
another of my suggestions for a new motto for our state, and one I
am particularly fond of: "It Could Be Worse"). There could be no
boundaries at all, which depressingly would be far more accurate and
reflect the true nature of the Plains.

The thing is, there is another way of defining things besides setting boundaries: You can describe the nature of something by designating not where its edges are but rather what is at its heart, its
center, its most common or prevalent focus and locus, away from
which the nature of this thing slowly fades and dissolves into something else. For example, consider the "boundaries" of the regions considered the home ground of the various Plains Indian tribes before
the white man imposed his infernal, incomprehensible, and madden-
ingly illogical straight lines and right angles.

It was this feature of the white man's culture that Indians
found—and to some degree still find—utterly disorienting. The Indian
world is curved and round . . . round tipis, round earth lodges, round
religion, round dances, round round round . . . But the white man
considers anything other than straight and right-angled to be crazy
(note the finger spiraled around an ear to signal nuttiness) or even

dishonest: "*straight* and narrow, *straight* shooting, *straight* guy" versus "*crooked* politician." Look around you. If you are in a white man's context, everything around you is laid out in straight lines and right angles—the ceiling tiles, the floor mat, the desk, the shelves, the windows, the room, the halls, the buildings, the streets. That sort of relentless rectilinearity would have been unthinkable in the Indian world.

The city of Lincoln's pride is that it has the longest straight main street in the world, running almost from the Missouri River in the east, at the town of Union, 60 miles west to an intersection north of Milford, straight as an arrow. Have you ever noticed that as you travel our north–south highways and roads, again laid out in a ruthlessly square grid, every so often there is a jog a few hundred yards to one direction or the other? That's because of the problems that arise from imposing a square grid on a round earth. No kidding. Try pasting a sheet of grid paper smoothly on a basketball. Doesn't work. But nothing was going to stop the inexorable march of the white man's T-square and ruler, not even the unavoidable shape of the earth! Nowhere is that problem more evident than it is on the Plains and in Nebraska, because there's not much to get in the way of a straight line.

Not Edges but Centers

If you look in some history books or textbooks dealing with the Plains, you may find a map showing these Indian territories; the image is a fairly common one, even today, even considering that it is utterly wrong. A spider's web of lines swirls across the state, and in the oddly shaped boxes and triangles there are the words OMAHA, LAKOTA, PAWNEE, OTO, PONCA, and maybe CHEYENNE-ARAPAHO. Okay. Well, that seems clear enough.

But therein lies the fallacy of that map: There never was such clarity. What you see on the page before you is a total fantasy reflecting no sort of reality at all. No Indian ever stepped up to a line running over a hill, down along a creek, over a ridge, and through a copse and demonstrated his defiance to the tribe occupying the land across that line by sticking one foot over it, tapping a toe several times, and yelling tauntingly "Nyah nyah nyah nyah! Pawnee are party-poopers! And I laugh at the sanctity of your property lines, even if you did just pay a bundle to have them resurveyed last year!" That's not the way it worked. There were no lines designating tribal territories. Not straight ones, not curvy ones, not even vague or disputed ones. There were none. *Nada, nichts, rien* . . . A tribe's "territory" was defined by its center of power, away from which the group's hegemony gradually faded out in all directions until it blended slowly, inexorably, indistinctly, utterly without delimitation into some other tribe's "territory." No lines *ever*. No boundaries.

A bunch of young Omaha Tribe hotheads might decide that it would be fun to put together a raid on a Pawnee village, for example. Confident, brave, even arrogant and reckless here in the heart of their home village, in the center of their hunting lands, deep in their country, far from any other tribes' home villages, they would organize a raiding party of some friends, some experienced warriors, maybe a wise elder or two, and some youngsters who needed to get out of the village, out from under their parents' thumbs, and count a few coups themselves to establish a reputation that would make a favorable impression with some of the young ladies of the village. They would get their weapons and traveling and warring gear together and announce their intentions. There would be a pep rally to build up spirits, demonstrate intentions, and rally the troops, and the band would set out in a triumphant, glorious, and bold show of pomp and circumstance in the direction of those accursed Pawnee. No one . . . noooo ooooone! . . . is afraid of the wretched Pawnee!

The first night on the warpath, they would set up camp, build a good campfire, sing war songs, shout threats and boasts, maybe tell of some previous victories on other such raids, and then go to sleep full of confidence and bravado. The next day, farther from their village, a bit closer to the Pawnee, they would show more caution, and at that night's camp the fire might be lower and the singing less boisterous.

The third night out the fire would be damped before "Taps" was blown, one person might be designated to stay up and keep watch just in case a similar Pawnee war party was somewhere in the area, stories were told in quieter tones, and sleep was almost certainly a bit less easy. The fourth night out there was no fire, only hushed conversation, fitful sleep, and sentries set at a distance to detect any enemy approach. The fifth night there was no sleep or fire, rations were eaten cold, there was little conversation, and the guards were almost as many as the sleepers.

Now the party moved quietly and cautiously through the day, avoiding hilltops where they might be spotted. Scouts traveled ahead of the main body, creeping to the top of each rise to make sure another camp was not being approached. And that night, with the Pawnee villages now within easy approach, no one slept, no one talked, and the new, would-be warriors in the company were warned about the importance of stealth and obedience to orders. The time for noisy boasting was over for the moment, and everyone knew it.

Now they were no longer within Omaha lands; they had slowly but surely transitioned without the crossing of any particular threshold from Omaha land into Pawnee country. In fact, even the veterans couldn't be sure exactly where the balance of power had shifted from one year or season to another because it was all in constant flux: Sometimes the Omaha were particularly strong—perhaps because of an easy winter, or a good hunt, or some new technology—and their scope of their power had expanded even without them knowing this with any certainty. Sometimes the Pawnee were stronger, for the same or other reasons. Or a tribe was weakened by hunger, illness, or simply bad luck, and they grew weaker at even shorter distances from the center of their power.

When the Omaha raiders launched their quick, mostly symbolic raid on the Pawnee village, it was their audacity that scored the points, the fact that they were exercising power far away from their own gravitational center and precisely at the heart of that of the Pawnee. They "counted coup"—little more than an insulting slap across the "enemy's" face, perhaps stealing a horse or a parfleche of dried meat hanging on a rack outside an earth lodge entry—and retreated quickly toward the safety of their own "territory." As the Omaha ran from the Pawnee earth lodges to the Missouri, the Pawnee might pursue them, hot in their passion and courage here at the very heart of their own psychic strength. As the chase moved farther and farther away from the Loup Rivers and the Pawnee village and ever closer to the Omaha villages, the confidence and power of the Omaha grew ever stronger. And that of the Pawnee waned. Until finally the Omaha confidence was greater than that of the Pawnee, the balance tipped, and the Pawnee turned and retreated to their village, probably to brew up the courage to organize a raiding party of their own on the Omaha villages.

The closer the Omaha war band came to its home village, the brighter its evening fires were, the louder its victory songs and cries, the more boisterous the celebrations, until it arrived back home and marched triumphantly into town to receive its well-deserved accolades for courage and skill. Without ever once having crossed a line of any sort whatsoever at any point in their travels, the Plains of their world having no lines.

The Center of Everything

One of the reasons the world of the Plains Indian tribes operated in this manner was because this is the very nature of the Plains. There are few lines, and even where there were geographic designators like the Platte River, these were and to some degree still are more ephemeral than we white folks might imagine. There is a Nebraska, but its boundaries on a map have nothing to do with anything. Only the center counts when it comes to honest definitions. And Nebraska is in the center of the Great Plains of North America.

It is that center out of which the Plains character radiates in all directions, fading imperceptibly into other regions that surround it . . . across the shortgrass and tallgrass "boundary" to the woodland prairies to the east, the mountain fortress to the west, the Canadian tundra in the north, south to the Mexican desert. Nebraska is smack in the center, like the continent's keystone. There is an old joke here that runs, "Nebraska is in the middle of everything . . . a thousand miles from the San Francisco Opera, another thousand from the Museum of Modern Art." And yet like so much humor, that jibe has a good deal of truth to it. We *are* in middle of Everywhere, which is to say, in the middle of Nowhere. It was the Lakota Black Elk who saw the reality of it all with stunning clarity: When John Neihardt asked him in what way Harney Peak in the Black Hills was the Center of the Earth in Lakota cosmology, he explained that we live on a globe, and on a globe . . . *everywhere* is in the "Center." And nowhere is the center. That is, our white man view of things in a linear relationship with clear boundaries simply does not reflect the reality. Certainly not the reality of the Great Plains.

Nebraska is not a Hinterland but a *Mittelgrund*. We are not behind, removed, or remote from anything. We are in the exact center of the arena. Nebraska is the pivot not just for the Great Plains, or for the United States, but for the continent. My God, are we important, or what? No wonder we're the target of less fortunates in such backwaters as Texas and Detroit! And if you are still a doubter, I invite you to come visit my little town of Dannebrog, Nebraska. Step into the town tavern, right in the middle of the main drag, Mill Street, and order up one of the best burgers and draft root beers you'll find anywhere. Then sidle over toward the front door and lift or push aside with a casual foot the doormat . . . yeah, there . . . close to the door, over on the left side as you look out. See that plaque embedded in the floor? It's pretty well worn so you may have to bend over or even get down on your knee to read it. Can you make out the words now? It says, GEOGRAPHIC CENTER OF WESTERN CIVILIZATION. And that makes it official as far as I'm concerned.

Now, here's where I am going to run into a lot of trouble, because there are still well-intentioned but hopelessly misguided souls out there—some of them even really smart and professorial, with PhDs and everything—who insist on trying to define the Great

Plains by drawing lines around the region. I don't know how to say
this more plainly or simply: There are no lines. Not only are there no
lines, any effort to draw lines is nonsensical. Lines have nothing to do
with what the Great Plains are. If you want to know what the Great
Plains look like, stand somewhere in a pasture in the middle of
Nebraska and look around. That is the Plains. You are at the heart of
it and what you feel is the Plains. If you can't get to Nebraska, then
get as close as you can—Kansas, South Dakota . . . Every foot you
move away from that plaque in the floor of the Dannebrog Tavern,
you are just a touch farther away from what the Plains are, but the
closer you are to that plaque, the closer you are to the Plains. If
you're in Des Moines or Laramie, you're not on the Plains. If you are
in Salina or Sioux Falls, you're sort of on the Plains. All other under-
standings of what constitutes the North American Great Plains are
misunderstandings, believe me. When you see lines, disregard them.
They're nonsense.

As you drive westward out of Minneapolis, or Des Moines, or
Columbia, or eastward out of Denver, Cody, or Helena (hopefully not
on an interstate highway), you will see the landscape around you
slowly morphing into . . . the Great Plains. Somewhere around
Ogallala you can pretty much say you are "on the Plains," and about
the time you reach Omaha, you are well on your way out. If you are
a white man, you will probably feel some discontent with the notion
of no-line geography; if you have any Indian blood in you—you
know, that Cherokee princess your great-grandfather married—you
will not just understand what I am saying but figure that's the way it
should have been all along anyway.

The regions within the state of Nebraska are exactly the same
boundaryless entities. Where do the Missouri River Valley and its rich
alluvial bottomlands fade into the tallgrass woodlands? I suppose
somewhere around the top of the valley as you climb up out of it
through the washes and canyons. The Sandhills, the largest sand
dune area in the Western Hemisphere, in this entire half of the
world, blend into the Pine Ridge to the north and the Platte and Loup

River complexes to the south pretty much the same way: a slight rise
to a valley wall or a declivity into a greener valley. That's it. There's
not much by way of dramatic landmarks to signal the transitions . . .
fewer or more trees, cornfields becoming pastureland, bluebirds
growing even rarer, or eagles and Sandhill cranes appearing . . . Cacti
and Sandhill tortoises can be spotted if you look closely at the road-
sides, or suddenly there are no more antelope or sagebrush.

Terms of Endearment

Even those of us who have lived here all our lives don't quite know
what to call ourselves. When I was younger it seemed that everyone
wanted to refer to our region as the "Midwest," but then Ohio and
Indiana started using the phrase, wanting, I suppose, to associate
themselves with that magic phrase *the West* but looking, if you ask
me, pretty silly in the effort. Ohio and Indiana are not by any stretch
of the imagination *the West*, let alone the *Middle* of the West. A term
like *Mid-East* would make more sense for that region. There are no
end of places that consider themselves to be "Where the West Begins"
(and, you might note, not a single pretender to the title "Where the
East Begins!"), which may be a good way to fool tourists but doesn't
express any sort of reality, there being no place "where the West
begins." I suppose you could make a case for the Missouri River's
west bank—"the Nebraska Coast" as it was called in the nineteenth
century—being "where the West begins," or, as another assertion had
it, the 100th Meridian (once thought to be Cozad, Nebraska's, main
street, but displaced by modern surveys somewhere outside that frontier town). But that doesn't make a lot of sense to me, even though a
line here comes close to a divide between the tallgrass and shortgrass
prairies, the farmers and the ranchers. But then the population east of
that line would be ten times that to the west, with forty-two state senators coming from the eastern half, four from the west! That doesn't
seem fair.

Or maybe a better dividing line between East and West should
be the 98th Meridian running, significantly, through *Central* City,

Nebraska, but I could just as logically and reasonably advertise that the West begins just west of our back door, somewhere between the yard fence and Linda's studio door.

For my own convenience and by way of reflecting my own vision of our state (remember . . . the title of the book is *My Nebraska,* so I get to set the terms!), I will refer in these pages to Nebraska's regions as

1. *The Panhandle,* that area projecting out of the larger bulk of the state from about Ogallala westward.
2. *The Sandhills* (and I don't care about dictionary protocol—I capitalize the word and make it one unit out of respect and love for it, the same way I generally slug anyone who pronounces the word *coyote* as *kai-OAT-ee,* an outrageous sissy-pants blasphemy, rather than the God-given official pronunciation *KAI-oat*).
3. *The Missouri River East,* pretty much the first one or two tiers of counties along the eastern edge of the state.
4. *The South Center,* mostly the Republican Valley from the Missouri River East to the Panhandle, south of the Platte.
5. *The North Center,* from the Platte north, between the Missouri River East and the Sandhills—in other words, the Loup River complex where it is not within the Sandhills.

What with the areas being undefined by any actual physical features, there are a lot of places that obviously don't fit. The Pine Ridge doesn't quite belong in the Sandhills. You could argue that the Platte Valley is a region unto itself since it differs from the areas immediate to it and is even more cohesive now strung together on I–80, much as it always was on the railroads before, the Oregon-Mormon-Oxbow-Overland Trails before that, and primeval Indian and bison tracks before them.

Even more dramatically and significantly, I can't honestly see or say that Lincoln and Omaha—especially Omaha—fit into Nebraska and the Plains at all. No offense, but I'm only being honest here, and I presume I am among friends. Those two places are the closest we come to urban life, and urban life is not really the nature of the Plains or Nebraska. When I grew up in Lincoln, insofar as I grew up at all, it was a small town but even then, it was an education center, with clean industry like insurance companies and government. Not really Nebraska stuff.

About Omaha

And Omaha . . . well, Omaha actually has black people! And factories! A symphony and crime! Omaha is a *river city* in a region that has neither rivers nor cities otherwise. Omaha has traffic and Italians. People honk at you in Omaha, and when they wave at you, they are not always wishing you a long life and a nice day. One good flood, a little shifting of alluvial silts, some minor changes of lines drawn on pieces of papers, and most of the city east of 20th Street would be in Iowa. As it is, it might not even require that much trouble. Eppley Airfield could wind up back in Iowa without so much as inconveniencing the Iowa State Patrol—which already has representation on the Iowa lands around the airport, on the *west* side of the Missouri, *within* what is only nominally called Nebraska at that point. You have to drive through Iowa property and past Iowa radar speed traps just to get from downtown Omaha to the Omaha airport. A lot of sense *that* makes.

I suspect that some folks in Omaha might huff and puff at this suggestion, but there are others who desire this change with all their hearts if not their official statements. In fact, a sizable proportion of Omahans—I prefer the nineteenth-century pioneer designation for those who live in Omaha as "Omahogs" and "Omahens," but that terminology seems to be presently out of favor—would rather be annexed to Connecticut or upstate New York than Iowa. When I was doing my "Postcards from Nebraska" essays for CBS's *Sunday Morning,* I could pretty much count on regular complaints—always from Omaha—that my standard on-camera costume of Key overalls was an insult to our state because, they said (and this always knocked me out), it made Nebraska look . . . *rural!*

No kidding, that's what they wrote to me and even had the nerve to tell me to my face. The first couple of times this happened, all I could do was sputter and spit in complete disbelief, but eventually I managed to deal with it by suggesting that the complainant get into a car the next weekend and drive in a straight line north, south, or west for 50 miles . . . and then write and tell me what they saw. Wow! I'll be damned! Nebraska *is* rural! Who'd have guessed?

Then I would suggest that this same person pack up a suitcase before long and venture out for a weekend west out one of my favorite highways, Nebraska 2 or 92, for six hours. Just get on Center Street and drive west to Arthur or Alliance. I don't know if anyone from Omaha ever followed my advice. I suspect that if they did, they just withered away and never could bring themselves to return to Omaha's city limits.

Not everyone, but a lot of people in Lincoln and Omaha (1) are embarrassed by being rural and Nebraskan and (2) do what they can to give the appearance and manner of being somewhere else. They don't want to be rural, they don't want to be agricultural, they don't want to be Nebraskan. They think they can buy a new persona and therefore new respect by investing in a bigger football program at the university, thereby making themselves even more laughable because only an idiot thinks football has anything to do with a university, where—unless the institution is run by fools—the priority ought to be education. These sorry My Nebraskans deny the weather, the landscape, the people, the nature, the culture, the folklore, and history of the state in hopes of somehow transforming themselves into something they clearly are not. It's sad, if you think at all about it.

What's even more sad is that as I've traveled the world and presented Nebraska and the Plains to a larger national and international audience, I have discovered that the rest of the world envies what we have here, even while some Nebraskans deny and reject it: low population, productive agriculture, crisp skies, distinct seasons, a rich history, an incredible literary heritage, on and on and on . . . You won't get any of that from me. I love Nebraska not for what it might be or might have been, for what it could or should be, what I wish or dream, but for what it is right here and now.

Regionalities

When I sold some land in Colorado—the price of gas went up, the speed limit went down, a marriage dissolved, and, as Linda put it so well, in Colorado you can't see any scenery because it's all cluttered up with trees and mountains—I was looking for something in Nebraska, where I knew I would be comfortable. Something on the Platte River, maybe, or in the Sandhills. As so often is the case, things didn't quite work out that way, and while I may have been initially skeptical because I wasn't getting quite what I thought I wanted, as the great British philosopher Mick Jagger once said, "You cain't always get what you wa-hunt . . . you cain't always get what you wa-hunt . . . you cain't always get what you wa-hunt . . . but if you try some time, you just might find . . . you get what you neeeed!" I wound up on the Middle Loup River—a much better choice, as it turns out, because the Loup enjoys something a lot of Nebraska rivers don't have: water. I am not a farmer, but I live among farmers, and that's where I should and want to be. And while I'm not in the heart of the Sandhills, I'm at the very southeasternmost extension of that wonderful region. Our place is pure sugar sand and Sandhills biology, but from the top of our own sand dune behind the house, we can see the last of the Sandhills dunes to our east, Mumpumpey Hill.

So I take some pride and comfort in being no longer in Lincoln, a dubious Nebraska context as it is, and out here on the dividing line between ranch and farm, between Sandhills, North Center, and South Center, squeezed between sky and earth like a pumpkin seed squirted from between pinched thumb and forefinger.

While I insist that Nebraska is the heart of the continent's Great Steppes, that doesn't mean that it is therefore of a single character. My concept of how one defines such things, in fact, dictates that as the Plains taper away in all directions from that center, the dynamics are moving in *opposite* directions and therefore grow ever less alike.

This means that the hardwood forests of the Missouri River bottoms in the east of the state are dramatically different from the character of the Panhandle. Not only are the plants dramatically different, and the fauna and even the weather, but I honestly believe that the people who live there are different. You can see it even in the historical character of the First Nebraskans: The Omaha and Hochunk (aka Winnebago) were peaceful farmers, villagers, earth lodge people. And the Lakota and Cheyenne-Arapaho 400 miles to the west were nomadic tipi dwellers and fierce warriors. Just ask Brevet General George Armstrong Custer.

Something of that persists today. I simply don't believe that people west of where I am sitting at this very moment are the same as those to the east. As I sit here facing south out my study window, overlooking the sandy Loup River, I know that to my left, farmers predominate, and to my right, ranchers. But that occupational difference, in my opinion, is not so much the cause of differences as it is one of the products of the differences in geography. Just as weather clashes over the Plains, the warm, wet fronts from the Pacific and Gulf of Mexico meeting the dry, cold arctic fronts sweeping down from the north—meeting somewhere, I would guess, about 15 feet south of our back fence—so, too, do mentalities and personalities. Again and again in these pages, I qualify what I say with a caveat about where my point of reference is, because to one side of this central focus you may find one notion while to the other side of the spectrum the colors are dramatically different.

The first tier of counties along the Nebraska Coast, overlooking the Missouri River, were the first explored and visited by white European explorers. They are the oldest in terms of settlement: at the latest, the mid-nineteenth century. Even Nebraskans are often astonished to learn that the western part of the state wasn't opened for homesteading until 1904. While the west part of the state has a very short history—I have talked with *homesteaders* in Arthur and Arapahoe—east of Lincoln the frontier is practically archaeological. That first row of Nebraska counties along the Missouri River expects close to 30 inches of rain a year, while the westernmost row along the Wyoming and Colorado borders would not be surprised to get only a third of that. I have stumped a few of my university classes with the question "Where would you draw a north–south line to divide Nebraska's population in halves? (1) Grand Island, or (2) York?" The correct answer is "Neither of the above." Half of Nebraska's population lives east of Lincoln, in that first tier of counties along the Missouri River. We can fairly say that the land 50 miles west of the Missouri's banks is settled. West of that . . . well, we have yet to see how that works out. Time will tell.

The highest population density of most counties west of Grand Island occurred in 1904, when the area was opened for homesteading and settlers rushed in to take up residence on every quarter or half section on which they could throw up a quick shelter. Since then— only a century ago, after all—we have figured out that, well . . . uh . . . you can't survive on a quarter or half section of Sandhills or even high Plains ground. Nor on a full section, for that matter. Or, as it turns out, two sections. (For those of you who are used to measuring lots in square feet or ranchettes in square yards, a *section* is a square mile; that is, a square measuring 1 mile on all four sides.) And now we wonder about the viability of a family subsisting on ten sections. As a result, there are fewer and fewer residences, fewer and fewer people. We simply don't know how many people can make a living out here—if any. The most dramatic evidence I have ever had of this was when I once flew over the Sandhills late at night, after a long, hard, but fun-filled day with State Senators Loran Schmitt and Don Wesely. As we looked out the windows of the airplane, we saw something amazing and a bit chilling. What we saw was . . . nothing. No lights. None. Then one small cluster. And then again, pitch dark. On and on . . . nothing but pitch darkness. And this was on a deep winter night with the snow and wind buffeting our plane. Our mutual realization silenced our laughter: If something happened and this plane went down, we might not be found until spring, because there was no one down there to find us. Realities like this necessarily mold the personalities of the people who live with them.

The air is different from Nebraska region to region, too. That probably isn't noticeable as you drive across the state, but all you have to do is step out of an airplane onto the tarmac in Omaha, and then Grand Island, and then Scottsbluff to sense it. I could do that exercise blindfolded and know exactly where I am. The heat and cold feel different. The sky and colors are different, and yet all these things are different enough, too, from areas outside the Plains or farther from this center of gravity that what is Nebraska is clearly and still Nebraska, and what is not *is not*. It's a long way from one end of Nebraska to the other. Pretty much a world, in fact.

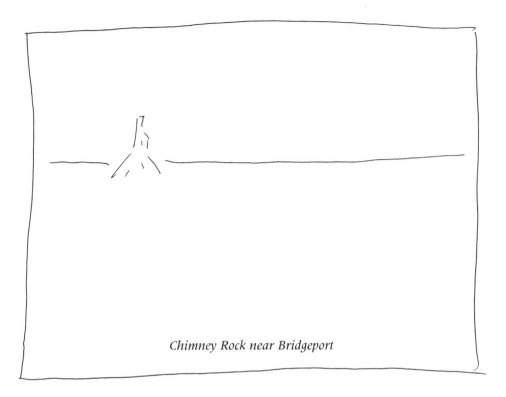

Chimney Rock near Bridgeport

CHAPTER THREE

Weather, Sky, and Seasons

Of all the features of the Great Plains and Nebraska that I am going to discuss in these pages, why on earth would I start with the weather? Because everything in Nebraska starts with the weather, that's why. Walk into any country tavern or cafe any day of the week or year and strike up a conversation. It won't be long—probably mere minutes— before the topic turns to the weather. Twenty years ago I took absolute glee at visitors' amazement that our local evening news opened with . . . the weather. That struck me as a declaration of Nebraskan-ness, but then the broadcasters figured out that we all watched the weather report and forecast, and then turned our televisions off. War reports, crime waves, impending plagues, even sports . . . all that is of no particular consequence to Nebraskans. All that counts to us is the weather. Everything else is ornamental.

Now broadcasters delay the weather until after reports on the purchase of new all-weather tires for the Gretna senior citizen handi-van, graphic coverage of the Husker first-team quarterback's diarrhea problems, and the opening of a macramé crafts shop. They do it because they know we true Nebraskans will sit through absolutely any amount of nonsense to get to the weather report.

Nothing amuses Nebraskans more than televised weather reports on news broadcasts on the East or West Coast or, even more hilariously, in Europe. "We expect some cloudiness in Yorkshire. Possible thunder in Kent. We have reports of the usual daily sprinkles in Aberystwith. Thus concludes today's weather broadcast. Sorry to have taken up so much of your time but we thought you'd want to know about that thunder . . ."

Man, when you get a weather report in Nebraska, you get a report to a fare-thee-well. I remember the time thirty years ago when I strolled into the Chew-'n'-Chat Café up in town and made two enormous mistakes. First, someone said to me, "So . . . how much rain did you get down at your place last night?" and I said obligingly, "Three-tenths of an inch."

Well, the place erupted in absolute uncontrollable hilarity. Scared the hell out of me. I wondered if maybe my fly was open or something. Once everyone gained their self-control, they explained that (1) they were amazed at my stupidity in answering the question at all (never . . . *never!* . . . be the first to give a rain gauge reading, because the first liar doesn't have a chance), but (2) even more idiotically, I had given the reading in—get ready to laugh until root beer comes out your nose—I had given it in *tenths!* In Nebraska rain doesn't come in tenths. It comes in hundredths. Always. I might just as well have said "About a third of an inch," or maybe "Seventy-six millimeters." I had exposed myself worse than if my fly *had* been open. I demonstrated that I was a city puke, maybe not even a true Nebraskan.

It Was the Best of Weather, It Was the Worst of Weather . . .

Probably the most tiresome cliché there is about weather is, "Yeppers, you gotta say that about San Diego [fill in any other place-name—*any* place-name apparently] . . . if you don't like the weather, just wait a minute!" Puh-*leez!* You don't even have weather if you don't live on the Great Plains. You may have *severe* weather . . . hurricanes in Florida, heat in Arizona, rain in Seattle . . . but take it from an expert, you don't have the variety and severity of weather we have here on the Plains. You may have the worst of one world, but we have the worst of all worlds. The common complaint when some event draws a smaller-than-hoped crowd is, "There are two problems with scheduling something in Nebraska: bad weather . . . and good weather." When the weather isn't so bad that it drives people into their storm cellars, well, then it's way too nice to go anyplace but out in the backyard to enjoy it.

What's more, the extremes of best and worst, good and bad weather often happen within one and the same week. Or day. Or hour. Predicting weather in Nebraska is a matter of rolling the dice. Another name for "meteorology" on the American Great Plains is *guesswork*. I have seen record lows and highs within days of each other. One morning classes were called off at the university in Lincoln because a blizzard had brought everything to a dead stop. I washed my car in the driveway that very afternoon. My buddy Dave and I once took my new Christmas canoe out for a trial float on a local lake . . . on February 29. We had to push our way through the ice to do it, but it was so hot, we finally shed our shirts to get some relief. At one point Dave stepped out of the canoe to push aside a huge floe of ice and fell into the water. He came up blue from the cold . . . and then complained all the way home about the pain of the sunburn he had gotten when he wasn't suffering from hypothermia. It has snowed every month of the year in Nebraska except July. I suspect it has snowed in July, too, but no one wrote it down. Or maybe it's just a matter of no one wanting to admit that they've seen snow in July. This past week a contractor was putting in some new windows for us, and everything seemed to be going wrong. He said, "Well, at least we don't have to worry about a hurricane"—this was during the disastrous destruction of New Orleans by Hurricane Katrina in 2005. Lovely Linda's response said a lot about her experience as a lifetime resident of Nebraska: "The day is still young."

Few weeks go by in Nebraska, and almost no months, without new weather records being set. Few of us think about the implications of that constant statistical revision, however. It means that we really don't know yet what the nature of this place is. We don't know yet how hot it can get here, or how cold, or how windy, how much snow or water we can get at any one time or in any one year, or how little, how . . . well, how anything. All we know is that whatever we have seen so far is only the beginning. One thing is certain: In our century-and-a-quarter tenure on the Plains, we ain't seen nothing.

Most residents of the Plains have become so accustomed to the severity of the region's meteorological conditions that it isn't easy to impress them. The most astonishing events happen, and a year later they are forgotten. For years Nebraska had the record (at Potter) of the largest hailstone ever recorded in North America, a steer-killing block of ice the size of a softball. Then to our disappointment—at least mine—Kansas took that record away from us. With typical Nebraska determination, however, just a couple of years ago we out-disastered Kansas when a monster hailstone fell near York, Nebraska, not all that far from our place here.

I love weather. Even extreme weather. My Omaha name is within the Konce or Wind Clan. (Isn't it interesting that the name *Kansas* means "wind"? As in the song by the group Kansas, "Dust in the Wind"? Oooh . . .) But the one thing that truly unsettles my stomach is tornadoes. I once wondered why I have never run across a Plains Indian story about tornadoes. I mean, surely they witnessed them, were impressed by them, and must have had something to say about them. So . . . ? Then I realized that there *are* stories about huge, mystic, powerful, terrifying gods called the Thunderers who crush humans with inexorable, inexplicable, unpredictable force, reaching down from the sky in destructive fury. Hmmm . . . sounds like tornadoes to me.

Tornadoes are horrifying. We spend many nights each year in the cellar under our stairs, cowering, worrying, listening to the wind and hail batter our house, worrying about ourselves, our friends, our family, praying that the Thunderers take mercy on us again this time. But even at that, even with the blizzards, rainstorms, straight winds, prairie fires, droughts, floods, hail, lightning . . . and tornadoes, I still count us in Nebraska to be lucky compared with people in the path of tsunamis and hurricanes, earthquakes and volcanoes.

I have been in storms with plum-size to tennis-ball-size hail on two different occasions, and you can take it from me, it is terrifying. My car was pounded to a pulp both times. I managed to maneuver a sleeping bag over the windshield in hopes of keeping it from caving in and then crawled into the backseat to avoid being killed if the windshield should give way. What surprised me and added to the horror of it was that out the car windows, I could see the hail hitting the ground . . . and then rebounding 10 or 12 feet into the air, and then falling again, doubling the chaos. A major tourist attraction of my little town of Dannebrog is the nationally renowned—well, okay, some people in Iowa know about it—National Liars Hall of Fame, a kind of tall-tale Smithsonian Institution. Last year someone generously donated to the Hall of Fame a box of golf balls the size of hailstones.

How Bad Was It?

That little gag line is more significant than you might think because it is representative of the traditional method of dealing with the brutality of Plains climate. It is a time-honored, effective way for human beings to deal with adverse conditions. It's a well-established principle of psychology that we laugh at things that bother us, frighten us, or haunt us. We can disarm even horrendous things—like weather—that threaten our health, welfare, and even lives with laughter. And that is why tall tales, especially about weather, have flourished on the Plains.

Tall tales have been common all around the world through all of time insofar as we know, but I would contend that no soil has been so fertile for the whopper as that of the Great Plains, at the heart of which is Nebraska. And that's because the basis of the tall tale is an extension of reality to the point of a ludicrous extreme: *It was so cold, I saw two cottontails pushing a jackrabbit trying to get him started . . . It was so hot, we turned on the furnace to cool it down . . . It was so dry, I saw three cottonwood trees following around a dog.* To compose an exaggeration that goes so far beyond the already ridiculous weather extremes of America's Great Plains—well, you really have to go some! The reality itself all too often approaches the ridiculous. As I write these words (July 2005), Chadron, Nebraska, set a record high temperature one day. Then in the same week, a record low. October 2, 2005, we had a new record high temperature for the day in Nebraska: ninety-five degrees. Exactly one year to the day from October 2, 2004, when we set a record low for the day: twenty-eight degrees.

Contrasting extremes like these are not at all unusual on the Plains. In fact, it would seem strange to live in this region for *any* length of time in which the limits are not reset to even wilder extremes. That seems to be the pattern: The record low temperature in North Dakota was sixty-two degrees below zero, set in January of 1936. And the record high of 121 was set in July . . . of 1936. Six months after the Plains reached a temperature that would earn the respect of Inuit in the Arctic, poor Scandinavian immigrants in North Dakota withered in a Saharan inferno. I love to point out when citing these extremes that the absolute temperature range in those six months was 181 degrees. Between freezing (32 degrees Fahrenheit) and boiling (212 degrees) there are only 180 degrees. The range of temperature extremes for North Dakota is more than the range between freezing and boiling. I mean, good grief . . . is that nutty or what?

Now, Nebraska's record in this regard is respectable enough: A record high of 118 degrees has been reported on several occasions at sites from Geneva and Minden in the South Center to Hartington way up in the northeastern corner of the state; the record low for the state is minus forty-seven degrees near Bridgeport, Nebraska. And we have only been keeping records for a bit over a century. Imagine what this place can deal out in a period of, say, 1,000 years. What can our children expect? What did the Pawnee and Lakota experience? Highs of 150? I wouldn't doubt it. Lows of seventy below? Years with less than 2 inches of rain? More than 60 inches? Maybe 30 inches . . . in one day? None of these possibilities can be ruled out.

I never cite or consider the savagery of the long catalog of records of both heat and cold set on the Plains in 1936 without thinking of my dear mother. I was born in 1936, in the middle of the most brutal weather year yet recorded here; she and my father didn't have so much as the $2.00 it would have taken to buy a fan, but as she—a true Nebraskan—says, "It wasn't so bad. We were all in the same boat after all. No one had anything so none of us knew any different."

No wonder then that Plains humor runs to narratives like the one about the three Swedish brothers who migrated to and settled in America, one in Pennsylvania, one in Colorado, and one in Nebraska. And as fortune would have it, all three died on the same day, and in accordance with their wishes they were cremated together. After an hour the Swede from Pennsylvania was ashes, and after two the Swede from Colorado was gone. But after a week and a half the Swede from Nebraska stepped out and said, "You know, another week of weather like this and we won't have a corn crop this year!"

In my opinion—and I think I am theologically correct here—the tallest tale of all in Nebraska starts something like this: "The average temperature for this date is . . ." Or maybe, "The normal rainfall for July in Nebraska is . . ." Nothing, but nothing, is more idiotic when talking about Nebraska weather than averages, normals, usuals, and ordinaries. The usual, average, normal for Nebraska *is* the extreme.

And what's more (and what's worse, I might add) is that we still don't have a very good idea of what those extremes might be. As I mentioned before, new records are set for all manner of meteorological phenomena every week. Wouldn't you think that by now, after a century and a half of observation, we'd have some idea of what the parameters are? Well, you might think that, but you'd be wrong. We simply do not know what the limits are. Just when we think things are as bad as they are going to get . . . they get worse. Man, how long is this going to go on?

If the tall-tale teller is then going to exaggerate what God has already taken to the ridiculous, he has to push even farther—hence the extraordinary accomplishments of Plains mendacity (which I have vainly tried to introduce as an Olympic sport, by the way). And then the unavoidable question has to be . . . why? Why would you *want* to exaggerate what is already beyond the ridiculous? Why would you emphasize what is clearly the very worst feature of a landscape? What is funny about making the already miserable perfectly dreadful? Nineteenth-century booster materials distributed to lure settlers out onto the Nebraska Plains sure didn't take this approach. Their exaggerations tended toward mitigation of the extremes; they wanted to make this place seem like a heaven on earth that we had somehow missed noticing in the past. Crops flourished here . . . plant nails and harvest crowbars! Toss out that corn seed but then you'd better jump back before the plants rocketing out of the ground catch you by your overall straps and carry you so far into the ether, you'll have to survive on biscuits shot up to you from the barrel of a 12-gauge shotgun wielded by a do-gooder on the ground!

The Fact of the Fiction

One gorgeous spring morning we enjoyed a casual Sunday breakfast with our old friends John and Annie and were about to see them off on their way back to their home in Lincoln from our central Nebraska farm. As we said our good-byes in our kitchen, the room suddenly went dark. Unseen by us in our home with a southern exposure, a storm had swept in from the north, and literally in the span of a minute we were completely buried in a blizzard so dense we couldn't see 10 feet out of our windows. In utter astonishment, we turned to each other and . . . well, nothing. We didn't do or say anything, because there wasn't anything to do or say. John and Annie dropped their overnight bags from their hands; it was clear they weren't going to be going anywhere on that day. No one was going anywhere on that day. Nothing was going to be moving at that point, certainly not that day, perhaps not for many days.

From contemplating a pleasant drive for our friends and a day of enjoying spring for us, we suddenly were thinking about survival. *Will our generator work? Where are the candles and kerosene lanterns? Are the dogs in their porch and safe from the cold, wind, and snow? Do we have enough wood inside for the fireplace? Are the emergency supplies of water and food enough to keep us going until we can get out of our farmyard, or till rescue workers can make their way in to us from the highway?*

We didn't ask those questions out loud because there wasn't time. We just stood there in the darkened room, looking out at the raging white fury, openmouthed, utterly flummoxed. All four of us— John, Annie, Linda, and I—are lifelong Nebraskans. You'd think we would have developed some kind of mechanism to prepare us for weather stunners like this, but we sure hadn't. And I'm not sure any human being can. The body adjusts to the ferocity of the extremes on the Plains and the insane, violent jolts as those extremes impose themselves on top of each other with far too little time for a comfortable segue, but the mind struggles to come to grips with it all.

In less time than it took me to write the previous paragraph or for you to read it, there was suddenly sun streaming in our kitchen windows again. The foot of snow so suddenly dumped on us was already melting. We went out into the farmyard, still staggered by the violence of the unbuffered transition from one season to another and back . . . springwinterspring . . . just that fast. And off to the southeast we could see a pitch-black line of clouds moving off at incredible speed, disappearing over the trees by the river at the bottom of our land and then over the distant horizon, on its way to shock others somewhere downwind from us, I presume.

We picked up John and Annie's luggage again and traipsed out to their car, having delayed their departure by less than an hour when only moments before we were making plans for them to hunker down with us for a week or so until we were dug out. My recollection is that we talked about what had just happened only briefly. What was there to say, after all? We had all been there. We had all seen it. We all knew how utterly insane this weather event had been. We all knew that the others were feeling the very same astonishment. So . . . we simply loaded John and Annie into their car and sent them on their way, not far behind the blizzard-squall, for all the world realizing Ole Rolvaag's description in his *Giants in the Earth* of exactly that personality in Plains weather.

Rolvaag is telling the story of a Norwegian family, far from their native fjords, sea, forests, and stone, trying to adjust to the conditions of the northern Plains (near Sioux Falls, South Dakota, but it doesn't matter . . . it's the northern Plains). And he depicts the geography as a living, breathing, monsterlike entity determined to crush those who would crush it:

> And endless plain. From Kansas—Illinois, it stretched, far into the Canadian north, God alone knows how far; from the Mississippi River to the western Rockies, miles without number . . . Endless . . . beginningless. A gray waste . . . an empty silence . . . a boundless cold. Snow fell; snow flew; a universe of nothing but dead whiteness. . . . Monsterlike the Plain lay there—sucked in her breath one week, and the next week blew it out again. Man, she scorned, his works she would not brook. . . . She would know, when the time came, how to guard herself and her own against him!

Gulp!

And again later,

> . . . That night the Great Prairie stretched herself voluptuously; giantlike and full of cunning, she laughed softly into the reddish moon. "Now we shall see what human might may avail against us!
>
> ". . . Now we'll see!" . . .

Double gulp!

If that doesn't stop you dead in your tracks and make you want to double the size of the firewood pile on your porch this coming winter, one of Rolvaag's chapters has a title that constitutes, to my mind, the most chilling twelve words in all of Plains literature: "The Great Plains Drinks the Blood of Christian Men and Is Satisfied."

Triple gulp! Now that I think about it, reading *Giants in the Earth* right before you contemplate a move to the Great Plains might not be the best idea.

Rog-Nook of the North

One night when I almost died I thought of that Rolvaag passage and even in the middle of my dire situation, considering that grim narrative, I had to laugh at the rich irony and truth of it all. I was single and footloose at the time. I had gone up to town for a couple of beers at the local tavern, and since it was a perfectly lovely day, I drove the closest thing I have to a sport vehicle, my beloved Sweet Allis, a 1937 Allis Chalmers WC tractor. I met some buddies, downed a few brews, and then as dark approached decided to be on my way back down to my riverside cabin . . . my old tractor not having any lights and all.

As I drove down Depot Street and past my pal Russ Powers's house, he waved at me from his living room window and motioned that I should come on in, which I did. He had some things he wanted to talk about, so we had a couple more beers at his kitchen table. I noted that I shouldn't really have much more because I hadn't eaten, so Russ, always an accommodating kind of guy, whipped up some scrambled eggs, toast from some bread he had just baked, and some fried ham. And we talked as we sat at his kitchen table. About ten or ten thirty I thanked him and said I really should get back down to the cabin. Since it was now dark, Russ loaned me a big flashlight to light my way down the road but also to warn other motorists that I was out there moving fairly slowly since I was, after all, on an antique tractor. We said our good-byes and I opened Russ's front door to go on my way.

And I stepped . . . directly into one of the most ferocious blizzards I have ever seen. Both Russ and I stood there in his doorway, actually disoriented. Snow was 3 feet deep even on his porch. We couldn't see beyond that because of the wind and blinding snow blowing horizontally. Oh man, now I was in trouble . . . not only was it dark, and snowing, and blowing, but there I was going to be on the road home through this mess on an open antique tractor with no lights!

I pulled myself together as best I could, turned the crank and brought the old machine to full roar, held the flashlight futilely up at arm's length, and started tentatively into the pitch-black night shrouded in the suffocating whiteness. Suddenly right before me there was something I couldn't make out. As I recall, I had the impression there was some kind of wall across the road, but with the wind, dark, and snow, I really couldn't see all that clearly. Still, I did know that nothing had ever been there in that road before and right now something simply was.

I pushed in the clutch, and the old tractor ground to a stop in the deep snow. I moved the flashlight around trying to make out what it was. I inched closer. I still couldn't figure it out. I could see what looked like a car stopped dead in the road . . . but only part of a car. The rear half maybe? I took off my glasses and scraped the snow from the inside. I got down off the tractor and waded through the snow still trying to determine what was in the road directly in front of me. When I got there—just a couple of dozen steps, but a major effort through the blizzard—I still couldn't believe what I was seeing. It was indeed a car, Tim Hostettler's car in fact, but only the back half. The front half was buried in a snowdrift . . . 12 feet high. Right there, across Depot Street, stretching south from the Schroeders' house. In just the few hours I had been at Russ Powers's kitchen table, Depot Street had not just snowed shut, it had snowed shut to a depth of 12 feet! I later learned that Tim hadn't been as cautious or slow as I was on Sweet Allis and so even with full headlights he had plowed directly into the solid snow wall and been brought to a complete stop, right there, where he'd had to abandon his car.

I therefore had to make a half-mile detour north into the wind and snow, and then down the highway, terrified that someone might come behind me going faster than the couple of miles an hour I was traveling and not see the flashlight I was now pointing backward, since I couldn't see anything ahead of me anyway. I kept to the shoulder of the highway by watching the reflector posts pass immediately to my right on the approach to the river—and my cabin. I only made it halfway to the cabin down my heavily wooded river road, where I finally had to abandon Sweet Allis to the elements and fight my way to the warmth of my woodstove.

Altogether now: "Beautiful Nebraska, peaceful prairie land . . ."

Surprise, Surprise!

That kind of meteorological surprise is in itself something of a surprise: Even though we sit here on our little tree farm almost at river level in the broad valley of the Middle Loup just before it joins the North Loup at St. Paul, Nebraska, we see the weather coming at us from a long way off. There is a tall sandhill right behind our farmstead, and I put up an old windmill tower high on the hill above our house just to have a place to go for a wider view still, but even from our back door, about 12 feet above the river itself, we can see towering cumulus clouds building 50, sometimes 100 miles to the west. We see storms gathering in northern Kansas on the weather service radar screens . . . and then look out our kitchen window to see the clouds themselves. At night lightning is reported nearing Lincoln, and from our bathroom window we see that selfsame lightning on the eastern horizon. Although the sky is clear when we wake up on a December morning, we get a warning that a blizzard is headed our way from South Dakota, and as I drive into town to get the mail I can see that blizzard approaching from 100 miles away. We literally see the weather around us in a huge circle with a radius of anywhere from 20 to 200 miles, depending on where we happen to be standing at the time and the altitude at which that weather is forming. I never get tired of looking at it, and I never cease to be amazed by it.

It doesn't take long in Nebraska to acquire a kind of constant uncertainty about the weather, and a healthy skepticism about a

weatherman's predictions—even about what our own eyes seem to
be telling us. My experience is not unusual; if my impressions seem
particularly and peculiarly dramatic, that's only because I make a
point of noting such things, and because I have consciously worked
at inoculating myself from the numbing that most human minds suffer after even a short exposure to Nebraska climate.

Now a moment of pain for me . . . an admission I try to avoid.
You know how I told you about North Dakota's records for temperature highs and lows and how much I envy them? Well, South Dakota
also has Nebraska—and everywhere else in the world—outclassed in
another category. I'd like to ignore this but I am too admiring of the
event, even if it did happen just a few miles over the Nebraska–South
Dakota state line. It's still *Plains* weather, so I'm going to claim it anyway. I speak of the day of January 22, 1943, a day that will live in
meteorological infamy. Imagine living that day in Spearfish, South
Dakota . . . a lovely town in the beautiful Black Hills. You wake up
and step out your door at 5:30 in the morning to cold but seasonal
temperature of four degrees below zero Fahrenheit. Then you are
surprised when the temperature rises to a balmy forty-five degrees
above zero. At 5:32 A.M. No, you didn't read that wrong. Two minutes later. According to the official records, the temperature in
Spearfish, South Dakota, rose forty-seven degrees in two minutes.
But you are just happy you aren't in Rapid City, where the temperature at 5:30 that same morning was five degrees below zero but at
9:40 had reached fifty-four above.

Had enough of that kind of teeth-cracking weather? Well, the
weather hasn't had enough of you. Less than an hour later, it was
down to eleven degrees again, but then in another fifteen minutes it
rose back up to fifty-five (it is now 10:45 AM). At 11:30 it was a frigid
ten degrees above zero . . . but at 4:00 that same afternoon it was
fifty-six. That evening at 7:30 it was five above. Plate-glass windows
in the town of Lead cracked with the insane temperature shifts, and
I'm betting that thermometers just gave up and quit recording temperatures altogether. I have a feeling I would have felt the same way.

If I'd been that person I said was headed across the yard to the out-house at 5:30 that morning, I think I would have given up, too, and just spent the day in bed hoping no one was filling out forms to have me involuntarily committed.

This is something of an extreme case, to be sure, but extreme is the game here on the Plains. I sort randomly through my files . . . Here's a clipping from the Lincoln newspaper, a historical item reminding us of what happened in our not-so-distant past: June 12, 1913: "Five inches of rain fell in ten minutes in Newman Grove. Because of a water shortage in Lincoln, an ordinance was passed forbidding use of water on lawns or gardens."

Rain *and* Shine

And remember, we can't just look at phenomena like this (or like so many others) through our own jaded eyes. Imagine what all this was like for the average immigrant settler to the Plains from Norway, Germany, or Czechoslovakia, or Pennsylvania or Delaware. The average rainfall in Germany is 34 inches, Norway 39 to 100 (!), Vermont 38, Indiana 40 to 46. Nebraska? From 27 along the Missouri River to 12 in the west. Is it any wonder this was not simply called but considered to be the Great American Desert? If you're accustomed to 30 or 50 inches of rain a year, 12 is going to look one hell of a lot like a desert to you.

Oh, it rains here. Sometimes quite a bit. One June afternoon we got 9 inches of rain on our main street in about two hours, shortly after which Oak Creek decided not to make its usual turn north of town and instead ran directly down the main drag and out the other side of town. That was the last time it rained on my ground that year until late September. The Omaha newspaper, not a particularly reliable source of information about anything, including the weather, reported that we had a wet summer. Rained once. Nine inches. Wet summer.

Rainy season? Even seasons don't make any sense or follow any logic here. I once spent some time in May in my cabin down at the river, and it was so idyllic I couldn't believe that I had somehow missed this glorious time of year previously. The river was clear and cool, the temperature balmy. I speared fish for supper and lounged in absolute perfect comfort for almost two weeks.

I resolved that henceforth, for me it would be May-At-The-Farm. The next May I brought Linda out here to spend the month with me in my Hawaiian Heaven in Nebraska. It rained and was cold twenty days straight. It seemed like an inconvenience then but now, deep into a twelve-year drought, I would be happy if it rained one day straight. Still, as a Nebraska farmer told a reporter who asked about the drought, "The way I figure it, every day of drought is one day closer to a good rain." If that isn't typically Nebraskan . . .

When we were hit by a ferocious hailstorm one summer, my farmer friend Marv Casperson once laughed like only a farmer can laugh that he was all set to face his insurance adjuster to request a claim for the hail damage but he thought he might have some trouble explaining that what corn hadn't been pounded into a feathery pulp . . . had frozen overnight under the coating of ice balls. A corn crop frozen out in July? It can happen in Nebraska, and I know for a fact that it did.

Despite religious crackpots who somehow see *intelligent* design in all this, I consider Nebraskans and their grasp of the weather the clearest evidence of evolution. Our otherwise normal human memories, you see, have been pounded into a new format by all the heat, cold, wind, hail, snow, et cetera, et cetera, et cetera, resulting in what I call Plains Meteorological Amnesia. Briefly, this means that Nebraskans never remember what happens in terms of the weather for more than a few months or even weeks.

We remember all kinds of other things . . . some people remember how much rushing yardage the Cornhuskers made last year in the third quarter of the game against Missouri, or how many bushels of milo per acre they got even without irrigation in 1956 . . . even though it only rained 18.63 inches that year, or when it was that that Welsch guy and his buddy Russ cut down the trees and knocked down the power lines north of town, blacking out half the county just five minutes before the kickoff of the Oklahoma–Nebraska game . . . twice (I don't want to talk about it), or exactly how much that catfish weighed that Archie Goodwin caught under the Mill Bridge just before they tore it out and put up the new one . . .

But these very same people will sit in the tavern in February and with all the innocence of a three-year-old lay the plans for an outdoor wedding in Nebraska the following August. Or swelter in the struggling air-conditioning of the tavern in August while planning the spring church picnic down by the river next March. Somehow they've forgotten the heat, cold, bugs, hail, storms, tornadoes, sleet, and lightning . . . well, you name it and they have meteorologically forgotten it. See what I mean? Great Plains Meteorological Amnesia.

What's even more amazing, when the planners, hosts, and participants in these ill-timed events realize the mistake they've made in planning any sort of event at any time of year in Nebraska, *they are clearly and honestly surprised!* It's as if they've never been in Nebraska in August or February even though they have spent their entire lives here. Or even May or October, if you think about it, because no matter what your intentions might be, whatever you think you are going to do outdoors in Nebraska is sure as billyhell going to encounter foul weather. A winter sledding outing on January 20? It'll be seventy-five degrees and there won't be any snow anywhere in the state. Count on it. An outdoor concert on June 5? I don't care what the almanac says, believe me, there will be an "unseasonable frost" or raging floods on rivers that haven't seen water in decades. Or cyclonic winds, or a plague of toads, or swirling clouds of locusts. The very word *unseasonable* is a self-contained exercise in irony in Nebraska.

Doing Something about It

I have suggested in other writings that this one certainty of Nebraska weather—its uncertainty—can be used to our advantage by those of us who are clever enough. It may be as simple as leaving your car windows open to ensure a rainstorm, or it could be more elaborate, as with our Danish Festival here in Dannebrog, an annual event with the romantical Danish name Grunt Love Fest (variously altered to "Grunge Love" and "Grudge Love" by cynical locals).

Or at least the festival is annual *now*. When I first came out here in 1975, the festival had been discontinued for many years. Old-timers explained to me that they had noticed that every time they planned the traditional observance of Danish Constitution Day for the usual first weekend in June, it rained. In fact, it not only rained, it poured; Oak Creek, which surrounds the town on three sides, inevitably went out of its banks; and if you look on the west wall of Harriett's Café, you will indeed see a panorama of photographs from various years of people standing around on the main street in water up to their belts . . . on Grunt Love weekend. So wiser heads of the community decided to call a stop to the annual flooding by calling off the annual festivals. The festivals stopped, and so did the flooding, pretty much as expected.

But then twenty years ago or so we went into a period of major drought and a new generation of thinkers came up with the plan of reinstituting the festival, ostensibly to draw tourists but realistically to get some water on the ground. Back came the festival, which during almost all years since has been graced with substantial rainstorms and a couple of major floods. As dry as it's been of late, I can't help but wonder if we shouldn't consider having the festival a couple times a year. And maybe we should move our annual Danish Christmas festival, usually held on the second or third weekend of December— when the temperatures run around seventy-five degrees and the sun beats down on shoppers—to August, when we could use temperatures like that. Then we could move the Fourth of July to February. If it weren't for Memorial Day and Labor Day weekends when everyone plans picnics, ball games, and other outdoor activities, we'd never get any rain around here.

There is another factor of Nebraska weather that is rarely noted or discussed but is just as real to those of us who live here as cow-killing hailstones the size of grapefruits; you can see it in the title of one of my own books, in fact: *It's Not the End of the Earth, But You Can See It from Here*. As I have previously noted, from the parking area north of our house but even more from the sandhill up behind the place, we can see weather in Kansas, South Dakota, and almost to Iowa. I'm not kidding. It never ceases to amaze me when the weather report says ferocious storms are brewing over northern Kansas, or northern Nebraska, or maybe right over Lincoln, and we can step out the door and see the towering clouds and even flashes of lightning. That doesn't mean weather doesn't sneak up on us from over the tall cottonwoods along the river a few hundred yards south of us, or over the hill to the north toward town, but on a clear Nebraska day you truly can see forever.

And at night . . . I have repeatedly suggested to people who are supposed to be in charge—from the governor's office to flunkies working on the highways—that at some place along the interstate through Nebraska we should forget all the phony crapola like that idiotic arch at Kearney and instead built a short path at right angles to the highway from a rest stop well removed from any town lights and at the dead end built a small shelter where people could just sit, look up, and admire a Nebraska night sky.

From our own yard we have been awed by the shimmering curtains of the northern lights, by a Milky Way so crowded with galaxies and stars that it becomes a luminescent blur made up of indistinguishable spots of light. We Nebraskans are missing a real bet in ignoring one of the most spectacular of the gifts of scenery Wakan Tanka, "the Great Mysterious," has given the Plains: our night sky. And it wouldn't hurt to hire a choir of coyotes to do guest appearances every night on schedule to sing their version of the Howl-a-lulu Chorus, that incredibly ornamented Baroque composition only they have mastered.

Decamping

My bedroom is actually a porch with windows all around. I sleep with them wide open pretty much all year 'round, not just to enjoy the wonderful scents and temperatures of the night, but also the rattle of the cottonwood leaves shuddering not 20 feet from my pillow, the sound of the coyotes singing, owls hooting, deer coughing, cows mooing, and once a mountain lion's roar. Don't believe anyone who tells you about the quiet of the rural Nebraska night . . . it's nothing but a cacophony all night long, and I for one love every squeak, rattle, roar, whistle, and hoot of it.

I once almost cried in front of a large class when somehow we came upon the topic of camping out in Nebraska, or sitting in a boat all night long fishing and hoping you don't get a bite that would disturb the calm, or sitting around a campfire with a tin cup of good bourbon, with just a faint chill in the air, the sound of a river not too far away . . . and some of my students expressed an uneasiness about these ideas. I was surprised. Hadn't they ever camped out? To my utter dismay, a sizable proportion of them admitted that they had never in their lives spent a night outside walls, without a ceiling over their beds. I cannot imagine a worse life, a more squandered existence. I could once honestly say that I had probably spent more nights sleeping outdoors than indoors, and I considered every night I'd slept indoors a misfortune.

In fact, I don't even like sleeping in a tent if I can avoid it. I make a habit when sleeping outdoors of pointing my feet due north at Polaris, the North Star. As I crawl into my sleeping bag I check my watch, if I have one, and note the time and the position of the Big Dipper in regard to Polaris. I know that the Earth revolves one full 360-degree turn under that sky each day—that's what a day is, after all—so the sky is like a twenty-four-hour clock, with one big hand, the Big Dipper, making one complete turn each day; a half turn each twelve hours, albeit counterclockwise. So if the Big Dipper is sticking out straight to the left as I go to sleep, if I should wake up and find it pointing straight down, having covered a quarter sector of the complete circle of the sky, it is six hours later. I am in effect sleeping under one gigantic clock projected on the only ceiling I have, the sky.

When I was traveling rivers with companions and more than one canoe, I got real tricky about my sleeping arrangements. I put one canoe upside down oriented east to west. I then put my sleeping bag at right angles from the middle of it, feet to the north. I pulled a second canoe up and made a T of it, placing its nose on top of the first canoe, making a small shelter under which I could sleep. I crawled into my bedroll and pushed the top canoe's nose to one side, sliding it along the keel of the other canoe until it didn't obscure my view of the sky and Polaris. If it should by chance rain, I simply reached up and over and, without so much as getting out of my sleeping bag, slid the top canoe back over the top of me, thus giving me not only shelter from the rain but also the wonderful sound of raindrops on aluminum just over my head. I grew so fond of this arrangement, in fact, I made a point of installing a sheet-metal roof on the porch of my cabin and on a patio porch just outside my bedroom window so I can enjoy the music of rain even when suffering the misfortune of having to sleep indoors. If you haven't taken your kid camping, you should be arrested for child abuse; if you haven't spent at least fifty nights of your life sleeping outdoors yourself, you shouldn't be allowed to vote in Nebraska elections. At least teach your kid how to pee outdoors. I consider nothing to be more a sign of an effete and degenerated younger generation than the poor, miserable, pale, namby-pamby child who hasn't even learned how to pee outdoors. Any parent whose child is not accomplished at this exercise should be imprisoned.

By "camping" I do *not* mean hauling campers, motorcycles, ATVs, and every other damned thing you own to a paved park where you hook up to the electricity and sewer outlets and look out your window at the trailer sitting next to you at arm's length. I'm talking about setting up a tent—at most—out of sight and sound of anyone or anything human. Maybe on an island in the Platte River, or among the bluffs along the Missouri, or along a quiet stream out in the Sandhills. (Don't trespass, mind you. Be sure to get permissions before doing anything like this, or even so much as hiking across someone's property. It's not just a matter of courtesy; it may be a matter of safety. Some of us do not take kindly to trespassers.)

If you can't go camping, consider simply walking along a river-bank. Or even across a pasture. Or an unplowed field in spring. When I was a young teacher, I once had a conversation with an anthropology teacher on the same faculty and I mentioned to him that I would just love to find Indian artifacts, but didn't know where to look. "Anywhere," he said. Anywhere? Anywhere. He explained that Indians had hunted this ground we call Nebraska for thousands of years. They camped, built villages, worked, killed game, fought each other, prepared food all over the place. At one time or another they had pretty much been everywhere. "Next spring," he said, "let me know and we'll go for a ride some weekend day. All we need to do is find a field that a farmer plowed the fall before so that there's been some snow and rain on it. We'll find something if we spend a couple of hours walking. You can't miss. I'll check into a couple of places we can go right around here." And that's what we did. I was astonished. We found some broken arrowheads and a metal trade point, just lying there on the ground. (Please note that I do not approve at all of *digging*—not just digging at village sites, but most assuredly not at burial sites, a desecration that is immoral as well as illegal.) Since then I've found that village sites are not rarities, either; there are several within fifteen minutes' driving of here. Here on my own small bit of Nebraska ground, I have found a Pawnee scraper and hand stone or *mano*. Near here I have found many bits of pottery and bone, a buffalo horn, shell ornaments, bone beads, game pieces, arrowheads, scrapers, on and on.

But all that aside, just walking the ground step by step is a reve-lation. You not only *do* not see nature from the window of a speeding car, you *can*not see nature from the window of a speeding car. I have been walking the same path on this land of mine for more than thirty years now, and there is not a single time I haven't seen something new in my walks—a feather, a plant, a bird, a snake, an animal, a track, a sound, a scent . . . I suspect that a lot of hunting and fishing has nothing to do with killing and most assuredly, most absurdly, nothing to do with food. Such activities are merely ways to appear macho and tough while doing something that is actually quite sensitive and thoughtful. That is, you can look like a "real man" while doing something you suspect is vaguely sissy.

Well, if you really are a man, you should be able to do what you damned well please without any consideration of what others think. Save yourself a lot of expense and jeopardy this autumn by climbing into a deer stand without a rifle and just sitting there from before dawn until late morning. You will find your life refreshed without all the trouble and expense of lugging a gun, firing shots, falling out of the stand, gutting a beautiful animal, and on and on and on. You'll be amazed at what you see and how good you can feel without killing something.

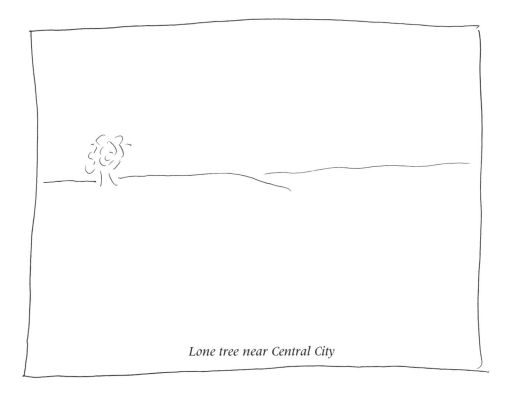

Lone tree near Central City

CHAPTER FOUR

Sand, Stone, Soil, and Seasons

Okay, okay, so I exaggerate a little bit. Exaggerating is the Nebraska thing to do. There *are* seasons in Nebraska, and as is the case with almost everything else here, we have seasons *in spades*. A dear friend of mine of more than fifty years now lives in Hawaii, and I have bad dreams about his life. Another lives in Phoenix and I burn candles for him. What a perfectly hideous existence—life without seasons. They both boast that they never have to shovel snow and somehow think they are taunting me when they are in fact underscoring in my mind the own emptiness of *their* climatological lives. I love winter. Absolutely love it. I love the cold, I love the snow, I love the wind, and I especially love that just about the time every year when I am thoroughly sick and tired of cold, snow, and wind, it goes away, the geese and cranes fill their sky above our farm with their raucous squawks, and we wallow in the pleasures of another Nebraska spring, which usually occurs sometime between noon and four o'clock on some May afternoon, whereupon the thermometer instantly spurts up to ninety-seven degrees and it is summer. And it is hot, dry, and humid for a few months, so that just about the time we are about to load a revolver and play Nebraska roulette—five of six cylinders loaded—the cottonwood leaves turn brilliant yellow and fall to the ground and the geese and cranes do a return flight . . . again sometime between noon and four on an October afternoon. Then it freezes, snows, and blows, and there we are again. Which once again is fine with me, since I have the psychological advantage of a terminal case of Great Plains Meteorological Amnesia.

Again, I am only kidding. *I* remember with absolute glee the most radical of Nebraska's seasonal brutalities. Because that's the part I like. For me it's a kind of self-abuse. I love it when Nebraska makes me feel that I am special because I have survived it . . . and can still laugh. I know it sounds nuts, but I love walking across my Sandhills when even the cacti wither. And nothing tickles me more than walking through a raging blizzard when dying is a real possibility. Maybe it's just a matter of being like the guy who bangs his head against a brick wall because it feels so good when he stops. I enjoy the cold only because I know that I will soon take off my arctic parka and stand in front of the warming fireplace or woodstove listening to the wind roar *outside*. But no, I simply enjoy weather that leaves little doubt about where it stands. I am probably the only person you know who has taken his spring vacation in northern Greenland, north of Thule, at the northernmost human habitations on earth, Qaanaaq and Sioropoluk.

See, I'd dreamed about Greenland and its 3-mile-thick ice cap since I was seventeen. Of course it was an impossible dream, and it became ever more impossible as I traversed my youth and crossed into middle age, indulging in a respectable number of midlife crises

without the topic of Greenland so much as even coming up. Then I
emerged into my seniority and pretty much gave up on the notion.
Which of course is precisely when the gods like to smile on the
doubter. It's too complicated to go into in detail here, but I corre-
sponded by e-mail with a fellow about my tractor books, blah blah
blah, and then I noticed his return address, something about . . . *oh
my God!* . . . Thule, our airbase far above the Arctic Circle in northern
Greenland.

I explained to him my lust to go there, drooled and begged, and
wangled a chance to visit this highly restricted military installation
ostensibly to entertain the troops, which I dutifully did, but mostly to
wallow in a winter even more dramatic than that of the Great Plains.
And man, did I ever. It turned out to be one of those rare vacations
where every single moment is more wonderful than that of I had
imagined the entire time there would be. There was not a moment
when I was not a-tingle with the experience of brutal cold, stinging ice
crystals, whiteouts, polar bear warnings, an ocean frozen solid, Inuit
hunters setting out with dogsleds to kill whales with sticks, seal steaks
for supper, whale blubber for dessert . . . To some degree this has
spoiled me for Nebraska winters, of course, but I am enough of a loyal
Son of the Plains to know that "Arctic" is only an ideal and there is
every chance that this coming winter in Nebraska will rival anything
the North Pole could throw at me in Qaanaaq. Or not. (I will have to
admit, however, that my pride in my lust for the cold took a severe
blow recently when I boasted to my friend Dick about my love of winter and cold and reveled in memories of my far-too-short a visit to the
Arctic, when he replied, "Cold? Believe me, I know what cold is! I've
forgotten anniversaries before, so . . . *I know cold!*")

Well Seasoned

My old friend and cartoonist Paul Fell once did a book titled *Nebraska's
Five Seasons*, which was instantly understood by all Nebraskans.
There's the obvious and usual four—spring, summer, autumn, and
winter—but in Nebraska there is also Football. We don't have a rainy

season, but we do have football. And probably a few others, too. I'd guess that most Nebraskans calculate the year by divisions other than those customary four listed above. Because I went off to school almost every autumn all of my life, from the ages of four through fifty, the year always started for me sometime around September first, not the first of January. For me there is asparagus and morel mushroom season, chokecherry and ground cherry season, ham smoking season, and powwow season. For me there is shorts-and-Hawaiian-shirts season, and the more cherished and traditional overalls-and-work-shirts season. Our year is further divided into two parts by our dogs . . . north of the house in the shade season, which we call summer, and south of the house in the sun season, which we call winter.

Some of my friends measure their year in terms of hunting seasons: pheasant, deer, turkey . . . These days, out here in the rural countryside, there is planting season, harvest, laying irrigation pipe, picking it up. There's calving season, and the days the Sandhill cranes come and then again when they go back. I see the year in terms of when the produce stands at St. Libory start carrying sweet corn and then the sadder days when the end of summer is signaled by the mounds of pumpkins stacked within sight of Highway 281. I welcome harvest season because it signals the approach of winter but also because it is such a dramatic statement about the fecundity of this wonderful land. Town streets and railheads start to grow mountains of corn and milo piled on the ground because the elevators, our Cathedrals of Plenty, are stuffed full. In contrast with some drivers—who consider themselves way too important for such nonsense as speed limits and appropriate caution, and who pound their steering wheels in frustration as they have to slow down for the "moon machines" that take over Nebraska's byways . . . combines, groaning farm trucks, swathers, rakes, tractors, grain carts—I laugh at the idiots who even for a moment consider themselves to be more important than what makes this state truly great: not a bunch of hired goons at the university playing a boys' game on Saturday afternoon, but *harvest*, the feeding of the world!

Flat-ulence

One of the most inaccurate of the many misconceptions about what Nebraska is comes from motorists who see nothing of the state beyond quick glances to either side of I–80. Beginning just east of Grand Island, the interstate runs mostly right alongside the Platte River all the way to the state's borders. Well, most valleys are flat, but the Platte River's is so notably horizontal that it was labeled by the French the *platte*, or "flat," river, and before that by the Omaha and Ponca *niblantha*, or *nebraska*, also meaning "flat river." It stands to reason therefore that the highway on its banks is also flat. That makes for easy highway construction and easy driving. But not much for scenery.

So whose fault is it then when some dumb-ass drives that one concrete slab and thinks he has therefore seen the entire state . . . and hey, boy, it's really flat? Nebraska is *not* flat. If you think it's flat, you're an idiot. In fact, some of the vertical definition of our geography is dramatic. The stabilized dunes of the Sandhills are most often gently sloped on one side but steep on the other. There are actual, no-kidding, honest-to-God cliffs along the Niobrara and Missouri River Valley walls, and notable promontories scattered everywhere in the region. Think about it: What are the chances of them building a major highway up the side of a steep butte and down the other? Not good. (Although there *is* a remarkable road to the top of Scotts Bluff, with Nebraska's only automobile tunnels. Frankly, I wish it were still the way I saw it in my youth when I had to climb on foot to the top with a geology class. We camped on the summit that night and had a view of the Platte Valley, and the towns of Scottsbluff and Gering, that was worth every drop of sweat it took to get there.) So, to get such views you may need to go a bit out of your way. If you like your scenery rolled out for you on a screen and spread on your windshield . . . well, I'll admit that Nebraska may not be for you, so yeah, go ahead and believe that it's flat.

One night I camped in a park near Bridgeport and before dawn headed out to Courthouse Rock and Jail Rock to do some folktale research. There are various Native stories about a band of hunters being trapped atop Courthouse Rock by a larger and more hostile group of warriors (probably Lakota—those guys were always looking for trouble). The narrative went that the cornered group went up the butte on the gentler slope of the north side and then, one night, cut their leggings into a rope and lowered themselves quietly down the steeper south side, where the siege party would never have expected a successful escape. I wanted to see if such a thing would have been possible.

At dawn I had easily scrambled up the north slope of Courthouse Rock. It was anything but a stroll, requiring some handwork, too, but it certainly would have been an easy climb for the agile hunters, and defensible. I reached the top and edged to the southern rim, leaned over, and looked down. Well, two things struck me. First, about 20 feet below me was perched a golden eagle, even more surprised to see me than I was to see him. I had never seen an eagle before. (This was in the early 1970s; these days we can pretty much expect a few eagles to winter right here on our own land, much farther east.) He screamed a bone-chilling scream and swooped down into the valley below. The *deep* valley below. That was the second thing I noticed. I don't know—it sure seemed to me like a long, scary drop to be rappelled with a fragile rope made of torn and braided leather leggings, but I suppose if a horrible death was the alternative . . .

I clambered back down to my car just below the north slope. It was still early, and a lovely day. I eyed Jail Rock, a much smaller, much steeper prominence nearby. Jail Rock has no gentle slope on any side; it is just a sheer-sided thumb to Courthouse Rock's hand, rising straight from the valley floor, like those steep-sided buttes you see in all the old western movies and occasional cigarette ads in Monument Valley. Except smaller.

I was in pretty good shape those days and was doing quite a bit of mountain climbing, mostly the Colorado "Fourteeners." I'd never done any technical rock climbing but, well, this seemed tame enough, and since I was here . . . Going up Jail Rock was a challenge—groping for hand- and footholds, reaching, stretching, scrambling. But, as it turned out, it was nothing compared with coming *down* Jail Rock.

I reached the small flattish area on the top, took in the stunning view, congratulated myself for my skill and agility, and then, spotting a quickly gathering thunderstorm approaching from the east, and considering the crescendo of thunder and lightning it was bringing along with it, and knowing that my own father had been struck by lightning and almost killed only a few miles from where I was standing at that moment, I decided that maybe it would be a good idea to get back down off the highest thing for 50 miles in any and every direction.

Uh-oh. As I looked around, I couldn't even see for sure where I had come up the steep soft-rock wall. What if I started down, groping with my toes for a hold, not able to see a thing below me, and I hit a dead end where there simply were no more footholds? No wonder climbers are warned never to climb alone, I mumbled to myself. Jeez . . . here I was, all alone, in the middle of nowhere, high atop a narrow rock pillar, in increasing wind and rain—and lightning—and with no idea how I was going to get down. At that moment, from that height, it seemed like my car was a good 300 miles away, so help me.

As I inched my way down over the now wet soft sandstone, absolutely terrified and dripping with sweat, I eased over the sharp lip of the rock and clutched my way down the ever more slippery wall. When my feet were once again on the solid floor of the Platte Valley at the foot of the rock, I swore a series of promises, sent up a flurry of prayers of gratitude, thought up a couple of dozen new names for myself, and learned a lesson I can guaran-damned-tee you I have never forgotten.

Yeah, Nebraska . . . it's flat. But take it from me, while it may indeed be mostly flat, it isn't all that flat everywhere!

Stalking My Quarry

The soils of Nebraska say a lot about its origins and history. There isn't a lot of rock in the state, for example, nor were there many trees

when the frontier first moved through, and so the old building traditions to the east of the Missouri of rock, brick, and stone petered out
and died here on the Plains and we became the Land of the Soddie—
the sod house. And later, when the frontier moved beyond suitable
soils for sod, pioneers resorted to building their homes with baled
straw and hay, and even railroad ties. The hahahahaha "soil" here on
my own ground is nothing but a fine sugar sand, blown up out of the
Loup River millennia ago, as were (according to most theories) the
sands of the Sandhills, out of the Platte and other Pleistocene rivers,
lakes, and glacial outwashes. The fine clays and loess of the eastern
quadrants of the state are also windblown, giving rise to the inevitable
metaphors of the Great Plains as a "sea." The surface of the sea, after
all, is formed by exactly the same force as the soils of the Plains: wind.
What's unsettling during periods of drought like the one we are expe-
riencing at this writing in the first decade of the twenty-first century is
the image of those vast clouds of blowing dust and sand that obviously
once ruled this region and which will almost certainly hold sway yet
once again, perhaps sooner than we can hope and pray.

When I was but a lad, I spent my weekends, terminal nerd that I
was, prowling Morrill Hall on the university campus, looking at fossils, rocks, artifacts . . . To this day I can show you the exact classroom door that I once peered through to see students sitting around
in a geology class and I can feel again the stirrings . . . the *lust* I felt to
be sitting there myself. And not many years later I did exactly that,
sitting in an intro to geology class in that very same room. There was
never a doubt in my mind that I would fulfill my arts-and-sciences
science requirement with classes in geology. I love rocks. I have
always collected rocks. I still collect rocks. Ask Linda how often she
has had to stop the washer or dryer to take out a stray rock I have
picked up somewhere along my way during the day and left in an
overalls pocket.

It's not easy being a rock enthusiast in Nebraska, there being
after all not a lot of rocks here. At least not rocks easily noticed.
Again, when I was a kid, I recall a deep sewer line being installed at a

new house a few hundred yards from our own home in Lincoln. It's amazing I didn't ever die, exploring storm sewers, snooping around construction sites, and, in this case, going deep into an unshored trench where no one would have found me for days had there been a cave-in. But I was there, and I was fascinated that at the bottom of the trench the diggers had hit rock—a loose, rust-colored sandstone. The Dakota Sandstone, like so much of Nebraska's substrata, was laid down by the same forces that are still shaping the Plains topography: wind and water. That same sandstone is exposed around Lincoln at sites like the Children's Zoo, in the narrow gulch carved by Antelope Creek along the zoo's eastern edge, or out at Pioneer Park at the base of the statue *The Smoke Signal*.

Along the eastern and southern edges of the state, there is limestone suitable for construction, a nice solid ivory-colored stone, exposed in places like Roca (Spanish for "rock") south of Lincoln, in cuts along the Salt Creek, near Ashland and Union, where it was historically quarried for building purposes, and Louisville and Weeping Water, where it is still harvested for cement, roadbed material, and construction. ("Yes, Virginia, there *was* a rock at Table Rock!") The limestone at these sites was laid down by an ancient sea, an extension of what is now the Gulf of Mexico. We came that close to having oceanfront property in Nebraska! This rock is made up in large part of fossil creatures, ranging in size from microscopic up to fairly substantial and easily identified on sight—crinoid stems, foraminifera, gastropods, brachiopods, snails, clams, little creepy crawlies . . . The goo piled up at the bottom of the sea was compacted over thousands of years and eventually was pressed into layers of rock. It's nice stuff, very pretty in house construction—although you have to be careful not to use it in fireplaces exposed to heat and flame and the weather, because it has a nasty propensity for exploding when small amounts of moisture in it turn to steam and blow open the rock around it.

When I was old enough to drive a car and especially once I acquired some basic knowledge of geology, my nerdiness was transferred from Morrill Hall's display cases to the limestone quarries from

which the specimens in those cases had originally come. I never tired
of roaming abandoned quarries, especially in the Ashland and
Murray areas, looking for fossils. I don't know how many geology
hammers I wore out chipping apart layers of limestone on weekends.

Mine, All Mine!

Once while scouting along the road from Ashland to Louisville on the
north side of the Platte, I spotted some old, faded WARNING signs that
appeared to have been originally intended to close off an old quarry,
one I hadn't previously explored. So I stopped the car, demonstrated
yet again my contempt for authority by ignoring the signs, climbed the
fence, and entered what was, yes, a small, very old, long-abandoned
quarry, and a good place to look for fossils that might have weathered
out of the matrix over the years. I climbed a small dirt incline to the
face of the rock to do a quick check for exposed fossils or layers that
might contain fossils and . . . *hey, what's this?* At the top of the incline
there was a low, narrow slot of an opening. I peered in. Hmmm . . .

And wow! What I saw astonished me. In climbing the hill, I had
obviously scaled a pile of dirt and rock that had been scraped up and
into the mouth of an enormous cavern; I was at the roof level of a
gigantic opening maybe 50 feet wide and 30 feet high. I cautiously
lowered myself through the opening and then down the slope into the
huge subterranean room. The narrow entry slot didn't let in much
light, but I could see what was indeed a very large passageway. The
rails still on the floor told me that unlike all the quarries with which I
was familiar, open pits with high rock faces from which rock was
blasted, this one was actually a limestone *mine* dug back into the
Platte's valley wall, going far enough back into the darkness that I
couldn't see any end to it. I walked slowly and carefully into the darkness, slipping on the slimy rocks. Water dripped from the ceiling, and
huge slabs of limestone on the cavern floor told me that there was
some reason to doubt the solidity of the walls and ceiling, rock or not.
I went farther and farther into the gloom, down a slight incline.
Suddenly I stepped ankle-deep into cold water, so undisturbed that it

was crystal clear, utterly invisible to my eye, and I could go no farther.

Years later I returned to this hidden and mysterious (to me) site with teaching colleagues Bill Kloefkorn, Leon Satterfield, and Vic Lane, with lanterns and a canoe. Two of us—I think it was Bill with me—launched the canoe and set off cautiously across the shallow, clear water into the pitch dark. It was creepy beyond my abilities to describe. The cavern was completely dark aside from our lanterns, the water was absolutely transparent, there were clear, long-abandoned signs of human mining activity, and not a sound could be heard but the scrape of our canoe on rock slabs that had fallen to the floor and the splashes of our paddles.

We found to our already substantial uneasiness that the underground cavern was not a simple, single tunnel going back into the hill. Soon there were side galleries branching off to either side of the main tunnel we were in, and we could see that we were in not a single tube but rather a kind of grid of passages, with huge pillars of limestone left in place to support the overburden. We worried about the possibility of getting lost in the maze, not having any idea how big this underground complex might be, after all.

Finally, we retreated, awed by what we had seen and where we had just been. There's not much more to the story. I suppose that's a pretty puny conclusion, but the chill I felt deep underground in that dark wetness is still with me. When we came back out of the hole, we found a changed world. When we had gone into the quarry-mine hours earlier it had been a sunny, warm, autumn day, but—Nebraska being Nebraska—it was now snowing, blowing, and cold. As it happened, for some reason Vic Lane just happened to have a large, unopened bottle of Benedictine and Brandy liqueur in the trunk of his car, and its sweet warmth was just the thing we needed to cap an adventure that had left a real mark on our psyches. Wow . . . spelunking in Nebraska. Who would have thought . . . ?

Is that quarry still there? I don't know. I've never been back, and that was forty years ago. I suppose it's there, however. God knows, it still exists in my mind.

There have been and are other mines in Nebraska. There were once tentative efforts to profit from the low-grade, thin coal seams within the same limestone layers along the Missouri River bluffs, for example. I suspect that even more substantial coal deposits are being laid down at this very moment by the flotsam dropped from the thousands of coal trains passing through Nebraska every day, moving from the vast coal deposits of Wyoming to power stations all over the eastern half of the United States. Like all coal, Nebraska's is composed of the settlings of huge swamps and marshes again associated with the shallow seas that once stretched up onto what is now the Great Plains from what is now the Gulf of Mexico.

Salt of the Earth

Another mineral that showed some early promise for exploitation but faltered and failed was salt. Indeed, Lincoln was established where it is precisely because of the natural occurrence of salt under and near it. Thus, Salt Creek, was known well before white incursion onto the Plains by Native tribes who came to the flats northwest of town, just south of the airport, to gather salt. To this day the Omaha know Lincoln by the name *Niskithe*, or "salt."

If you can slow down on I–80 just west of Exit 399 without being killed by some half-wit going 20 miles an hour over the speed limit, take a look a couple of hundred yards to either side of the highway shoulder. During a dry spell you can see a kind of white crusting on the soil, especially at the end of the airport runway coming toward the highway from the north. That's salt. The groundwater beneath Lincoln is so salty it is not potable and can't even be run through air conditioners without damaging them. As a result—and another fact even most residents of the capital city don't know— Lincoln's water is brought to the town in gigantic pipes from well fields in the Platte River gravels from near Ashland, just upstream, I might note, from the confluence of Salt Creek, the outlet for Lincoln's septic water systems. Funny how that works.

The Morton family (as in Morton's Salt) began an operation

with evaporating pans to extract salt, and there was some hope the water would have curative capabilities. An artesian salt spring near 9th and O Streets in Lincoln and wells at the old Capital Beach amusement park swimming pool drew on the saline water, but eventually infinitely larger and more easily exploited salt sources in Utah—the Great Salt Lake and the salt flats—and subsurface salt deposits in Kansas that can be harvested by the millions of tons with bulldozers, conveyor belts, and trucks the size of Vermont made any thought of fooling with the piddling amounts in Lancaster County not worth the trouble.

Rock On!

Another source of what rocks we have in Nebraska is all the detritus hauled down here from the Far North by various glaciers that have scraped their way down, at least into the northeastern quarter of the state. It's an old joke, but like a lot of oldies, it's one I love:

> Gent: Where did all these rocks in your fields come from?
> Farmer: They tell me a glacier brung 'em.
> Gent: Where's the glacier?
> Farmer: Went back for more rocks, I reckon.

I think what's really funny about that is that it's true. You will see in some field and pasture corners from Lincoln on northeast an occasional red, gray, or black boulder, usually granite. Pleistocene glaciers broke loose and dragged those rocks down this way from what is now northern Canada. As the ice melted, the rocks were left behind. Incidentally, the hills between Seward and Lincoln down to around Crete and Milford are the terminal moraine of those glaciers, the farthest point in their southward push; here they ground to a stop, piling up a ridge of geological wreckage like a gigantic bulldozer.

When I was a callow youth and, as I have noted, a real rock hound and developing Nebraska curiosities enthusiast, I was poring over a Nebraska road map when I spotted something in the southwest part of the state that puzzled me. And surprised me. And interested me. Somewhere on the map down around McCook a small legend said WORLD'S LARGEST SILICA MINE. Silica mine? In Nebraska? Wow. I hadn't heard of any kind of mines in Nebraska, let alone a silica mine. Whatever silica was.

Well, we were planning our annual August family trek west at the time. We never headed out of Lincoln in any direction but west, for some reason. I was twenty years old before I knew there was anything east of Lincoln. We had relatives in Wyoming—maybe that was the reason. And we always went in August, the hottest, most miserable travel time of the year. Again, the only reason I can imagine for that bad sense of timing is that we are German. Whatever the case, while I normally just went along with whatever my parents decided by way of a vacation trip, this time I put in a request: I wanted to visit the World's Largest Silica Mine. I saw it on a map. And Dad agreed to go a few hours out of our way to do exactly that. I have no idea if Dad had any idea what a silica mine is, and he is gone now so I can't ask him. It would have been like him to go to the extra effort just to let me make a fool of myself.

Well, when we arrived there and took one look, I figured out pretty quickly that *silica mine* is a fancy term for "sand pit." Man, was I ever disappointed. But not for long. I discovered at some point that for me sand and gravel pits, where huge suction pipes sluice out water and gravel and sand solids, running them through sorting screens for use in making concrete, road cover, cat boxes, whatever, are an absolute playground. To this day I am content sitting for hours—even days—at the refuse pile of a sand or gravel pit. Because that's where things like fossilized turtles, camel ribs, bison skulls, woolly mammoth teeth, on and on and on, are culled out of the usable rock, gravel, and sand and discarded. It's like excavating a fossil treasure except without the labor of digging.

Seeing the Elephant

Most Nebraskans are unaware of what a treasure store of fossils this state holds. Mike Voorhies, a paleontologist at the University of

Nebraska and an old friend of mine, once astonished me when I told him I had actually found ancient ivory in the gravels delivered to spread on our road from nearby "silica mines." I even found some elephant bones when the foundation was dug for our house here near Dannebrog. In essence, Mike said, "Big deal. There are elephants everywhere in Nebraska." He then gave me a figure my mind has consistently refused to accept. Every time I want to tell someone how many elephants (counting mastodons and four-tuskers but not Republicans and other geezers) there are per square mile in Nebraska, I have to contact Mike again and have him reassure me because his educated, conservative, and informed estimate is . . . sit down . . . brace yourself . . . I'll give you time to prepare to be astonished.

Mike adds, "For background, by *elephant* I mean fossil remains representing one individual animal . . . a full skeleton [rare] or a skull and jaws, a femur, or just a wisdom tooth. Archie's [the largest elephant in the world, on exhibit in the Nebraska Museum on the University of Nebraska campus] 300 bones and teeth count as one 'elephant,' two left tusks count as two." Here it comes . . . dramatic pause . . . it's all in the timing . . . Mike Voorhies, an expert in the topic, estimates there are . . . *3,000 elephants per square mile in Nebraska*. Three thousand! Per square mile! That means there are more fossil elephants in Nebraska by far than there are people. That's almost five elephants *per acre!* Not only are there a *lot* of elephants in Nebraska, Nebraska is downright jammed up with 'em. Dig a hole in Nebraska . . . find an elephant!

Every year or so there is a major television report about the astonishing find of a mammoth or mastodon skull, a skeleton, or even just a tooth somewhere in Nebraska. The story is reported with awe, as if it were the most remarkable thing the reporter could imagine. That's because like me, he or she doesn't know any better. Mike Voorhies added to his note to me: "Last year with very reduced field crews, we managed to recover about 1,200 identifiable 'elephant' fossils representing no fewer than 87 individuals."

Tell me again how boring Nebraska is!

Nebraska is a treasure trove of rhinoceroses, saber-toothed tigers, primitive horses and camels, huge ground sloths, ancient rodents and reptiles, and even bison twice as big as the modern animals. I was once skinny-dipping in the Loup River along the southern border of our land and felt something solid against my delicate behind, kind of like a rock. Well, we don't get a lot of rocks around there, not even a lot of logs stranded in the river. So I wiggled this bit of whatever a little and finally pulled it from the water. It was a huge cow skull. Okay . . . that makes sense, I guess. I put the skull on the roof of my cabin for no particular purpose. Not long thereafter a farmer friend came visiting and asked me about the skull. "It's an old cow skull I found in the river," I said.

"I don't know what that is, but it's no cow skull," he laughed.

Hmmm. So I took the skull back to Lincoln with me and one day when I was going to the university campus I stopped by the Paleontology Department in Morrill Hall and showed it to Bert Schultz, another old friend. I told him I wondered if maybe this wasn't a buffalo skull. "Not quite," he said, "but sort of." The modern "buffalo" is designated scientifically *Bison bison*, but what I had in my hands, Bert said, was a *Bison antiquus*, a 30,000-year-old Pleistocene forebear of the modern *Bison bison*—much larger, perhaps 6 feet high at the shoulder, with horns pointed forward rather than upward because it tended to be a solitary rather than a herd animal. Herd etiquette among buffalo apparently dictates that goring of one's friends and family, even accidentally, is taboo. "Okay, everybody, if we're going to travel en masse, it's going to be . . . *horns up!*"

After that I had some idea what I was looking for by way of fossilized wonders and knew that I didn't need to go far from home to find them. Or wear any kind of particular paleontological outfit for the search or have specialized equipment other than my bare buns. Whether it's in rock quarries or simply in soils and sands, a good part of the ground beneath us in Nebraska is made up of the remains of the mighty and small creatures that came before us. I find that to be impressive and moving.

Even our clays may be fossils of minute microorganisms that once swarmed in the warm, shallow, nutrient-rich seas that covered the region. Their microscopic skeletons sank to the bottom of the waters in incalculable numbers, building up thick layers of fine-grained, sticky soils that when baked become as hard as any rock. Early efforts in Nebraska to "burn brick" were short-lived and not particularly successful, since it was hard to accumulate enough fuel to bake much brick or to bake it very well. Such brick produced around here in central Howard County was so soft it showed noticeable erosion—even substantial damage—after only fifty years of exposure to the elements.

But once there was enough fuel for firing the kilns, the industry took off and is still doing well to this day. Major brickworks are in operation near Yankee Hill just southwest of Lincoln and at Endicott near Fairbury. The clay is obtained from pits in the immediate area of the works and produces excellent, hard, and handsome brick.

Liquid Assets

Perhaps the two most important mineral resources of the state are the least appreciated and recognized: water and soil. One of the largest bodies of fresh water in the world— the Ogallala Aquifer—lies beneath us, under most of Nebraska and extending into states around us, especially south as far as Texas. Or at least so it used to be. Texas has already squandered its portion of the aquifer and, having learned nothing, the rest of us are about to do the same.

As thousands of huge pumps pull up water built up over tens, maybe hundreds of thousands of years, and the water table drops, small streams on the surface and more and more wells go dry. Exploiters of water resources feign ignorance of the obvious cause-and-effect relationship, dismissing concerns as the nonsense of them dadburned tree huggers. What do they care? They won't be around to deal with the consequences. Jesus will come back sooner or later and fix everything. A particularly painful consequence of such a betrayal of our obligations of stewardship, in my opinion, is that

some of the remarkable and occasionally enormous artesian wells of
the Sandhills are sinking and disappearing as the subsurface sources
for the deep reservoir that supplies them are drained. I have had the
rare good fortune to have access to some of these incredible phenomena and I can tell you for a fact, if we lose these things, we will have
lost something very dramatic. These gigantic gushings rival the gey-
sers of Yellowstone. I had heard of these things for many years but
still I wasn't prepared for the big one—the Big Blue Hole—that I had
a chance to visit in a remote area north of Sarben, Nebraska.

First, there were a lot of smaller gushers, pushing gallons of
water up out of the ground, on the path to get to the Big One. And
they were impressive enough. But when we reached the deep bowl
in the middle of which was a huge boiling pool a good 30 feet across
with millions of gallons of water boiling up out of the earth . . . wow!
There is no way I could have anticipated the wonder of it. Water is
pushed from deep within the Ogallala Aquifer by the pressure of
even more water and the earth and sand burden above it; the water
is of course incredibly pure, but it also carries with it a heavy burden
of sand, which is held in constant suspension by the powerful pushing of the water from below.

As my group and I stood there with our mouths open at this
amazing phenomenon, I noticed some things much larger than grains
of sand boiling up occasionally and sinking back down into the sand
curtain hanging in the water. The objects looked like . . . well . . . as
stupid as this sounds, they looked like *rocks* bobbing up and down in
the springs. Rocks don't float, though, right? And these things were
floating up through the sand and water almost to the surface and
then sinking back down, too quickly in the water made opaque by
the sand to be clearly identified.

Somehow we managed to snag one of these UFOs (Unidentified
Floating Objects) before it sank back down and it was—good grief!—*a
rock*. Somehow the suspended sand grains in the water increased the
buoyancy of the water, I guess like the dissolved salt of the Great Salt
Lake increases buoyancy of swimmers. That, combined with the pres-

sure of the water from below, was actually "floating" rocks that bobbed up and down in the bottomless pool.

We had a discussion about what the heck it would feel like for a human being to get into this washing machine turmoil of rocks, sand, and water, but being sensible adults, we did the wise and mature thing and did *not* so much as entertain the thought of getting into the roiling pit. No, we talked a young girl in the party into going in instead. She bobbed like a cork and reported that the feeling was absolutely creepy since she was struggling to balance on the column of pressure from under her that seemed to want to reject her altogether and throw her completely out of the pool. Yikes. Thanks, but no thanks.

During the summer of this writing, blathering half-wits have suggested that hundreds of huge, deep wells be used to pull up water from this geological dinosaur—water buried thousands of years—to fill up Lake McConaughy near the town of Ogallala. Why? Well, so fishermen can catch a few bass on a lazy Saturday, so water-skiers and Jet Skiers can skip around polluting the air and water while burning fuel we don't need to waste, and so farmers downstream can irrigate corn to make fuel to run the oversized SUVs, RVs, motorboats, and Jct Skis that give clods mindless pleasure, that's why. Never mind the future. We'll eventually just come up with some substitute for water when we run out. "Let 'em drink Budweiser" seems to be the motto of those for whom ignorance is truly bliss. We should be treating this stuff like gold, or at least like petroleum, but instead we are throwing it away like garbage.

The Dirt

So it goes, too, with our agriculturally productive soil. This stuff is precious. It feeds us, and the world for that matter. And yet we are mining it to grow fuel for oversize automobiles and silly recreational noisemakers, all the while not paying nearly enough attention to the stewardship you would think common sense and the majority theology require. Farmers are miners. But just as the coal and salt resources of the area petered out or were eventually forgotten as commercially valuable resources, our soil can be destroyed if we are careless or thoughtless in how we use it. It's like firewood. I'm amazed that people speak of wood as a renewable energy source, which it is, without considering that the only way that makes any sense is if we renew it. We can't just cut down trees and burn the wood forever without replanting the trees. Same with our soil. With fairly easy and inexpensive care, the soil and water resources of the Great Plains can feed us forever. Minus that care, however, our time here may be short. And we'll have no one to blame but ourselves.

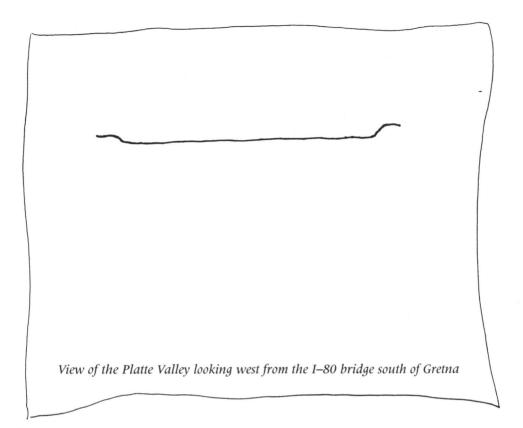

View of the Platte Valley looking west from the I–80 bridge south of Gretna

CHAPTER   FIVE

Water and Rivers

To a remarkable degree, Nebraska, heart of the "Great American
Desert," can be defined by water. And I don't just mean the Missouri
River that forms our eastern boundary—although that isn't simply a
matter of trivia. The frontier smacked up against this formidable
watercourse and was stopped dead in its tracks for a few decades. It
couldn't be bridged, it most assuredly couldn't be forded, and a ferry
. . . well, as I have suggested elsewhere, go down to the edge of that
river sometime and look across its incredibly wide, roiling, angry
water and imagine trying to row or pole your way across it on a shallow raft or boat. Thanks, but no thanks.

    The Missouri River was notoriously unpredictable, the channel making wild swings from bank to bank with no warning, sometimes devouring entire towns, or moving from one side of a town to another, putting it in a completely different state or territory from where it had been the week before. Pioneers sometimes called the Big Muddy "the Old Harlot" because she changed beds so often! She was described as "too thick to drink, too thin to plow." It was a grave-yard of shallow-draft steamboats that slammed into new islands where there had been a deep channel on the previous trip, caught on gigantic snags and sawyers, gigantic trees that washed out of banks during floods and washes, one end sometimes catching the bottom so that the end bobbed treacherously up and down in the current like a man sawing wood—thus a "sawyer," disappearing in front of a steamer and coming back up right into the paddle wheel or tearing the bottom out of the keel. The Missouri was a treacherous mistress, providing a relatively fast and easy roadway from St. Louis to the new frontier at Kansas City, Nebraska City, or Omaha but also destroying as many men as she made rich.

An old friend and his son once invited my son and me to join them on an inaugural Boy Scout canoe float of a stretch of the Missouri from the Fort Randall Dam outwash to the end of running water above Lewis and Clark Lake behind the Gavins Point Dam near Yankton. Well, okay, I guessed that would be fun. But it turned out to be much more than okay: It was remarkable. First, it hadn't occurred to me, but the river between these dams was not the murky, roiling beast I knew from Blair or Omaha or Nebraska City. I probably should have reasoned this, but the dam above us stopped the water and settled out all the murk and mud, so the water we were on was crystal clear. We could see the bed of the river 12 feet below our canoe.

But an even bigger surprise was that if we wanted to look at that riverbed, we were going to have to look fast, because it was pass-ing beneath us at a rate that took our breath away. And while it was surprising how fast we were going over the river bottom, it was absolutely terrifying how fast we were going past the riverbank to our starboard. The Missouri River is big, deep, sometimes muddy and even violent, but in looking at it from high bridges and banks, from a distance, and out of airplane windows, I simply hadn't realized how fast it moves. The Missouri is *not* a "lazy river." Negotiating a turn into the current and trying to nose the canoe into the bank and stop was not an insignificant consideration. You couldn't simply grab a tree branch or sunflower stalk—either you would be torn from your canoe, or the canoe would be swept out from beneath you. Any effort to beach a canoe on the bank was sure to result in disaster, wet gear, a wrecked canoe, and possibly scattered survivors in that ferocious water. We quickly learned to turn our canoes upstream, paddle furiously to slow our momentum, and then ease over to the bank while still paddling hard to maintain a relatively even pace with the bank. Most of all, we learned very quickly to have a new respect for the Mighty Missouri.

I taught at Dana College near the Missouri River town of Blair, Nebraska, for four years in the early 1960s. I loved the college and the town, but most of all I loved the quick and easy access to the Missouri and the oxbow lakes (cutoff bends of the river that have kept their water) along its banks. Most of all I loved the ancient bridge that crossed the river at Blair, carrying the old Lincoln Highway, US 30. For many years that bridge was the last bit of toll road on the Lincoln Highway because the family monopoly that profited from it managed to find new repairs the bridge needed whenever it seemed to get anywhere close to being paid off and thus reverting to public ownership.

I loved that rattly old bridge because, for one thing, it was very high. But what really captured my heart was that the floor of the road on the bridge was . . . how do I describe this in words . . . ? If you saw it, you would understand immediately what I am trying to tell you. I'll give it a try and you work at understanding what I am struggling with, okay? The road was a grid made of steel on edge, a couple of inches thick, and therefore more air than substance. As you approached it and drove on it, it looked solid because you were seeing most of the metal from its side. But if you looked straight down at it, you saw its thinnest dimension. And if you were moving in a car, even at a slow speed, and happened to open your car door just a little and look down, the grid vanished from sight and all you saw was . . . a straight drop of a couple of hundred feet to the river below. It thus became my total delight to take visitors to our Blair home to see the river. I'd drive up that old bridge approach, pay my toll of a quarter or whatever it was, then slowly drive across the span. At some point I would tell my passengers to crack their door ajar and look down. The horrified reaction was always instant and always the same—a jarring spasm of vertigo and nausea like you can't imagine without having the experience. It was like suddenly going into free fall over that huge river without any chance of pulling a ripcord to save your life. I lost a lot of friends like that.

The Nebraska River

To my mind the real Nebraska RIVER—in capital letters—is the River Nebraska, our Platte River, the spine of our state and its namesake. In fact, I would love to see some bold politicians assert themselves (yeah, right . . . politicians assert themselves!) and declare that the truly ugly name *Platte*, for all the world a precise depiction of the sound of a cow pie slapping onto the earth, be changed back from its French form to the original Native word and the original name of the waterway, the *Nebraska*. Let Colorado and Wyoming do what they will in naming their segments of the river—it's not the same river at all in either state, and in fact once it comes out of the mountains it isn't a river in Colorado at all. In Nebraska, however, that waterway should be officially called *the Nebraska*. It's only a matter of common decency.

The Platte is a unique river. The word *unique* is painfully overused these days, but not in the case of the Platte. It is an abrading river; that is, it is not cutting its way down through rock and earth to form a canyon but is instead dragging billions of tons of rock, gravel, sand, bones, and flotsam out of the mountains and highlands of the western Plains to deposit them ever deeper on the lower Plains well downstream in Nebraska. Its valley is therefore broad and shallow, and its banks, low. Most distinctively, it is laced with islands—thousands of islands, from tiny islets scarcely big enough to root a tree to gigantic tracts big enough to contain fields and pastures and even host center-pivot irrigators.

I often hear snide comments about the name of the city of any size closest to us here in Dannebrog: Grand Island. *Grand Island*? Where's the island? And exactly how grand is it? Well, pretty damned grand, actually. In fact, gigantic. If you approach Grand Island on I–80, note the first time you cross a bridge signed PLATTE RIVER. During most times of the year, when there is water in that river, take just a glance and note which way the water is running. Okay. Got it? Now, no matter which direction you are headed, you will soon cross another bridge . . . hmmm . . . also designated PLATTE RIVER. Did you notice? The water is running in the same direction as under the last bridge. And then another. And then another. All Platte River. All running under the highway in the same direction. Now, think about that: If the water is running in the same direction in all those channels, that means the highway (and therefore you) is on islands out in the middle of that river. For miles and miles you are actually on islands out in the middle of the Platte. That's a bunch of pretty grand islands, if you ask me.

I love the section of the Platte from Grand Island to Fremont, primarily for these islands. It is a canoer's paradise. When it has water in it. Sadly, for nature and those of us who love nature, Nebraska's namesake is sucked dry to irrigate fields to grow more corn to make more fuel for monstrous vehicles that are destroying our lives and our environment. We can always devise new fuels and new ways to employ them, but when the water is gone, so are we. I wish the water squanderers who drain the Platte every year would give some consideration to their self-destructive madness.

I am crushed those summers when the Platte goes completely dry, because it means everything around it and in it dies . . . crawdads, minnows, tadpoles, catfish, carp, turtles, algae, water bugs, reeds, cattails,

arrowhead arums, everything. And that means cranes and herons suffer, too, and raccoons, possums, deer, bobcats, muskrats, beaver, snakes
. . . everything dies or just goes away. Everything goes except the
morons who trespass up and down the river on ATV four-wheelers,
creating dust and noise, destroying habitat, disturbing what wildlife is
left and those of us who love that wildlife and the peace and quiet.
Squandering fuel, manufactured by squandering water to grow corn to
make the ethanol to fuel ATVs that squander the fuel . . . It's nuts.

A friend and I were once canoeing the Platte near Central City.
Over the couple of days we'd been on the float, we'd seen a veritable
zoo of wildlife, including the one and only loon I've seen (and
heard!) in Nebraska. We were sitting on a bank enjoying the calm of
the river when from somewhere far off upstream we heard a horrible
roar coming our way. It came ever closer, until it was deafening.
Then around the bend came an airboat, with a roar so loud it hurt
our ears. This atrocity came right up to us and finally went quiet, the
occupants obvious pleased with themselves for having called our
attention to them.

"Watcha doing, fellas?" the moronic pilot shouted.

"We *were* enjoying the wildlife," we yelled back in disgust.

"Wildlife?" the boat driver sputtered. "We ain't seen no wildlife."

My friend and I could only sit there in amazement at this
exchange, wondering whatever happened to the laws dictating the
nonsurvival of the unfittest. Where's Darwin when we really need
him?

The Platte River is a favorite of mine not only because it is
unpredictable in terms of whether it has water in it or not, and
because it's piling up sediment rather than wearing it down, but also
because it exercises a similar independence of spirit in where it does
and doesn't go. The Platte's geological history is in itself interesting. I
have gone on trips with physical geologists and had them point out
various abandoned ancient channels, some a long, *long* way from
where the Platte now flows . . . through the Sandhills to the north,
cutting across landscapes south and west of where we now think the

Platte has always run. A glance at a topographic map of Nebraska and certainly of the current Platte Valley shows clear evidence of the vagaries of what seems otherwise a pretty sedate river. At one time or another, the Platte (and for that matter the Middle Loup Fork right here at our place) has strayed a long way—even miles—from where it now peacefully flows and, for the moment, seems so permanent. Whenever I spot these abandoned riverbeds, I try to imagine what the landscape must have been like way back then, way back when . . .

While it doesn't take a lot of imagination to see how the Missouri River could be a pretty formidable barrier for westward travel across the continent, the Platte seems less likely a candidate as a major obstacle. Don't fool yourself. It wasn't all that long ago that the Platte was damned near uncrossable . . . too wide to bridge, too shallow to ferry, too soft and marshy to ford. If you want a real adventure and some appreciation for this reality, just try sometime to cross the Platte River on foot. Where the water is only a foot or two deep, the quicksands and holes are much more of a hazard. If you were trying to cross on horseback or, worse yet, with a wagon, there were dozens of islands to be skirted or traversed. Imagine slogging through a river's quicksands for a couple of hundred yards, then having to heave your wagon up onto a bank, cross a heavily wooded and brush-clogged island, lower it back into the river, and then go back to fighting quicksand. No fun. No fun at all.

Even today there aren't a lot of bridges crossing the Platte, and motorists may still need to go out of their way to find a crossing. Even interstate bridges can be washed out, as happened near Ogallala not long ago, and people can be killed as their vehicles fall into a raging flood where yesterday there was only dry sand. And where again the next day the sand will be only damp. There was in fact a lot of talk during the early years of this state about splitting Nebraska in half right up the middle along the Platte, a North Nebraska and South Nebraska, to avoid all the problems the people on the wrong side of the river were certain to have once a capital was established either north or south of that uncrossable Platte.

There's more. The Platte is truly a Heyoka River, a trickster clown river, if there ever was one. Nebraskans rarely give it much thought, even if they are more familiar with a map of the state than a visitor or newcomer might be. Think about it—the town of Fremont, just west of Blair and north of Omaha, is on the Platte, right? And so is Ashland, just north of Lincoln. Hmmm . . . and quite a way *south* of Omaha. Good grief! After leaving the Grand Island area, the Platte River moseys on up steadily northeast with a destination around Sioux City apparently well in mind. But then she changes her mind and makes an abrupt turn to the south in Lincoln's direction, changing her mind and direction again at Ashland, going straight east to enter the Missouri at Plattsmouth. Having apparently also lost her *e* somewhere along the line.

So to some degree Oregon and Mormon Trail followers didn't start west along the Platte at the Platte's mouth because that would have involved one heck of a detour north before heading in the intended direction of straight west. But there was a lot more to the decision than that, and it is another feature of this contrary river that few Nebraskans note or consider. The next time you cross the Platte River near Gretna on I–80, try to glance to both sides as you enter the valley from either side. Look quickly both ways up and down the river. Do be careful, because I–80 between Omaha and Lincoln is without question the home ground of Nebraska's very worst drivers; I have often petitioned our state legislature to require all automobiles with Omaha and Bellevue license plates to carry rotating amber caution lights on their rooftops so other drivers have some idea where the next accident is about to occur. I would prefer to take all Douglas and Sarpy County drivers out of automobiles and put them on roller skates, but I have been assured by experts that considering how they handle traffic, there would almost certainly be just as many casualties. It's not cars that empower these nut cases, but wheels.

Where was I? Oh yeah . . . if you can do it safely, the next time you come down into the Platte Valley near Gretna on I–80, look to either side. And think a moment about what you see. To the west is a sweeping, shallow valley 5 to 10 miles wide. Well, okay, that figures. We all know that a river's valley grows wider and wider the farther it travels downslope in its bed, until at its mouth it's at its widest. Yeah, well, that's what other rivers do. Not the Platte. To the east as you look down the Platte from Interstate 80, you see a very narrow valley, not much more than a mile wide, with high limestone cliffs and canyons on both sides. What the heck is *that* all about? What happened to that broad, shallow valley you saw stretching off to the west? It's the Platte, that's what.

Try to imagine, furthermore, what that valley was like in early or mid-April when migrants were about to launch off on their travels across the Great Plains from their jumping-off place at the Missouri River. Most Oregon, Oxbow, and Mormon Trailers shot for a departure date of April 15 to get the best spring grass for their livestock yet miss spring flooding. You sure didn't start off for California, Utah, or Oregon in July or August. Things went bad enough for that Donner outfit when they got a bit of a late start and fell behind in their schedule, you may recall. In April that narrow slot of a canyon-valley of the Platte between Ashland and Plattsmouth might well be wall-to-wall flooding, and even if not, it was a very narrow passage badly clogged with forest, rock, and already settled and farmed ground not friendly to folks in wagon trains. As a result of this bottleneck at the end of its flow and the peculiar northward detour once it exited that bottleneck, overland trails started from north of Omaha, or from Nebraska City, or out of Independence, Missouri, instead and angled across the open Plains to join the Platte between where we now see the towns of Grand Island and Kearney.

Not even when those who would use the Platte as a way west were through that initial bottleneck was the road an easy one, however. Travelers on the Oregon Trail were on the south side of the Platte River. At North Platte the river forks, the South Fork heading west, then southwest, then south to Denver and west up into the mountains of the Front Range. The North Fork goes westward into Wyoming, entering the canyons and mountains. Oregon-, Deseret-, and California-bound travelers wanted to go west, but here they were, on the south bank of the South Fork that was about to turn fairly sharply southward. That meant that the Crossers had to ford the South Platte at some point and get back over to the south bank of the *North* Fork of the Platte again. Things are never simple.

California Hill in Nebraska

As I have already noted, crossing the Platte is not an easy task under the best of conditions, but these people with horses, oxen, and heavy, by-now-battered wagons reached the forks of the Platte, where we now find the town of North Platte, relatively early in summer, probably around early June. There was still water in the Platte, more than likely; it might even have been in spring flooding stage. If you take a look at even a road map, you will see that the South Platte and North Platte Forks parallel each other just a few miles apart for more than 50 miles farther west, all the way to where the town of Ogallala now lies.

Keep on imagining being on that wagon train on the south bank of the South Fork of the Platte contemplating crossing over that river, and then over that long, narrow strip of land between the rivers . . . what do you suppose that feeling was like? Well, that narrow spit is between two very low-banked rivers, for one thing. And since it was still spring or early summer, that ground was almost certainly recently flooded. It may still have had standing water on it. It is one of the few places on the entire Plains where fire and buffalo have not savaged the botany, so this strip of ground is heavily wooded, choked with brush and downed logs . . . even snags washed up onto it by centuries of annual flooding. Infested with mosquitoes, snakes, muck and mud . . . This was *not* a good place to cross from the south bank of the South Platte to the south bank of the North Fork.

Once again the devious Platte was throwing a curveball—or perhaps more precisely a beanball—at those who would take advantage of her fortuitous direction. The travelers therefore had to keep going along the south bank of the South Fork another 70 or 80 miles—that is, another week or two at a covered wagon pace—to a spot between where we now find the towns of Brule and Big Springs, ford the South Fork of the Platte, and then head directly north over the rise of ground between the two forks of the Platte . . . called California Hill because that's where the trail over it was headed . . . and then back down the steep canyon wall into the valley and south bank of the North Platte at Ash Hollow near where the town of Lewellen now lies.

I wish with all my heart that we could rename the Platte River the *Nebraska*. I have a feeling that the travelers on the Oregon Trail had a few other names for it. It may have initially been a complimentary metaphor when our three-time presidential candidate William Jennings Bryan was labeled "the Boy Orator of the Platte," but it wasn't long before some wag and political opponent noted that Bryan was indeed like the Platte . . . "an inch deep and a mile wide at the mouth." (I should note for my own satisfaction, however, that I am an admirer of Bryan despite the sad circumstances of his final crusade in the Scopes Monkey Trial in Tennessee against science and evolution in the name of hysterical religiosity, a national joke that unfortunately continues to this very day.)

Lake McConaughy, or Big Mac, near Ogallala, is formed by Kingsley Dam, one of the largest earthen dams in the world, across the North Platte River. The North Platte drains a good part of the Rocky Mountains in Wyoming, and I suppose that when it was built, everyone figured that that water was pretty much going to flow forever. Well, as the earth has warmed recently, as glaciers have disappeared, as less moisture has fallen to replenish them, the Platte has brought ever less water to Big Mac, too. Lakeside marinas and boat piers now sit high and dry, and while 1,000-acre sand beaches may be nice for sunning and picnicking, the lack of water really cuts into the lake's other purposes: water recreation like fishing and boating, power generation, irrigation, wildlife maintenance, river regulation for downstream agriculture, and natural phenomena like the annual migration of geese, ducks, whooping cranes, and Sandhill cranes. I love the Platte and I hate to see it die, but at this writing—2006— things don't look too good for my Platte River.

Looping the Loup

Next in primacy of Nebraska rivers—at least in my mind—is the Loup
Forks System, sometimes described as a "ladder of rivers" draining the
Sandhills sponge in a series of parallels, finally entering the Platte . . .
uh, the Nebraska . . . near the town of Columbus. I love the Loup
Rivers—all of them: the most beautiful North, the reliable and
wooded Middle, and the more junior South Fork. I love the Loup
Rivers not only because I have a quarter mile of their banks here on
our farm but also because they never go dry as the Sandhills trickle
out their watery wealth over the year (occasionally the South Loup,
perhaps, but never the Middle or North Forks); because they are
wonderfully clean (albeit heavily sandy), given that they are not the
recipients of the effluvia of any city or even large village; and because
they flow through some of the wildest, least populated lands of the
Plains. And I tend to grump when people carelessly call them the
Loop Rivers. They don't loop. But they were the home of the *Loup*—
French for "wolf"—or Pawnee people.

The fact that I am now situated here within easy strolling distance of the Middle Loup is in fact one of those remarkable bits of
serendipity—"coincidence," as the white man insists on calling it,
"destiny" as much wiser Native people see it. I can't remember
exactly what year it was, about 1966 or 1967 I would guess, when I
was sitting in the daily faculty coffee circle at Nebraska Wesleyan in
Lincoln and we got to talking about how we really should do something to celebrate the end of the school year and our annual, brief
release from servitude. You know, maybe a camping trip, or . . .
what? a river float? I had gotten a big old aluminum tub of a rowboat
from my father-in-law, easily capable of carrying four or five people
and their gear. How about setting out on a float on some Nebraska
river for a couple of days? Seemed like a pretty good idea.

But which river? We had never looked at Nebraska's rivers with
an endeavor like this in mind. What Nebraska rivers are floatable?
We didn't know. Is it possible to get to the rivers with a boat and
camping gear? Maybe at a bridge? Where would we leave our cars if

we spent a couple of days on the water? No idea. So we looked at some road maps, and it would have been pretty hard to miss the obvious network of the Loup forks. Leon Satterfield, an English professor, and I took a Sunday drive to the Nebraska midlands to take a look. We looked at the South Loup—pretty small and shallow for my boat, which I had dubbed *Diamond in the Rough*. It probably didn't draw more than 6 to 8 inches, but what we saw on the Platte and South Loup Rivers was mostly sandbars and shallows. The North Loup was pretty enough but maybe a bit fast for us river novices, and the longest drive, considering that we would be launching our expeditionary force from Lincoln. So we looked at the Middle Loup downstream from where I now live, at a bridge near Fullerton or Palmer, I can't remember which. Wow . . . the river we were looking at seemed very promising. There was plenty of water, it was moving along but not at a pace faster than we or the *Diamond ITR* could handle. It wasn't all that long a drive from Lincoln . . . just a couple of hours each way. Leon and I decided the Middle Loup it would be for our first faculty spring float.

The Loup River Expeditionary Farce

Our party consisted of four friends: Bill Kloefkorn, now our Nebraska state poet, Bill's brother John, also an English teacher; Leon Satterfield, now a gadfly newspaper columnist; and me, now a . . . well, whatever I am now. We gathered our gear: a cooler of Man Food (steaks, mostly), lots of beer, canned beans, coffee, a tent, sleeping bags, a hatchet, and not much else. Early one morning we set off with light hearts and empty heads to place our destiny in the hands of The River. We parked a downstream vehicle at an all-night eatery near Columbus, where the Loup empties into the Platte and where we planned to end our three-day voyage, got to the bridge south of Palmer, unloaded our boat and gear, found a friendly farmer willing to let us leave our vehicle . . . and set off into The Unknown. And in total and blissful Ignorance. (A good part of this narrative has blurred over the years because of my years, the obliterative capacity of alcohol, and the mind's natural tendency to erase pain, so Bill—Leon—John: I may be conflating several of our Loup River floats into this one. Don't bother correcting me. It won't do any good. Besides, I may have some of the circumstances wrong but you'll have to admit I have the consequences down pat.)

We had, we found, made a couple of miscalculations. First, we hadn't considered what the speed of a river's current might be. In subsequent years we learned that a flooding river moves one hell of a lot faster than you might think and while it may seem like fun, ripping along a riverbank with floating debris like hog houses and cottonwood trees becomes very scary very quickly. And even when a river like the Loup is moving along at its *regular* pace, what looks like 50 miles on a road map becomes more like 100 on the water. And at a couple of miles an hour, that's a lot of days of floating in the sun.

Ignorance Is Blitz

Insofar as *floating* is the operative term. Our second mistake was that we hadn't checked at some of the other Loup crossings between Columbus and Palmer—figuring, I suppose, that a river is a river, and what goes in at the top pretty much has to come out at the bottom. Makes sense, doesn't it? Our first day was blissful—a jolly crew, a yare boat, incredible scenery, a serene river . . . We found a gloriously situated campsite as the day grew long, on a small spit of land jutting out into the river. We would sleep, we figured, with the gurgle of the gentle river flowing around us as we nestled warm and cozy in our sleeping bags and tent. We rustled up some grub for supper—pirates don't cook, they rustle up grub—and spent the quiet evening watching the sun set across the river as we sipped some good bourbon from tin cups at a campfire. It was the most perfect kind of evening possible for a bunch of good friends.

It got even better as far off to the west we saw faint flashes of lightning. Wow . . . wouldn't it be neat to lie in our tent with a gentle rain falling on the canvas, a kind of meteorological lullaby providing a nice tenor line to the bass and soprano ripples from the river? We wondered if the rains would even come our way, or get here before morning, since they were so far away on the horizon. Inspired by their love of nature, their attraction to Romantic poetry, and perhaps by the chilled bourbon in their cups, Bill, John, and Leon began to shout challenges to the gods, encouraging them to bring their storms this way, where the intrepid voyagers could share the dynamics of the storm. I went to bed. I already knew way too much about Plains weather to indulge myself in such hubris. I grew increasingly uneasy as my comrades' shouts grew ever bolder. And as the low rumble of thunder did indeed respond and approach our campsite, whose vulnerability was becoming ever more obvious. At least to me.

By the time my friends joined me in the tent, the wind was picking up and the thunder was almost constant. We had no more than dropped off to sleep, in fact, when all hell broke loose. The gods had decided to rise to my friends' shouted challenges, it seemed. We crawled out of the tent as the storm gathered its fury. We "deadmanned" it with cords tied to nearby trees and anchors made of sandfilled empty beer cans quickly buried in the sand and hunkered down to await the fun. The lightning became constant, the wind tornadic, and the rain a deluge. Exposed as we were on a narrow tongue of ground jutting well out into the river, we were set to enjoy every nuance of the storm slamming into us.

The tent suddenly shuddered and dropped down on its poles and strained at its tethers as the storm began to batter it. We could feel the water rising . . . inside the tent and into our sleeping bags. Turning on a flashlight, we could see that the rain was blowing not into the tent through an open vent or door but *through* the canvas in an ever heavier mist so that it was now raining *inside* the tent.

There wasn't much sleep that night, but we sure as billyhell learned a lesson about camping on a river in Nebraska and daring the gods to join us: It's not a good idea. You'd think that four guys who had read about the voyage of Odysseus would have known that. But there was more to be learned. We survived the storm, congratulated ourselves on not dying, and the next morning launched anew onto the again calmed waters of the Middle Loup. Everything seemed to be going fine. We swam in the river, floating alongside the *Diamond*. We ate and drank, farted at will, enjoyed with renewed vigor the life around us. Wooded banks slipped by. Occasionally we got out of the boat and dragged it over a sandbar back into a channel, but the water was cool and the day pleasant so it was only more of the fun of the float. We got to the bridge at Fullerton . . . somewhat later than we had planned, but not far enough behind schedule to give us reason to worry. One or two of our group walked a mile or so into town to get more ice and beer, and once again we set off on our trek, passing the Fullerton public landfill along the way, and composing and singing a chantey celebrating its grandeur.

Dam-nation

I don't remember where we camped that night, but I know that fairly early the next day we were hugging a bank, enjoying the passing scene, when we started to hear a strange sound—a kind of roar, like rushing water. Almost like . . . a waterfall. Now, a waterfall would have been a total absurdity in the landscape we saw around us. The river is languid, low, and flat. The banks are low; the soils, soft. There is not a rock to be seen along the Middle Loup River. We had not glimpsed so much as a ripple in the water other than when the river washed over a downed log.

But the roar grew louder. Almost threatening. We sat uneasy and upright in our boat, peering around each turn, puzzled by the sound. We hugged the bank in the event that we came unexpectedly upon a . . . Upon a *what*? We had no idea. We couldn't imagine what might lie ahead. We turned a corner and to our utter astonishment found . . . jeez, we still couldn't figure out what it was . . . some kind of dam?

Well, yes. It turns out that just west of Genoa, a low dam diverts almost all the water from the river into a mile-long basin where the heavy sand burden of the water settles out and is dredged and the water is sent on down an irrigation canal, which eventually empties through power turbines into lakes north of Columbus, then draining into the Platte. A consequence of this diversion was that as we walked the bank and looked down the Loup "River's" bed downstream from the dam, we saw nothing but a vast and empty stretch of sand with only the barest trickle of water escaping over and through the confines of the dam.

I almost wrote *damn* by mistake in that last sentence, and I'm not surprised. We checked with the people apparently in charge of the damn dam and they said no, we could not put our boat into the canal to float to Columbus. We *could* drag it and our gear a mile or so and then put into the canal once it exited the settling basin and was flowing free . . . but not in the settling basin. Or we could continue on down the "river." They reassured us that only a mile or so farther down, the Cedar River joined with the Loup, and perhaps that would give us what we needed to navigate the rest of our intended "float." Now not so much a float as a drag.

We dragged the *Diamond* over the low dam and onto the dry white sand that had been the Loup. And we started the long agony down "stream." Hours that seemed like months later, we came to the confluence of the Cedar. The painfully puny stream trickled out onto the sand we had been slogging across and spread out into a shallow sheet that within only a few hundred yards disappeared again into the sand. All that day we labored, dragging the boat until the hiss of aluminum on sand became an obscene curse. Where we could find a bit of shallow, green, warm water we took advantage of a bit of buoyancy and floated the boat, sometimes 100 yards, sometimes only feet. The day went from an idyll to a hell.

By the time we got to the Genoa bridge, a long, long way from our intended landing at Columbus, we were fried by the sun, exhausted from the heat and labor, altogether fed up with the adventure. We surrendered. I think it was John who volunteered to hitchhike back to Palmer and our car—we were still closer to our departure point than our intended goal in Columbus. We watched him start down the highway with the pinwheel on his straw hat spinning in the heat, absolutely certain that no one in his right mind would pick up what appeared to be a lunatic and we would probably still be sitting there in the shade of the bridge with the damned boat for another week waiting for John's return. But someone took pity on us—I can only imagine that John looked even more pitiful than he looked loony—and by the next morning we arrived in Columbus to get our downstream car and return to Lincoln much wearied, much abused and battered, and much chastened in our search for adventure.

But, apparently, not much wiser. For years we set off on LREFs (Loup River Expeditionary Floats). Then more decades after I had my own chunk of Loup and didn't need to float it, other generations of floaters discovered new mistakes, performed new accidents, entered more dead ends, and explored previously unimagined disasters.

The only thing that sustained me in the ten or fifteen floats that I was a part of was a story I read somewhere about a team of trappers who came down out of the mountains of Wyoming one spring with a fortune's worth of then enormously precious beaver skins . . . a couple of years' worth of work, probably. They hit the North Platte River somewhere upstream in what is now Wyoming, built a huge raft, and set off merrily on their way to the Missouri, St. Louis, and incalculable wealth and ease. You know, like Bill, Leon, John, and I set off that lovely May morning down the Middle Loup.

What the trappers didn't know was that the Platte in full flow is indeed a wonderful floating river. I have often canoed it myself . . . best canoeing river in Nebraska, as far as I'm concerned. For a month, at least. And then . . . it goes away. Simply disappears into the sand. So somewhere around where North Platte is now, I imagine, the trappers and their barge ran out of water. More and more, day by day, hour by hour, the water grew ever more shallow and the sandbars ever more of an obstacle. Soon the trappers were dragging their cargo as often as they were floating it. Then there was no more floating, only dragging.

By now summer had come on, so in addition to having become

a labor of monumental enormity, the days were witheringly hot. And of course the mosquitoes welcomed the new buffet with which they were presented. The pile of raw hides grew hot, too, as did the smell. Which drew flies, including biting deerflies that draw blood with every slash of their saberlike cutters. I imagine that the only thing that might have kept insects and maybe Lakota and Pawnee at bay would have been the blue cloud of ear-searing profanity that must have hung around that stinking, sinking mess for the months it took to get the load far enough downstream to pick up decent water, perhaps at the influx of the Loups or the Elkhorn—way too far downstream to do much good in any case.

I don't recall if the load, or even the trappers, ever made it to the Mississippi, or for that matter the Missouri. I'm afraid to do much more research into the question. I'm not sure my tender spirit can handle the ferocity of the review those trappers must have given their summer on the Platte, and "Beautiful Nebraska . . . peaceful prairie land . . ." I had only a couple of days of an experience only vaguely approaching their own ordeal, and, thank you very much, that was plenty.

Bull

On a later float we pushed off on the crest of a raging Loup River in flood. Within hours we had covered what had previously taken many days. We had major injuries and lost most of our gear when the *Diamond* and one canoe turned over and dumped everything from watermelons to sleeping bags into the roiling waters. My favorite recollection, however, was another idyllic day when absolutely nothing went wrong.

It was a glorious time—warm but not hot, the river high but not flooding. The beer was cold. We were on schedule. And after a wonderful day on the water, we were about to pull into bank and set up camp in a grassy and shaded lea, flat and clear . . . a perfect campsite if ever I saw one. Shortly before we were about to bank the boats, however, a huge, nasty, dirt-pawing, fire-breathing bull began to stalk us, walking along the riverbank eyeing us threateningly. Well, we decided that since this stretch of nice pasture went on quite a way and we could see a couple of fences coming down to the river only 100 yards ahead, we would float past the fence and thus have barbed wire (or *bobwahr* as it is known hereabouts) between us and Ferdinand.

Good plan. But as I said, we were near the end of a long day on the river, and deep into our beer supply. While we were scrupulous about cleaning up our campsites and carrying all our trash with us, to our amazement and dismay, even to the bafflement of John, who later confessed some sort of brain spasm, he emptied a beer and blithely bounced the empty can off the head of that bull, boinking him right between the eyes. To say that the bull was annoyed by this insult would be missing the point by far. He roared. He glared and pawed the ground. He made threats that we all knew he could probably keep. And we cursed John for his arrogance. And we thanked the merciful heavens when we went past the end of that fence coming down to and into the river and the bull was stopped, having to satisfy himself with fantasies of ripping us and our canoes to shreds.

We set up camp a couple of dozen yards downstream from the fence. We watched the bull, and he watched us. But he did not seem inclined to challenge the fence. He knew his limits, we were pleased to note. We put up the tents, built a campfire, put supper on to cook, poured some whiskey over the ice in our tin cups, and settled down to a peaceful evening in the grandeur that is Nebraska at night, more about which later. The bull gave up to the inevitable reality of our insult and intrusion onto his ground and walked off. As we watched his humiliated retreat, however, he did something we might have anticipated if we'd had even a scintilla of good sense. But we didn't. He walked around the end of the fence, which was only, oh, maybe 30 yards up from the river. And he strolled directly and casually right into the middle of our camp.

With amazing speed for out-of-shape schoolteachers, we all assessed the climbability of the trees surrounding our camp and with

an agility worthy of the Cirque du Soleil went up trees each individu-
ally selected to suit our personal tastes. We spent several hours there
on our respective branches, chatting and admiring the size of the bull
as he explored our supplies and equipment, and then wandered off
again around the fence, presumably to a more interesting environment, hopefully a barnyard a mile or so away. Eventually we came
down out of the trees, reestablished our lost primacy to our camp-
ground and property, and eventually even found the confidence to
enter our tents and sleeping bags and go to sleep.

I don't know what time it was when I woke up to a noise I had
never heard before . . . bull breath not 2 feet from my face, at the
door of my tent. Quietly, gently, I woke up whoever it was who was
sharing my tent and told him of our situation. We thought about quietly cutting a hole in the back of the tent with a knife and slowly,
silently exiting . . . but the tent was small and the bull was obviously
quite at home here on his own ground, even in the dark. We thought
about waking our companions in the other tents with as little volume
as possible, if for no other reason than to give the bull additional
moving targets from which to choose should he decide to play soccer
with our corpses. But soon I heard hushed whispers coming from the
other tents, too. Everyone was aware of our visitor. We thought
about asking for a volunteer to make a break for it, perhaps back up
the trees, to draw him away while the rest of us ran for the boats and
the safety of the water, but no one stepped forward.

There wasn't much sleep that night. Mercifully, however, there
was also no damage or injuries. I like to think that Mr. El Toro knew
quite well was he was doing, smelled the abundant fear of half a
dozen terrified men, and decided that this approach was far more fun
than simply killing us. As far as I know, no one on one of our Loup
floats ever again gave so much as a fleeting thought to bouncing a
beer can off the head of a fence post along the river's bank, let alone
a bull.

Nebraska's One Wild River

The most popular Nebraska river for floating is without question the Niobrara, skimming along just south of the Nebraska–South Dakota border, most particularly from the town of Valentine at the Fort Niobrara park access downstream to Rocky Ford, an easy two-day float. The Niobrara is classified as a "wild river" but it's that only if you've never been on an *actual* wild river. The Niobrara is not a particularly challenging float. But it is a beautiful one. There are some short, exciting "whitewater" stretches that take some care, thought, and skill with a canoe and which have dumped a lot of paddling beginners into the river's cold, clear water. I consider a canoe trip on the Niobrara to be the ultimate test for the strength of a marriage short of an affair. There are a couple of "chutes" where you can actually see the downward slope of the water and, man, are those ever fun. Except maybe the time I thought it would be fun to swim the long, deep chute just upstream from Rocky Ford without a life preserver and almost drowned. The rushing, boiling water took me right down to the bottom of the deep channel and simply would not let me back to the surface. After what seemed forever and almost too late I made it to the surface for a quick breath of air. At that moment and in precisely the right spot, Loren Wilson, the float manager, was in the water, saw the look of desperation in my eyes even at 100 yards, rushed out into the river, grabbed me by the hair, and pulled me up and out of the rapids before I went under permanently. I wear my hair long to this day in anticipation of the next really stupid thing I do.

The first few times I did Niobrara floats, in the late 1960s and early 1970s, there was one turn that featured a very impressive whirlpool, about 30 yards across, a huge whirling saucer perhaps 4 to 5 feet lower in the center than at its edges. It was great amusement to go through but even more fun to watch as other canoes spun, rolled, and beached in efforts to get through the hazard.

To my mind, the most attractive element of the deep, wooded, rocky, narrow canyon of the Niobrara is not simply its own crystal waters but the hundreds of waterfalls that plunge down its southern canyon wall to join it. The falls range from towering but delicate and lacy cataracts like Smith Falls or Fort Falls, probably the most famous of the side falls, to small stair-step tinklers, jewel boxes well back from the main river, visited by very few people, as spiritual and moving as a feature of a Japanese garden planned by a master gardener. Those who know such things also know that falling water doesn't have to be massive to stir the spirit.

Or for that matter, the carnal. I accompanied outfitter Loren Wilson on a couple of dozen Niobrara floats with groups who had hired him, his canoes, and his crew for a managed float. One of Loren's favorite waterfalls had its own special benefits. This waterfall is maybe 8 to 10 feet high and about the same across at the top; it features a narrow horizontal ledge all along the point where it hits the river's surface. When our group of thirty or forty canoers reached this particular spot on the river, Loren would have us beach the canoes and then explain that we were going to do something special here . . . a surprise that could only explain itself. Three or four of us on the crew would clamber to the top of the waterfall, sit in the shallow water at its brink, and spread our legs to partially and momentarily block its flow while all the other canoers stood in the shallow water on a shoal around the base. Then he would designate three or four of our guests to come stand below us on the ledge with their backs to the wall behind the falls. When they were in place, Loren would give the word and those of us at the top would lift up our rears and let the backed-up water, crystal clear, cold and clean, cascade over the edge onto those standing below on the ledge. It was a fun feeling, although not nearly as spectacular as Loren seemed to suggest it would be.

But Loren wasn't done. He had a little surprise up his sleeve. Or up someone's sleeve, at any rate. After a couple of goes at this, he would invite three or four young ladies from the group to step on up and onto the ledge under our human retaining dam. And when they were in place and we had plenty of water backed up, Loren would again give the word. It worked every time. Not until a good thirty seconds after that water poured over the nubile maidens below did it become evident that good ol' Loren had purposely selected ladies with generous endowments who were wearing halter tops or unbinding swimming suits. And the dynamics of falling water's hydraulic force were thus illustrated dramatically in a way no physics class could ever demonstrate. (Oh come on! Of course that is sexist and adolescent! I know that. But what's a little semi-nudity among friends? And isn't being silly a part of floating down the river?)

It Never Fails—There's Always an Idiot, or a Couple Hundred Idiots

Speaking of biology lessons, the canyon of the Niobrara stretching from its outlet into the Missouri woodlands of eastern Nebraska to the high Plains a couple of hundred miles west is an invaluable environment because it is an ecological bridge. Within this canyon the biology of the East meets that of the West. In this incredibly restricted context, plants survive when they cannot be found elsewhere . . . ironwood, aspen, paper birch. Here the western bluebird has an interface with the eastern. The Niobrara is probably the route by means of which creatures like the mountain lion travel into new areas, a kind of transfusion tube from one source of vitality to a weaker one.

And that IV tube is threatened with being slowly but firmly squeezed into not a flow, or even a drip, but a cold and dead memory. In the larger picture, political disregard for human contributions to global warming and increasing pollution is contributing to the jeopardy faced by the Niobrara, but there is the even greater and yet more easily controlled destruction of the river and its canyon from those who should be the ones to most appreciate it, those who float the river in canoes and inner tubes.

If you love nature, when you are a quarter mile downstream from the Fort Niobrara bridge southeast of Valentine on a clear, warm Saturday and there is nothing but the sound of the river, the occasional hiss of sand or scraping of a rock under your canoe, and birds and wind, you know for a fact that you have just entered the most splendid cathedral on God's green earth. If you are an ignorant clod, on the other hand, it's time to pop open a Miller Lite, yell obscenities at your buddies in the canoe downstream, and start looking for a broadcast of the Husker football game on your transistor radio. And turn it up loud enough so that everyone on the banks and river can share your crashing stupidity. Slowly but surely the abusers of the river have come to outnumber the worshipers such that the Cathedral of the Niobrara is now often little more than a sports bar. Since the river is a federally designated waterway, there are moves afoot to restrict the number of canoers and tubers who can be on the river at any one time by issuing permits and numbers, but the fact is, it is in part the government that has made the river ever more accessible to the boors and despoiled the best parts of it. For example, they have built an atrocious wooden bridge-walkway and viewing platform to Smith Falls. It's enough to make those of us who knew the Niobrara "back when" gnash our teeth and weep.

I will treasure the times I was on that river and didn't see another soul except whoever was in the bow of my canoe. The best was a late-September float I took with an old friend now gone, Dick Whitefoot. Of course the air was wonderfully crisp, the colors of the autumn trees were stunning, and—the best part—no one else was on the river, not one single other soul but us. At Smith Falls we camped in splendid solitude, cooked up a couple of wonderfully firm and clean catfish Dick quickly caught, and slept in worshipful peace.

Other Waters

Other floaters tell me that even more remote Nebraska rivers offer the same peace and spiritual beauty the Niobrara used to have . . . notably, the Dismal (and isn't *that* the most evocative name for any waterway ever?) and the Snake, although my son Chris cautions that the Snake is not for the casual tourist and camper. It can be a very difficult and even dangerous piece of water for anyone but the young, strong, and daring. (Nebraska's largest and most spectacular waterfall, by the way, is on the Snake, south and west of Valentine.)

The Republican River in the south has been badly drained by irrigation and water diversion at dams and has therefore clogged up with brush, sand, and islands, but I can imagine it, the Blue, Elkhorn, and plenty of other minor courses in Nebraska would be pleasant if labor-intensive (not necessarily mutually exclusive concepts, I might note) floats in spring, like the Platte, when the water is up.

The canoe has always been the favored craft for shallow, sometimes restricted Nebraska rivers, but increasingly other modes of buoyancy are finding favor. Automobile tire inner tubes have given way to larger tractor inner tubes, sometimes with net decks to support camping gear and coolers, the "passengers" bobbing alongside, hanging on to ropes and lines attached to the tube. I have mentioned the accursed airboats with their serenity- and wildlife-destroying roar, and ATVs ripping up the landscape and frittering away our soil reserves while similarly destroying the peace. I can't explain why, but for some reason I am not as offended by one of the latest and most inventive fashions in Nebraska river floating . . . "tanking." Maybe it's the obviously rural basis that mitigates the hooha-ing and general party atmosphere in a context that, to my mind, requires reverence. A stock tank—a gigantic sheet-metal dish 12 to 20 feet across and 2 to 3 feet deep, designed to water cattle—is hauled down to the river, loaded up with food, drink, and . . . maybe this is the charming part . . . lawn chairs. The floaters board and downstream they go, with absolutely no control, at the mercy of the elements, for all the world becoming a Zen metaphor for life. The tanks offer remarkable stability and have a very shallow draft with their gigantic, flat bottoms, but after my experiences on the Loup with the *Diamond ITR*, I sure hate to think of dragging one of those gigantic things, loaded with beer, fried chicken, and lawn furniture, off a sandbar and through a narrow channel of the Elkhorn! As I said, it might be a good idea to save this one river-gloating technique for the high waters of spring.

Nebraska has a reputation for drought, and with good reason, but that doesn't mean it is dry. Let me explain: Our strength is groundwater, and where that ground finds a surface exposure, it can be lovely indeed. Take a look at a map that shows the area's lakes. Look at the Sandhills to the northwest of Grand Island. See all those blue speckles and spots? Those are lakes. Thousands of them. Nebraska has more shoreline than any state other than Minnesota. Yes, the most obvious shoreline for Nebraska is that beside the Missouri River, but when you add up all those little shorelines along the Sandhills lakes . . . wow! There is also an impressive number of reservoirs behind dams built on various rivers like the Republican, the Loup, and even the Calamus, and along the south side of the Platte from Ogallala down to Lexington, but these are generally clogged up with homes and cabins, water-skiers, Jet Skiers, massive fishing rafts and powerboats, on and on and on, with a list including all of the most annoying devices available to people with way too much money and far too little regard for others.

The Sandhills lakes are too remote and too shallow for most of the blasphemous activities of humans and are therefore my favorites. If you enjoy observing wildlife, take it from me and spend a day or two sometime soon just sitting in a lawn chair at the edge of a Sandhills lake—any Sandhills lake—with a mug of coffee or a cold drink and binoculars . . . and soak it in. You will be amazed at what you see. Even driving by the lakes, especially on the remote highways where you can take your time and not worry about traffic—say, Highway 61 north of Arthur, or better yet any of the county, unnumbered, aggregate one-laners through the Sandhills lake country north of North Platte to Bridgeport—is an adventure in wildlife like you've never seen, a veritable Nebraska safari. There aren't a lot of roads up that way, so you don't need to be worried about taking the wrong one! The Crescent Lake Wildlife Refuge north of Oshkosh is a particular favorite of mine and definitely worth the trip.

I'll talk about this later when I discuss roads and the nature of Nebraskans, but perhaps I should mention here, too, that especially those of you who are not accustomed to the wilderness might be uneasy about launching off into the total unknown, a true desolation where there are fewer than two people per square mile, probably more like less than *one* person per square mile in most cases. Take it from me, you will never be safer in your life than you are when you're alone in the Sandhills. Yes, the people there are definitely loners, sometimes downright peculiar. They can be rough in manner and mien. But by far the biggest problem you will have if you stop for any length of time to enjoy the scenery is that of the one or two other vehicles you will see in the road in an hour—if that—almost everyone will stop to see if you need help. Far from being in danger from strangers on the Sandhills roads, you will have problems with them being way too helpful and friendly. You are far more likely to get an invitation to supper from a landowner or even a curious passerby than you are a threat or actual violation of your safety.

I'm sure that one of the reasons I like the Sandhills lakes is that they are often more wetland than water. Over the years I have found that the most interesting area of my own sixty acres of Nebraska here near Dannebrog is the periodic wetlands, sandbars, willow islands, and wet slough along the river rather than the dry, solid ground or the river itself. That's because that transitional area between land and water, kind of wet and kind of dry, is where things are really going on. It's where the interesting wildlife and plants are. It is in these land-to-water border regions that the real dynamics of life go on. And that's what the Sandhills lakes are. If I were to dream up a fantasy vacation, one element of it would be a week camped at the edge of a Sandhills lake and marsh, just sitting and looking. More about that later, too.

I don't have space here to list all the watery places you might go to find peace and wonders. There are too many of them, for one thing. When I first took an interest in wild foods, a neighbor of ours came home to suburban Lincoln with a couple of bushels of wild plums and gave us some. Wow, I was amazed. I didn't know there were such things as wild plums, or that they are so good. So I asked her where she had found them, thinking I would go and get some, too. She couldn't remember. What? How could you find something as special as wild plums and not remember where? I was baffled. Well, she didn't remember because wild plums aren't that special. In fact, they aren't special at all. There's probably not one linear mile of Nebraska roads that doesn't have wild plums growing alongside. They're a weed. They're everywhere.

Same with Nebraska's watery wonders. Yes, there are special streams like Long Pine in north-central Nebraska near Bassett, stunning in its beauty. But I've found the same kind of beauty and wonder smack in the middle of Lincoln along Antelope Creek within easy walking distance of some very urban areas. Modest and humble Oak Creek that flows around and through Dannebrog is anything but a special river, and yet it is home to gigantic catfish, a few blue herons, all manner of raccoons, red foxes, coyotes, and . . . fossil elephants, one of which is on prominent display in Elephant Hall at the university. And a variety of plants that will amaze you. And the best part about these remote, little-known, -recognized, or -appreciated places is . . . no other people. Elsewhere in these pages I suggest that you just pick a Nebraska town at random and visit it. There's not a doubt in my mind that you will have a good time and find new friends there. Same with Nebraska's waterways. Pick a river or lake at random. Stop at a bridge over a nameless slough or creek. Sit on the bank awhile. Mosey around. Haul out a sleeping bag and sleep over. Drop a line in the water. Once again, the odds are a hundred to one that you will have a good time . . . and find some new friends.

Nebraska National Forest near Halsey

CHAPTER   SIX

Flora and Fauna, Beasts and Weeds

Speaking of wildlife—and I don't mean the Night Before strip joint in Lincoln—pure nature has to be one of Nebraska's major assets. And in contrast with what the rest of the world seems to be doing, in spite of humankind's best efforts, Nebraska's wildlife resources are only getting better. The thing is, like so much of what is the best of Nebraska, it's not a staged entertainment that's jammed into your face. A good part of the joy I take in Nebraska's wildlife and plant life is not merely seeing it exhibited in a formal garden or zoo but *discovering* it in its natural context, being surprised by it, stumbling on it, having it appear when I least expect it. I'm rounding a corner into town on my way to get the mail with a tractor when—wow! A flash of red . . . it's . . . yes!

. . . it's a gorgeous fox, grabbing a snack from a bit of opossum roadkill on the shoulder of a highway! On my way down the gravel toward St. Paul to visit my mother, daydreaming, same old road, same old dust, same old soybean field, same old . . . yikes! It's a coyote, gorgeous in her winter coat, and so close I can see her amber eyes! And then . . . then she runs into the bean field, and instead of slinking down between the rows she bounds high into the air to scout out a path through the thick crop, bouncing like a tennis ball again and again and again, bringing me to a stop with laughter. Headed back to the house from my office, distracted, preoccupied, mulling over some problem . . . whoops! Almost stepped on a big, beautiful garter snake sunning on the sidewalk! What mysterious critters they are. I'm betting this is the one Linda screamed about the other day . . . lives somewhere under the porch stairs, I think. Circling in the sky—is that . . . yep . . . it's a flight of pelicans! Wheeling, huge, white, and stunning in their beauty and grace. Pelicans! In Nebraska! Last week it was a flight of turkey buzzards sitting on the town water tower. That was creepy. And what the heck is *that?* I've never seen one before in my life but sure as billyhell, that's a *woodchuck!* Where the heck did *he* from? I can hardly wait to get home and tell Linda . . . a woodchuck, not 3 miles from our own place.

As with the weather, the one truly predictable thing about Nebraska wildlife is surprise. Sometimes even when I know better and should be expecting it, the processes and cycles of nature in this state catch me by surprise. For example, I know that every spring the cranes and geese will pass overhead, filling the air with their whirrs and birrs. And yet their appearance never fails to stop me in my tracks. For me the wonder is in large part the gigantic mechanisms of nature, inevitable and (hopefully) inexorable. The cranes have been flying this route for millions of years, and I hope to all that is holy that they have millions more, in defiance of the ignorant who would destroy what little they ask of us . . . some water in the rivers, for example. It seems little for our descendants to ask.

Flying the Coop

These days I can't imagine not noticing the flight of the cranes, and yet for many years I didn't. For one thing, I didn't live out here in the country, but you would have thought that in my many travels I would have noticed the cranes camped by the millions along the highways in the Platte Valley. They are big birds, after all. On the other hand, even now with a sharpened awareness for such things, I nearly miss the arrival and departure of the birds in spring and fall. Not the cranes or geese but all the other birds. It was my old friend Dan Selden who called my attention to this one. He drove into our yard one day, cocked his head, and said, "Listen. What do you hear?"

"Uuuh, nothing," I said.

"Exactly," he said. "The birds left this morning."

The birds left this morning? What the hell is that supposed to mean? Well, he explained, birds like robins, thrushes, threshers, and so forth don't just trickle in and out one at a time, now and then. Nope, they all pack up their luggage at once and take off in one major fare-thee-well. Hadn't I ever noticed? Well, no, as a matter of fact, I hadn't.

But from then on I did, and Dan was right. One morning I wake up to the manic chirping of robins at sunrise, and the next morning there is nothing but a haunting, empty silence. The birds are gone. And then I can sit back, check on my supply of firewood, and anticipate the morning I wake up and can tell Linda, "Listen, hon! The birds are back!" It gives me a thrill just to be let in on that little secret of nature.

There is the first eagle of autumn, and the first goldfinches of spring. Spring brings turkey chicks to the back fence, and the first gentle cooings of our turtledoves. One autumn day I was walking in the woods down along the river when suddenly I had a feeling of vertigo, and the trees around me suddenly took on a curious instability and lack of focus. My God—it was butterflies! Millions of monarch butterflies swarming the trees, resting on their way to wintering in Mexico. Talk about feeling as if I'd been let in on a cosmic secret. I felt privy to God on that day.

My favorite time of year is winter. I suspect there is less nature going on then, what with so many birds leaving, some animals hunkering down and sleeping off the cold, that kind of thing, but nature becomes more visible when there is a bit of snow on the ground, and I do love that. First thing after a good snow, I get into my winter warmies and head down to the river bottoms to see what the landlords are doing. I honestly feel that way. Linda and I are squatters; the true permanent residents are the ones who leave the fresh tracks in that snow. It's important to get down there not too long after a snowfall, because before long the snow will be so trampled, it's hard to tell what's going on. There are always heavily traveled trails, but what's astonishing is the remarkable number and variety of tracks, headed in every direction, large and small, moving slow, moving fast, hopping, running, loafing, dragging along . . . We rarely see any of these souls in person—an occasional glimpse of the turkeys, lots of squirrels of course, a cottontail now and then, rarely a fox or coyote, deer occasionally—but once it snows and their tracks are left behind them, only then do we get an insight to the enormous amount of traffic that goes on silently and unseen around us. It's amazing. Far more useful to us than an animal identification guide is the book in our library that identifies animal tracks. Just about the only other way to see things otherwise unseen is when they're roadkills on the highway near our place, and there are plenty of those. The only place I have yet to see a porcupine around here is dead on the shoulder of the highway, so I know they're here even if I—or worse yet my dogs—are spared the misfortune of running into one. Speeding motorists and confused critters keep our coyotes well fed.

Speaking of which, there is another way we keep track of who the other occupants of our sixty acres are besides their trails in the snow: what they, uh, leave behind in the natural course of digestion, if you catch my drift. We have come to recognize raccoon poop, deer poop, rabbit poop, owl poop, and, especially, coyote poop. No poop is as interesting as coyote poop, and you can quote me on that. My friend Russ the Scientist cautions me to be careful about handling any of this stuff because it can carry disease with it, but stirring around in dry, older coyote poop makes for some interesting reading indeed. (My guess is that at this point you are wondering about exactly how much of what I have told you previously can be taken seriously, right? But I'm not kidding here.) You'd be amazed at what coyotes eat. And eliminate. Bug wings, feathers, hair of all colors and textures, grass stems, little teeth (eeeeuuuuuwwww . . . that *has* to be a coyote proctological problem!), bones, sticks, and mysteries that defy identification.

So there are the daily cycles of those who travel around this place. And there are seasonal flows, like the migrations of the cranes and geese and the changes in the bird populations. But the truly grand and wonderful changes I've seen in my thirty years of deep immersion in Nebraska nature having this access, and the twenty years of actually living here full time, are even larger than daily and seasonal . . . they are perhaps as vast in scope as geology, measured in millennia. In some cases we are enjoying the return of animals that were historically here but have been driven from this landscape by the press of human population: turkeys, bald eagles, kestrels and hawks, mountain lions, wolves, elk, moose, and bluebirds. It's hard to say why beings like this are making a comeback. It might be attributable to some degree to conservation practices (many of which are now under assault by greedy, ignorant people who should and perhaps even do know better); to changes in land use, so there are now more wildlife refuges along waterways; and to the clear fact that the population in many parts of Nebraska is decreasing as we figure out how few can make a living on the fragile and harsh landscape. Eventually I'd like to see the native parakeet back in the state. See? There are a lot of great possibilities in this direction.

Newcomers

Even more mysterious and impressive to me, however, are the animals venturing onto the mid-Plains that are *not* historically native here. That sort of invasion has always gone on and is completely natural. Possums were not historically present in Nebraska, but they have slowly but surely pushed their way northwestward through the state and now are so common they have become nuisances, easily recognized by everyone except maybe those who are totally unaware of nature around them. Now we are getting reports of armadillos and scorpions moving northward into Nebraska, perhaps only temporarily because of the drought of the 1990s and early twenty-first century. These two invaders are not equipped to deal with the cold, but there are signs they are learning. Armadillos are now wintering in haystacks as far north as Ord, putting Dannebrog in their territory, although I have yet to see one in the wild myself. Six months ago I could say the same thing, however, about woodchucks, so . . .

By far and away my favorite new animal immigrant to Nebraska is the *Onychomys leucogaster,* or (I'm not kidding you) the howling mouse. These cute little boogers are absolutely ferocious, staking claim to 10 square yards or so of territory and defending it to the death against anything and everything. They'll take on cats and dogs. If they get really, really hungry, they'll even pull down a bird! They are not a pest for humankind, however, because they don't bother crops or carry off women and children. But best of all—note their name—they howl. Like coyotes. They stand up on their back legs, tip back on their long tails, point their noses at the moon, and howl their little hearts out. In my life I just once want to hear the haunting cry of the howling mouse. I want to see one of these little rascals. I want to get to know one.

There is perennial discontent in the state with the admittedly dumb designation of our university athletes as "Cornhuskers," and the goofy mascots that label necessitates. Well, I suggest that we adopt as our Official State Rodent, team mascot, and personal favorite this wonderful little scrapper, thus becoming the University of Nebraska Howling Mice. Give me one reason why not.

There are increasing reports of introductions that clearly have a human souce—for example, piranhas caught in local lakes and even in the Missouri River by startled fishermen. The usual official explanation is that these are private aquarium denizens that have been dumped by thoughtless idiots, and that these flesh-eating fish-demons can't possibly survive Nebraska winters. But think about it. Say ten people—a preposterously inflated number—release their piranhas into the Missouri River because they either ate the cat or are unnecessary baggage now that the owner is moving to Chicago. And let's say just for conversation's sake that each of the ten people dump three fish. That's thirty fish. In the Missouri River. Where maybe a hundred people are fishing along its 150-mile Nebraska bank on any one day. Take a look at the Missouri River, as I have already suggested. It is E-double-damned-*nor*mous! Trillions of gallons of water. And we now have thirty fish in it. And a fisherman catches one of them.

Out of the billions of fish naturally swimming in those billions of gallons of water—catfish, goldeyes, carp, buffalo fish, paddlefish, crappie—this one fisherman catches one of the thirty piranhas in the river. The odds of that happening make the lottery look like a general and generous giveaway. My point is that the odds of piranhas some-how surviving—and multiplying—in our waters are far, *far* greater than those of someone catching one. Yet three or four were caught in one summer season. Think of that the next time you go skinny-dipping in the farm pond.

These developments in Nebraska's fauna inventory please me to no end. If we can't go to nature, well, it appears that nature is com-ing to us. For me it's like a wonderful dream: the return of the old residents, an introduction of new citizens. So while we're speaking of fantasies realized, how about some fantasies to be dreamed? Cloning is now becoming almost commonplace. There is no reason to expect it to become more difficult. I wouldn't be at all surprised if in my life-time scientists clone the Tasmanian wolf, now extinct. Or maybe the dodo. How about the passenger pigeon? I would like to see clouds of passenger pigeons once again darkening the Nebraska sky as they were doing during the first white invasions into the area (speaking of pernicious introduced species). I wish something would happen to reverse the retreat of the honeybee from Nebraska; to be sure, the honeybee is a white man's introduction in the first place—the Omaha Indians knew it as "white man's fly"—but now there are very few bee trees, where they were common as recently as twenty years ago. I would love to see that trend reversed.

Okay, here it goes, a flight of fancy making a landing approach, ETA hopefully within my lifetime: How about . . . cloned saber-toothed tigers in the Panhandle again, or woolly mammoths and mastodons back in Howard County? Speeders now recklessly careen around the corner of Highway 58, across the Loup River bridge, and past our gate, only occasionally losing a grille or fender to a deer or turkey crossing the road. I can imagine traffic slowing to a crawl around that curve if it were designated a Woolly Mammoth or Mastodon Crossing. It's not as far-fetched a notion as you might think, actually. In the August 2005 issue of the journal *Nature*, a team of ecologists suggest turning the Plains not into a Buffalo Commons but an Africa Redux, releasing elephants, camels, and even big cats into a removed but very natural environment. Count me in. I'm for it.

Turning Over a New Leaf

Precisely the same phenomena occur in Nebraska botany. There are, for example, wonderful plants way too many Nebraskans don't generally know about: penstemon, lady's slipper orchids, watercress, even things as humble but grand as elderberry blossoms and delicious as ground cherries. There are plants that were once commonplace but which have become rare because of the loss of habitat, climate change, agricultural practices, the loss of pollinator insects like the honeybee: calamus, groundnuts, gooseberries, wild potatoes, gayfeather. There are introductions like various thistles, spurge, kochia, Russian olive, mulberries—some bad, some good. Some plants that are native—like the prickly pear cactus—have come to infest large areas like our wretched sixty-acre sandbox here on the Middle Loup River, where it has become our main annoyance.

Just as I have established the case for animals, there are larger dynamics in what grows here and what does not with larger changes

in climate and weather; as we have come to know our small plot here
ever better, we have been able to notice subtle and curious changes in
what we see by way of plants from year to year. One year the woolly
mullein springs up everywhere. The next year it is gone but we see
more milkweed than usual, or ironweed. One year the morning prim-
rose takes over, and every morning we have a blinding flash of light
yellow covering our hillside . . . and the next year there is almost
none, but the wonderful blue haze of spiderwort blankets every hill
around us. How will the chicory do next year? Or the morel mush-
rooms? Last year that chokecherry bush in the uplands had branches
breaking down from the weight of the fruit . . . this year not a single
cherry. On any one day in any one season of any one year, Nebraska's
flora offerings may seem pretty monotonous. Not if you watch for any
period of time, though. The most distinctive trait of Nebraska's botany
is, in fact, change. The key phrase is *if you watch for any period of time*.
All Nebraskans should be required to pick out a piece of ground—if
only 1 yard by 1 yard—visit it weekly, keep a journal about it, and
keep track of all the wonderful things that go on in that bit of
Nebraska, whether in an Omaha alleyway or a Sandhills cattle pen.

I lament the day some goofball took it upon himself to discard
the state's designation as "the Tree Planter State." Nebraska Tree
Planters. What a noble way to be identified! Of all the contributions
Nebraska has made, Arbor Day is the best. There is no nobility whatsoever in being identified as the state that sells its children's education in return for a team of mercenaries playing football. But to be
the Tree Planter State . . . that speaks of grand and genuine idealism,
of a hope for and a contribution to the future.

And perhaps to inevitable futility. I was once talking with
"Young" Jules Sandoz, sister of author Mari Sandoz. We were dis-
cussing his family's long history of orchards, windbreaks, and tree
plantings in the Sandhills. He snorted, "Trees! This isn't tree country!
It's *grass* country." He was right, of course. Our ground here in
Howard County is designated an official tree farm, and we have
planted and nurtured (insofar as it is possible in what is after all

truly "grass country") many thousands of trees, and I do love trees, but I can't fool myself about what the Great Plains are. As Young Jules said, "Grass country. It's *grass* country." I imagine that when the white man finally does finish himself off and retreat from his temporary and ruinous occupation of the region, most of the trees we have planted will soon disappear before racing grass fires as they did through the previous millions of years. But for the moment, Linda and I will continue our futile struggle and plant trees. I can't help it . . . I love trees.

Of Trees

It is against the law in Lincoln, our state capital, to plant our state tree, the cottonwood. At least the female gender. People, it seems, get huffy about the female's "cotton" flying about and clogging radiators, air-conditioner condenser screens, and noses. I like the drifts of cottonwood fluff in road ruts and town gutters. Willa Cather called it "summer snow." I love the shimmer of cottonwood leaves in summer breezes, the rattle of the leaves in late summer and autumn, and the ferocious tenacity of cottonwood seedlings carpeting sandbars in the river, growing in the yard wherever they find a break in the grass cover, and persisting through the toughest winter, drought, wind, and hailstorm.

The Lakota considered the cottonwood sacred, using it reverently as a centerpiece of the annual Sundance. They felt that through the cottonwood leaf Wakan Tonka, "the Great Mysterious," gave us the pattern for both the tipi and moccasins. The Omaha appreciated the consideration of cottonwood not throwing sparks in the close quarters of a tipi or earth lodge. Cottonwoods have grown quickly in our yard here in some very difficult conditions, and yet there are cottonwood trees in the river bottoms that I noted as being gigantic and age-old when I first saw them thirty years ago . . . and they are still alive and probably growing, although now that I see them so regularly and because they are already so huge, it's hard to see. Some are described by old-timers in town as having been considered huge and old sixty years ago. How old can they be? They almost certainly ante-date white occupation. Bison may have rubbed against them in their lifetime; Pawnee perhaps camped in their shade. They are truly our elders and deserve our respect. Pushing down windbreaks planted thirty, maybe seventy years ago should be considered a crime against posterity. No Nebraskan should ever cut down a tree without planting two more in its place. It should be a law. I have spoken.

But at the bottom line, Young Jules was right—Nebraska and the Plains *are* grass country. Fires moving faster than a man could ride on horseback across the tinder-dry grass, more exploding than burning, and constant rubbing and horning by buffalo eliminated all but the most tenacious trees and those insulated by water on Platte River islands or in bends of creeks like the big, old oaks here in Dannebrog in a bend of Oak Creek and the Middle Loup River, prob-ably planted originally for food by the Pawnee.

If you think about it, Nebraska is largely still *grass* country . . . pasture to the west, corn, a kind of grass, to the east, milo and grain sorghum—more grasses—in the middle. There is other crop cover from soybeans to alfalfa, sugar beets to sunflowers and even milk-weed. A few wise agriculturists have decided that distorting the Plains to fit our crops may not be the smartest thing you could do and have instead adjusted crops to the land—substituting milo or grain sorghum, for example, for corn, which uses much more water, an increasingly scarce and expensive commodity, or developing grape varietals that are hardy in Nebraska weather, launching an absolute avalanche of wineries throughout the state.

But if man—or at least the white man—were to disappear from this geography, it would be a matter of only a few years before the whole region was back to its native grasses. Everything else, from corn to trees, is maintained artificially and only temporarily no mat-ter how persistent and pervasive it may seem now. Again, like the white man . . .

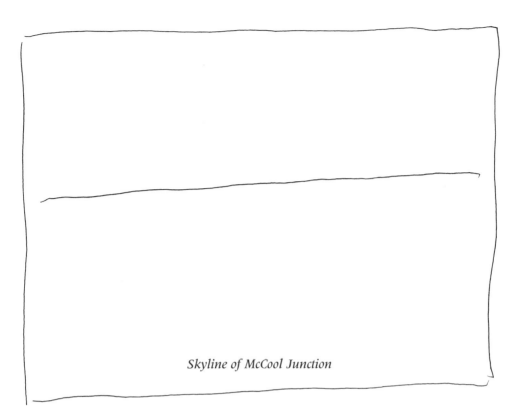

Skyline of McCool Junction

CHAPTER SEVEN

People and Folks

It may strike some of you as peculiar that I have waited so long in my discussion about Nebraska to get to Nebraskans. It isn't. The only human residents who have become so much a part and reflection of Nebraska geography that they actually have earned the designation of "Nebraskan" are the Native residents . . . the Omaha, Ponca, Lakota. The Hochunk, or Winnebago, are relative newcomers, too, and shamefully the Pawnee have been driven away (although there is some hope and promise that, like the bald eagle, they will be returning soon to their native homelands). We white folks simply haven't been here long enough. We still think of ourselves as conquerors of the Plains, as molders of the geography and climate rather than the opposite, which is the obvious truth. To this point, we non-Natives still don't know diddly-squat about the Great Plains.

Slowly but surely, however, I believe the Plains are having their impact on our psyches, clear evidence of Darwin's theories if there ever was one. If anything, it is test-tube evolution, hyperaccelerated when human beings utterly unaccustomed to this environment were injected into it in large numbers and not only without adequate preparation physically, emotionally, and intellectually, but in fact often dysprepared when they were given heinously incorrect information by boosters who wanted new settlers out here at any cost. At any cost to those who came, that is. As a result, to rephrase Mari Sandoz, either you were a homesteader, or you weren't. It was cut bait or die, as simple as that. You made it, or you didn't. Root, hog, or die, as the song of the time went. You were set up to get stinking rich and if you didn't—which was more often than not the case—you bought the pig in the poke and it turned out to be not quite the bargain you hoped. Not a doubt in my mind . . . I wouldn't have made it.

People prepared for balmy, idyllic conditions at worst, bearable at best, found themselves confronted by horrors they probably wouldn't have believed even if they'd been fully and honestly informed. So they died or folded up their tents and went back east, busted and fed up. A stunning number of homesteaders committed suicide—victims, it was said, of "wind sickness." Settlers learned to lock their barns because it was all too likely otherwise that when they came out to do the chores in the morning they would find that a neighbor, lacking anything of height or even a convenient tree stout enough, had used one of the barn beams as a gallows. When there weren't even barns, sometimes a well had to serve as the suicide's springboard to eternity. Then the railroads came through and provided sturdy trestles for desperate departures. The result of all this accelerated genetic selection has been an impressive distillation of spirit and body in those who survived, remained, and now descend.

Or perhaps more accurately, ascend, since those of us who survive consider ourselves strengthened by the forge of the Great Plains.

The Grand Mixmaster

All you have to do is look at places where racial and ethnic groups share an interface—Hawaii, for example, or the Asian–European historic frontier in southeastern Europe, or the Latino southwest of this country—and you will find it hard to deny that refreshing the gene pool generates some very handsome people. Whatever inbreeding there had been in the restricted and genetically degenerating European homelands of the settlers who came to the Great Plains was eliminated in spades when suddenly Danes who had never met another human being in their thirty or forty years of life who wasn't a Dane, suddenly here in Nebraska found themselves dealing with German settlers to the south, Poles to the west, Czechs to the north, a Chinese laundryman in St. Paul to the east, and, good grief, a black man right here in Dannebrog, the very heart of America's New Denmark . . . and he was the village blacksmith at that, utterly crucial to the economy of the village and impossible to avoid no matter how dubious the Danes who'd never seen so much as a Spaniard (let alone an African!) might be.

The frontier was a time of glorious mixing. Then as now the great majority swore that no child of theirs was going to marry a [fill in the blank: Bohunk, Negro, Polack, Chinaman, Catholic, Freethinker, Jew, German, Odenseer, Copenhager, Democrat, et cetera], but just as parents will be parents, children will be children, and the miscegenation proceeded apace. How do I know all this? Because I'm part of it. My grandparents had nothing but contempt for other German-Russians across town, yet any other nationality or race—anyone, in fact, who was not German-Russian—was labeled generically "Englischer Pieschiesser." Mexican, Japanese, Irish, Italian . . . to my grandparents they were all "English pie-shitters." Don't ask me why. Of course it makes no sense. Prejudice never does.

Me? Purebred German-Russian, Lutheran-born, I married my Lovely Linda, a Bohemian Catholic, and our child is so gloriously beautiful, she takes your breath away. It wasn't easy for the substantial number of black cowboys and homesteaders in Nebraska to fit in, if they ever did. But that's the way it goes. It happens, sometimes slowly, but also inevitably, inexorably. And it will happen with the Somalis now making new homes in places like Lincoln and Grand Island. Just as inevitable but less inexorable is the mindless and irrational hatred some people nurse for anyone who isn't precisely as ugly as they are.

Of Innocence and Ignorance

On the other hand, Nebraskans tend to feel more along the line of discomfort with people of unfamiliar appearance or culture rather than hatred. In his *God's Country and My People,* good ol' Wright Morris hit things square on, right on the nose once again, speaking of course of Nebraskans:

> A restrained optimism characterizes the inlook and the outlook of these pioneer people who welcome the visitor with a "Howdy, stranger!" and a friendly smile. Until a man proves himself bad he is considered good. . . . The state emblem, a stiffly pleated upper lip, symbolizes the spirit of its pioneer people in a new age.

I don't know how much of that Wright Morris wrote with a bit of sarcasm in his pen, but I don't think it makes much difference since, after all, it is gospel truth. Even the Nebraska Cornhusker football fan for whom I have so little regard is famous throughout the nation not only for his mindless passion for the game but also for his remarkable courtesy and goodwill toward the opposition's fans, being utterly bewildered when those on the other side of a stadium show rudeness, let alone malice.

As is so often the case, it was again Wright Morris who captured in his work *The Home Place* the trouble that Nebraskans have had (apparently for a long time) with crudeness:

> Simple folk don't know how to deal with vulgarity. They're puzzled by it, as real vulgarity is pretty refined. You don't come by it naturally. Maybe you can tell me why it is that simple folk are seldom indelicate, while it's something of a trial for sophisticated people not to be.

You can't put in an evening, with really smart people, without a good
deal of truck with what is nothing more nor less than vulgarity.

It is my impression that Nebraskans are not maliciously ugly
when it comes to religion, culture, politics, race, nationality, or language: The severe insularity of being here in the Middle of Nowhere,
the Middle of Everywhere, carries with it a natural consequence of
innocence about such things. Nebraskans believe a national health
program would be an evil thing because (1) that's what they've been
told by politicians, who incidentally avail themselves of federal health
benefits and medical care, and (2) they haven't experienced anything
even remotely like the kind of medical care that is accepted as a matter of course by the rest of the world. Nebraskans reject any notion of
public transit because they've never ridden a train in Europe.
Nebraskans take their coffee watery, with creamer and sweetener—
that is to say, bad—because they've never tasted good coffee. On and
on. You get the idea.

Similarly, Nebraskans are not pernicious in their religious imperi-
alism and oppression; they've simply never thought about it. I was
once sitting at the head table of a small-town banquet while a town
minister was delivering a blessing for the meal. He concluded, as is so
often the case at Nebraska gatherings, with the words ". . . in Jesus'
name we pray," and I muttered, as is also so often the case, ". . . and
tough luck to those of you present who happen to be Jewish." The
minister's wife was seated next to me and overheard my mumbled
comment and was surprised. She asked what I meant and I explained
that, well, since it was a rather large gathering—perhaps 500 people—
in a town of some size, it was entirely possible that there might be
some in attendance who were Jewish. Or even Muslim or Buddhist
or Deists . . . like George Washington and Thomas Jefferson, by the
way . . . and they might not want to be spoken for "in Jesus' name."

She said, "But . . . aren't Jews Christian?"

I thought, *Well, there you have it*. While there are ugly people
who see religion as a weapon they can use against others, a source of

power otherwise lacking in their lives, a hangover from superzealots who marched heathens to the river's edge and forced baptism at the point of a sword before they were sent on their way to heaven with an express ticket, more often than not religious bigotry in Nebraska is a product of ignorance and innocence, plain and simple.

Nebraskans, sadly, have forgotten that a great majority of immigrants came not to establish an official religion but to escape one. It's true that the Pilgrims did not come here to establish religious freedom but to escape what they considered excessive religious tolerance in Holland and to establish their own oppressive theocracy, as Roger Williams would tell his neo-Baptist followers. But some—maybe many—migrants came to Nebraska to get away from oppressive, state-sponsored religion. In many communities believers had problems building churches because their many neighbors who had come here to escape an enforced, majority faith burned any collection of materials meant for the construction of a new church. When Nebraska pietists speak of returning to the religion of our pioneer forebears, I can only assume that, as usual, they have no idea what they're talking about.

A friend's evangelical Baptist wife was once railing against those of us who feel there should be a separation of church and state (to protect religion, I might note) and insisted that prayer should be a standard part of public school instruction because "in America the majority rules," never mind that the Constitution was framed to protect the minority, not the majority. I said, "Well, then, you better get your kids to practice their Hail Marys, because the majority in this county is Catholic." She was stunned and silent. She had presumed that *she* was in the majority. That's why she felt the majority should rule. Somehow a majority theocracy where she wasn't in that majority didn't seem nearly as attractive to her. She simply hadn't considered such an unthinkable possibility. Few Nebraskans do. This means that those Nebraskans who consider themselves the most religious and who have therefore restricted their thinking to one narrow line of thought tend to be in fact the least spiritual. Like good Nebraskans, they do and believe what they are told.

Curiously, that makes them precisely what they are told they should abhor: humanists! That is, they put their faith not in the spirit of religion (or the Constitution) but in what some human agency—a bishop, priest, minister, council, or synod, a human figure or human agency of authority—tells them they should embrace. When there is a new threat to whatever they are being told to believe—a restriction of freedoms in the Constitution rather than the expansion of liberties the Founding Fathers clearly intended, or a more restrictive legalistic interpretation of the Scriptures as manipulated by remarkably narrow political notions rather than an extension or advance of Christian principles a la Jesus—Nebraskans will at least say what they are supposed to say.

And nonetheless do what they are supposed to do. And therein lies the basis for my trust and affection for Nebraskans, despite my dismay at the nutty things I sometimes hear from them. From the way Nebraskans talk, you might think they are just short of being bigots and fools, but their actual behavior says exactly the opposite. If you listen to Omaha or Lincoln AM radio stations, you may be shocked, as I have been, by the hate and venom that has become the standard: insults, invective, racial slurs, small-minded anti-intellectualism, crude and disingenuous dishonesty . . . I once heard a cultural throwback by the name of Michael Savage vomiting on radio KFAB that he was "sick and tired of this Ramadan crap." I had to stop my car and regain my poise. I had just spent the day with the Muslim community in Lincoln, and a kinder, gentler, sweeter, more generous, more spiritual crowd I have never seen. And here was a purported Christian spewing his filth, embarrassing me even while insulting my friends.

I complained to the programming director at KFAB, and his response made me want to cry: He said they air that kind of thing because that's what their audience wants. KFAB is, or at least claims to be, the largest broadcasting station in Nebraska, so he was telling me that my fellow Nebraskans want this kind of cultural pornography, and so he provides it to them. Michael Savage is one sick cookie, and I can accept that. But it is not so easy for me to imagine that there are that many sick people in Nebraska wanting to listen to him.

I'm still not over that obscene notion, but I think that my suspicions are right: Nebraskans may indeed agree with Savage's brand of ignorance, but it is out of innocence, not maliciousness. While Nebraskans may be slow to accept a new kind of immigrant, their appearance or religion, there is nonetheless a pervasive and genuine Nebraska disposition toward charity, acceptance, friendliness . . . that spirit that Wright Morris has in mind when he says that we Nebraskans accept people for what they are. Because that's what they are. As with all things, it seems, from clothing to music, from foodways to entertainment, from religion to politics, Nebraskans are anything but "trendy." Again, the words of my friend Wright Morris, speaking of Nebraskans in his book *God's Country* (that would be Nebraska) *and My People* (those would be Nebraskans):

> The people of the state, conservative by nature, living close to the soil and the round of seasons, are not swept by the tides of shifting opinion. . . . [They] both live longer and go mad sooner.

Ultimately, the most religious Nebraskans I have encountered are precisely those who profess— or who are at least perceived—to be the least religious. Maybe it's always that way, everywhere. I don't know. But I do have the distinct impression that it's the way things are here. If you want a conversation about the meaning of life, the mysteries of the universe, the perversity of life, the wonders around us, you don't ask the self-described "religious" Nebraskan, you ask the guy who is out fishing or hunting Sundays, or the farmer who may or may not go to church regularly, may or may not give a lot of thought to theology, but who works hard, raises his children well, and devotes his life to the most blessed pursuit there can possibly be on this green earth, growing food.

As for those who profess a religious faith in the heresy of Nebraska foot-Baal . . . well, by now you know how that story ends and where the heretics are headed.

Impolitic Politics

Nebraska politics defy analysis. The same state that elected Carl Curtis and Roman "Mediocrities Deserve Representation in the US Supreme Court" Hruska sent Bob Kerrey to the governor's mansion and eventually to the Senate. The very same people elected nominal Democrat Ben "Bend-Over" Nelson . . . and maverick Republican Chuck "Don't Tell Me What to Think" Hagel. The one decent and competent member of George W. Bush's hopelessly corrupt cabinet is former Nebraska governor Mike Johanns, elevated by President Bush to Secretary of Agriculture. He is a solidly right-wing Republican whom I, a raving liberal, nonetheless respect enormously for his civility, good sense, and honesty. Nebraska's right wing seems to be to the left of its left wing, while the state's left wing is often found to the right of its right. It's like a chicken turned inside out.

Given an increasingly desperate agricultural economy and ever weaker political voice as the strength and numbers of farmers and ranchers in America decline, who did Nebraska's third and almost totally agricultural district send to Congress? A popular football coach! A current best seller explores this same kind of political stupidity in Kansas and explains it as a self-destructive substitution of larger, more remote, less substantial smokescreen issues like guns, prayer, abortion, and so forth, for the much more immediate, obvious, and important *Kansas* issues like agriculture, the economy, civil liberties, and public services and infrastructure.

That same thing is to some degree true for Nebraska, too, but even more important to the Nebraska voter, in my estimation, is whom he knows and likes. Competence, experience, education, training, philosophy, record, effectiveness . . . none of that particularly matters to the Nebraska voter, who seems to ask first and perhaps only, *Do I like this guy? Do I even recall who he is?* That may not make for very good politics, but it does make everyone comfortable, and that seems to be what is most important to Nebraska. Who else? It was Wright Morris who said it so well (in his book *The Home Place*): "They take a man at his face value, as they figure it's his own face, a fairly private affair."

Who Are Nebraskans?

We are still mostly rural, for one thing, and then further divided into east and west, farm and ranch, as determined by the geography, tallgrass to shortgrass, dry to drier, corn to cattle. While most of the western part of the state is dominated by the Sandhills region with its very unique geography—the largest sand dune area in the entire Western Hemisphere, after all—it is my impression that there is still a slight difference between western Nebraskans and Sandhills Nebraskans.

It is, after all, primarily in the Sandhills that you find real isolation. Look at a road map. Look at the scarcity of roads through that huge area of land to the north and west, much more thinly populated than even the Panhandle or southwestern part of the state. I think that isolation, and the very thin population density, and the geographic severity of the region have molded a particular kind of disposition of its inhabitants. Nebraskans in general tend to be civil, personable, accepting, but blunt. Well, those characteristics go one step more toward the extreme in the Sandhills. Sandhillers are tough and hardworking, independent but eager to help when there is a problem, outspoken but taciturn, and not particularly receptive to the ideas, fashions, attitudes, and manner of those who are not from the Sandhills. Those who like the Sandhills tend to like the people of the Sandhills; the people of the Sandhills don't generally give much of a diddly damn whether the rest of us like them or not. I like 'em.

Farmers are not just people who live in the country. You don't learn how to be a farmer. You grow up a farmer. Farming doesn't only require an unbelievable inventory of skills and information; even more importantly, farming requires an attitude. I admire that spirit, but I don't have it. Our place here is officially a tree farm and we have planted tens of thousands of trees, but it kills me when we have a storm or drought and I watch helplessly as trees die. The trees weren't expensive to begin with, were planted in my spare time, and aren't really worth much even when fully grown, but nonetheless, when my trees die, a little bit of me dies, too. I know for a fact I couldn't watch a year's work destroyed by a storm, fire, wind, hail, freeze, flood, whatever, knowing that I depended on that crop for my very ownership of the land, or Antonia's education, or health care for Linda . . . Real farmers do it all the time. For them it is simply the way things go. I can't imagine walking that agricultural tightrope. I insist that all of us in Nebraska, however, are, like it or not, in agriculture. More about that later . . .

Cowboys and Indians

To my mind, the funniest misconception about Nebraska arises when a native of the state reacts to the naïveté of an outsider who reveals his ignorance by suggesting even vaguely that there are still cowboys and Indians on the Plains. There is hilarious laughter, perhaps even finger pointing and rolling on the ground. Man, how backward do you think we are? Wow . . . this idiot thinks we still have *cowboys* . . . and *Indians!*

Once things calm down a bit I take it on myself, sometimes in private conversation, to inform the ignorant dolt—the Nebraskan, not the visitor—that we *do* still have cowboys. And Indians. And not just for show. Cowboying is very much alive on Nebraska ranches, and it is not at all unusual to see cowboys at work in the Sandhills . . . insofar as you see anyone when you are in the Sandhills, that is. Yes, you will see men and women working cattle from the cabs of pickup trucks or ATVs—even with airplanes!—but to this day there is no substitute for a good hand on a good horse when it comes to moving cattle.

And not only are there Indians in Nebraska, but in fact the Omaha, Hochunk (Winnebago), and Ponca have reservations along the eastern edge of the state with substantial populations where many historical traditions are maintained with pride. Especially at powwow times nontribal members are invited to join in music, dance, food, and general celebration. Speaking of tightropes, many enrolled tribal members maintain a delicate balance between modern, mainstream life and a beautiful Native tradition that certainly deserves to continue at least as much as the cultural practices of Czech Sokols and the Sons of Italy. In the case of the Omaha Indians whose reservation lies an hour north of the city of Omaha, they are in fact still on land that has been their tribal area for 400 years, in contrast with the vast majority of America's Native population, which has been shuffled, forced, mugged, and robbed from and of their homelands. So, yeah . . . if there is a misconception about there being cowboys and Indians in Nebraska still today, it's the goofy notion of some Nebraskans that there are no cowboys and Indians in Nebraska today. They're here, and chances are they are going to be here a long, long time.

And Others

The bulk of immigrants to Nebraska historically came from Scandinavia, Germany, Poland, and Czechoslovakia, but there are also communities and neighborhoods that are still distinctively Italian, Irish, Welsh, and Greek. Increasingly, even in the rural countryside and small towns, there are clusters and neighborhoods of New Americans: Southeast Asians, Bosnians, Afghanis, Hispanics, Somalis, and Iraqis. I for one am wildly enthusiastic about the new blood. I have never found more enthusiastic Americans, harder workers, nicer, more honest, more decent, more friendly, more generous people than these New Americans. While there is still a general uneasiness within mainstream Nebraska circles about these strange colors, clothes, foods, and ways, there's only a bit of evil expressed a la Michael Savage toward our new neighbors. When the subject comes up among my Nebraska friends, the attitude toward New Americans generally seems to be something like "Well, yeah, sure, I like Jacinto and Isabella fine. I consider Pedro and Hermano some of the best guys I've ever worked with. I'm not crazy about *Mexicans*, you know, but sure, I like those guys. You know, they're not like really *Mexicans*, if you know what I mean." I find that Nebraskans are not quite sure how to deal with these new citizens, but to my delight, they are willing to give them a fair chance.

Not to mention that their foods are *wonderful!* While most of the newcomers and their cultural goods are a bit too peculiar for most Nebraskans at this point, as I have noted above, as slow as acceptance might be, sooner or later it comes along. When I was a child there was a sum total of *one* place in all of Lincoln, the capital city after all, to get "ethnic" foods, and that was Toni and Luigi's Italian Village (pronounced *EYE-talian*, by the way). In Omaha you could walk up a long, narrow flight of stairs to sample mysterious delights at King Fong's Chinese Restaurant, but hey, that's the kind of thing one expects of a big cosmopolitan city like Omaha. Now, in only a generation, "ethnic" foods thought extraordinarily exotic only a generation ago have become not just standard fare but *fast foods!* It's incredible to me. Nebraskans don't even think of tacos, pizza, runzas, egg rolls, pita bread, baklava, and salsa as anything but good ol' red-blooded American food now. I wouldn't be surprised if most Nebraskans couldn't even give you an approximation of a nation-of-origins for those dishes. They've become totally American. There's not a doubt in my mind that even though it is happening slowly now, baba ghanoush, nan, retsina, matte, and even menudo will enjoy the same familiarity. Even in Nebraska.

Bad Language

I was once at the Dannebrog Tavern with some friends and listened with interest as a local, well known for his bigotry, railed against these "damned Mexicans" and their perceived reluctance to learn "American." I didn't bother to mention on this occasion that the speaker himself didn't even have a masterful command of English, let alone a second language, so who was he to complain that Hispanics in the area weren't learning English fast enough for his standards? He wouldn't have sensed the irony, I'm sure. Nor did he show any sign that he sensed his own unintentional irony when he shifted cultural gears and began a sorrowful speech about how sad it was that here in the official Danish Capital of Nebraska one never hears the Danish language anymore.

I think that's where we stand with most bigotry in the state: It is silly. The worst thing you can do to a bigot is to not take him seriously, to laugh at him. Before anyone can raise an objection, bigotry will almost surely become the subject of nostalgia. "Remember those good old days when the guys over at the Azteca Bodega spoke nothing but Spanish? Man, that was great. Now it's nothing but punk kids who don't even know how to make a decent tamale."

Nebraskans demand that these guests and newcomers to our state make at least an effort to learn our beloved and God-given "American" language. On the other hand, should our National Guard troops hijacked to Iraq learn so much as one word of Arabic? Don't be silly. That would be an insult! Do Nebraskans make any effort at all to learn even a few words of Spanish for their annual winter trips to Cancún or Belize? Are you out of your mind? Of course not!

I suspect that the foods we now enjoy and think of as being ethnic specialties reflecting our various heritages may have suffered some in translation and transmission over the years. Is the Italian spaghetti specialty served at the Sons of Italy Hall in Omaha anything even remotely like what you would get if you ordered a pasta dish in Italy? How about the gyros at Jim's Gyros in Grand Island? Would they be recognizable to an immigrant newly arrived from Spanikopita, Greece? Do they even still make kolaches in a typical Prague bakery or household? And if they do, do they look like the ones in Dwight or Verdigris? We could expect, I suppose, that a burrito at Taco John's is not likely to be very authentic, but I have it on good authority that even the dishes at the truly Mexican eateries in Mexican neighborhoods around the state from Norfolk to Lexington are also not quite the same as what you might find in the country of origin. I can't imagine that dishes cooked up once a year specifically for town festivals and ethnic fairs, from Polish sausages in Loup City to German roulade in Eustis, would be identified as such back in the Homeland.

As a folklorist and eater of some accomplishment and practice, I have no problem at all with that. What's important in such things is not some sort of artificial standards of authenticity but taste and intent. The kringele and glogg served at Danish Festivals in Dannebrog are what we have come to accept here as kringele and glogg. Who cares if it's what they serve in Odense? If they still serve kringele and glogg in Odense. We don't pronounce the name of our town the way Danes pronounce the name of their flag, the Dannebrog, so . . . So, pass the kringele and glogg. I do know this: Checking on local specialties in Nebraska towns and neighborhoods is a good idea, no matter what the nationalities represented, no matter what degree of traditional legitimacy they represent.

A case in point: We patronize Havlik's, a sausage maker in our county seat of St. Paul, Nebraska. From the name I would guess that it was originally a Polish Czech market. Now, under the name Twin Loups, the friendly folks there still make superb Polish sausage and occasionally a Czech jaternice. They also make an exquisite Italian sweet sausage that transforms pasta dishes and sauces into absolute elixir. And they make German bratwurst. Havlik's, now Twin Loups, also makes buffalo sausage, which is neither authentically Italian, nor German, nor Polish.

Recently they have had some trouble finding enough cutting room labor for their custom butchering operation, so they've hired on some really great Hispanic workers. Someone at Twin Loups né Havlik's was bright enough to ask or notice that these new workers had their own ideas of what good sausage is, so they now make and sell a Mexican breakfast sausage that is exquisite. And that's the way America should work. At our best we're not a melting pot where every nuance and flavor blends into a neutral nothingness; we are a sausage display freezer with fifteen or twenty very different tastes to offer, each distinctive and delightful, each irreplaceable, each worth keeping as distinct as possible. And that's something you can still find in Nebraska. And God bless us all, each and every one.

Of Fancy Duds, Coffee, Red Beer, Overalls, and Pickup Trucks

Just one more thing about food: Nebraska coffee is terrible. Charles Kuralt loved Nebraska . . . hated our coffee. His theory was that pioneers carried only so much coffee with them, and their supplies had pretty much run out by the time they crossed the Missouri. I am reminded of a time when Oscar Henry, a curmudgeon I loved, was once offered a cup of coffee from a lovely old lady who was pouring it from a china pot into those little clear glass cups that sit on glass trays along with tasteless pastries at teas. Holding up the pot, she said, "Would anyone care for some coffee?" and Oscar grumbled, "Yeah . . . know where we can get some?" In Nebraska slightly discolored, vaguely off-taste warm water is what passes for coffee.

Another Nebraska potable is more to be relished: red beer. Many newcomers and visitors are mystified when they order a beer in a small-town tavern and are asked, "Plain?" Uhhh . . . "plain" in contrast with what? Plain in contrast with *red*, meaning draft beer with a generous dollop of tomato juice (or better yet, V8 or Bloody Mary mix) in it. It's an old European custom—*Bier mit Tschuss* in Berlin, *Alsterwasser* in Hamburg. All manner of fruit and vegetable juices are added to beer in Europe, especially when it is taken as an early-day drink. Same out here. If you haven't tried it, the next time you go into a Nebraska tavern, especially in a small town, look sophisticated and order a "red one." Other people in the tavern will probably figure you're a local and ask you how much rain you had over at your place.

Nebraska is not at the cutting edge of clothing fashions . . . maybe not even at the trailing hem. There have, however, been sartorial changes in Nebraska even within my lifetime. When I first moved into the rural countryside thirty years ago, for example, overalls were common garb. Now you don't see many fellows as dashing as me in my Key herringbone Imperials. Even for farmers it's now generally blue jeans, big buckles, western-cut shirts, and cowboy boots, the kind of thing you used to see in cattle country west of here. Cowboy hats enjoy wider popularity now, too, but are still by and large the fashion in western Nebraska; wearing cowboy hats while dining is definitely a custom of the west, and if you are anywhere that side of Broken Bow, you may want to be cautious about pointing, giggling, and making comments if you see some guy sitting eating at a table and wearing his hat while forking in his steak and spuds, even in a what passes for a fancy place in Nebraska. You may be the one who winds up doing the explaining if you're not careful.

Dress-up in most of the state is still a matter mostly of western wear—sport coats at most, more likely a bolo string tie with a silver or beadwork slide rather than a silk cravat cut to the width of the year's fashion. Anything fancier should probably be avoided. I once mentioned the possibility of wearing an ascot to the tavern here in Dannebrog and when one of my friends asked what an ascot is, another sputtered, "Well, you big dummy . . . that's the French word for 'snail'!" Dress codes run to shoes and shirts. When farmers used to arrive at my favorite steak house in a nearby town and ask the proprietor from the doorway if it was permissible for them to come in and eat in their overalls, coveralls, irrigation boots, branding clothes, whatever, the answer shouted from the other end of the bar always struck me as being wonderfully Nebraskan: "If that's the way you earned your money, then that's the way you can spend it! Come on in and sit down." Perhaps the biggest difference between urban and rural dress is that out here in the countryside we don't wear our baseball-style seed company caps backward. Ever.

In Nebraska's quasi-urban environments—that is, Omaha and Lincoln—automobiles are pretty much the same dreary clones you'll see in any city or town of size. But in the rural countryside the rule is the pickup truck. In a town like Dannebrog, population 354, it is not unusual during the morning rush hour to see nothing *but* pickup trucks on the main street—maybe ten or twelve vehicles parked while the drivers get the news over breakfast at Harriett's Danish or Tom's Bakery or pick up the mail at the post office. (By the way, it was my friend Eric who first told me when I came to Dannebrog that here the "rush hour" is when the Lutheran church lets out on Sunday morning!) While some of these pickups might be new and shiny with empty beds and spotless interiors, most rural Nebraska pickup trucks are tools as well as transportation: Fenders are battered

165

and bent; beds sport fencing tools, straw bales, and maybe a stillborn calf carcass; the cab is so cluttered with the detritus of prolonged occupation on the long drives to and from town and in between stints in the fields that there is scarcely room for more than the driver; the radio antenna, torn off while chasing cows through a plum thicket, has been replaced by a length of rusty barbed wire (said to be superior in bringing in the whining of country music, by the way); and a gun rack in the back window carries a shotgun, deer rifle, fishing rod, and maybe a .22 rifle . . . "just in case."

It is no more unusual to find a tractor parked on the main street than a pickup truck, grain truck, or passenger car. ATVs used in checking irrigation pipe or moving livestock aren't legal on state highways, but rules like that are considered minor annoyances and are disregarded by most farmers and ranchers, and for that matter by law enforcement officers who have any sense at all. It's understood by all but the most callow outsiders that the right-of-way in Nebraska is always given to agriculture. In Nebraska nothing else is quite as important. And that's the way it should be, in my opinion.

Walls and Roofs

I like to think that Nebraska is architecturally distinctive, from our incredibly gorgeous State Capitol to the most humble farm homes, historical and contemporary. In a fundamentally and pervasively horizontal state, our Capitol building is almost unique in its verticality—the principal and important exception being our grain elevators, which I like to think of as cathedrals dedicated to the gods of plenty. I'm not altogether convinced that there's not a connection between the two. There are jokes about the Capitol—wiseacres call it "the penis of the Plains," "Goodhue's most impressive erection," and so on. The smart remarks are encouraged by the fact that the large statue on the tip-top is *The Sower*, casting, uh, his, er, seed out over the, ummm, fertile Plains.

But no doubt about it, jokes aside, the Nebraska State Capitol is truly an architectural triumph from a time when government buildings were seen as symbols of collective pride rather than strictly utilitarian cereal-box designs to be tolerated and constructed as cheaply and quickly as possible. Just about the only reason I have ever imagined for wanting to be born somewhere other than Nebraska is my curiosity about what it would feel like to see that splendid building for the first time, inside and out, rather than growing up with it as I did.

Nebraska's architectural history is notable enough to be the subject of study and admiration. Once the frontier crossed the Missouri, what had always been construction traditions—brick, stone, wood, log—died. There was no wood here, or at any rate what little wood there was for log construction or firing brick was quickly used up by the first wave of settlers. There was little stone suitable for building beyond the easternmost extremes of the state. And yet hundreds of thousands of homesteaders were soon swarming out onto the Plains, and they all needed shelter, four to eight families per every single square mile. The architectural responses to the dilemma were fascinating. In newly opened lands, houses were constructed of used railroad ties, baled straw and hay, and most significantly of sod peeled from the naked surface of the land itself. While building with such materials began as an expedient—a temporary emergency response to the environmental and historical context, with every intention of putting up "proper" buildings when and if appropriate (that is, usual) construction materials became available—all of these devices eventually acquired a technology of their own, especially once it was seen that the sturdy materials offered real advantages in dealing with the severe conditions of the Plains and the frontier. The suitability and durability of baled straw, sod, and railroad ties can be seen in the fact that buildings of these materials are still standing and lived in today, a full century after they were built.

There was a time when I sniffed and snarled at the shoddy mobile homes and prefabricated "manufactured housing" that obstruct our highways these days and blight the countryside—homes that will almost assuredly not outlast the first occupant. But I've changed my mind. Or perhaps more precisely, had my mind changed. I was walking the streets of Regensburg, Germany, with a German friend once and was admiring the solid and stolid half-timber houses common to that area, and for that matter most of Europe. Occasional historical markers indicated that the houses were medieval, centuries old, built for the ages. And I began a diatribe about how miserable home construction is in America, or more specifically, in Nebraska . . . temporary cracker boxes stuck together with staples and sticks, hauled in on truck beds, and plunked down on little more than a few loose cinder blocks for a foundation. Instant slums . . . Tornado bait . . .

My German friend stopped me short. With a tone that suggested he was dead serious about what he was saying, he told me I was wrong. Dead wrong. He said that in Europe the stone, brick, and half-timber houses I admired so much had indeed stood for centuries . . . and were therefore owned and lived in only by the very rich. One of the things he loved most about America, in fact, was precisely what I was lamenting. The key word in his argument was one I used several times in the paragraph above . . . *home*. In America a *home* can be owned by everyone and anyone but the most abjectly poor. Passionately he told me that when he sees trailer houses and double-wides scattered around the American countryside, no matter how shabby and temporary, he sees a possibility of ownership that was precisely what brought European settlers to the frontier: a chance to escape servitude on the rocky, rootbound, tiny fields of Europe, inevitably owned by only the rich and powerful, and to come to the vast, open lands of America where they could *own* land. And a home. A Kinkaid shack . . . a sod hovel . . . a rough log house . . . no matter. It was a home. And it was owned by those who lived there. There were tears in my German friend's eyes as he spoke. And he was right. I have never been able to look at cheap housing the same way since that moment. This is America, land of the free, home of the brave. We need to remember the most neglected word in that abused ideal . . . *home*.

There aren't a lot of fine old buildings in Nebraska outside of towns and cities because, for one thing, the state is so young; buildings more than a century old are rare anywhere west of the Missouri

Valley. Our own home is ancient for central Nebraska—more than a hundred years old, in fact. And that is the accepted phrase to suggest antiquity in Nebraska: *more than a hundred years old*. Imagine trying to impress a German tourist who comes from a city founded by the Roman Empire before the birth of Christ, and where the church he attends was built in the early Middle Ages, with the information that some of the buildings he sees in Broken Bow, Nebraska, are "more than a century old." Yawn. Moreover, as the rural population declines in Nebraska, there are ever fewer houses, including old ones. Many old structures have been razed to reduce tax burdens on land now farmed by a neighbor living across the road, or in another section altogether. Houses that were once the pride of a builder dreaming of wealth and success have been abandoned and have fallen into disrepair, occupied only by raccoons and feral cats.

Or moved to another location. When we decided to move from our Lincoln home out to the country, being recyclers at heart, we started to shop for a nice old house we could transport onto our land. I had already found, dismantled, and moved an early-frontier log house to our place as a cabin retreat, so I presumed that when we needed a real *house*, we would do the same thing. Nonetheless I was surprised to find that there was no shortage of handsome and substantial old homes sitting empty, to be bought and moved. We had a choice from ten possible houses to buy and move to our place, in fact. We wound up purchasing a large, solid old house with wonderful woodwork, a stained-glass window, an etched window, interesting doors, and heavy framing . . . for a grand total of $350. Of course it cost a couple of thousand dollars more to move the house the 6 miles to our land, and a good deal more to rebuild it, roof it, rearrange the interior, and put a modern, solid foundation under it. But in the end getting a house this way was still cheaper than building from scratch—and as I like to point out, you don't get ghosts with new lumber.

Nebraska farmsteads west of Grand Island (and to a lesser extent even east) don't often sport the massive, rock-solid barns of the East. Abundant construction materials were never easily or cheaply available west of the Missouri River, and as farmland turned into ranchland, barns grew less and less necessary. As is true all across America now, the expense of maintaining old barns is prohibitive, a new roof on a large old barn potentially running into the high five figures, so of what few barns were originally built on the Plains, there are now even fewer.

Respect or Affection?

The farmstead of a century ago was built as a statement, a declaration of success, permanence, and a wish for respect . . . a large frame house in defiance of the inefficiency of such architecture on the open, windy, extreme Plains. The home and the farmstead buildings around it faced forward toward the road, with a large porch where the lord and his family were presumably to sit and survey the passing scene . . . which at that time went by on the road slowly enough for shouted greetings or at least a wave. The front door, or sometimes doors—one into the front, living room, the other into the formal parlor where it was assumed one would entertain the governor, should he drop by, or the minister—offered a measured welcome, and was usually reached through a front gate and a drive that circled past it. Inside the house, the kitchen was unseen; sometimes it wasn't even within the walls, being a separate "summer kitchen," a small building apart from the house proper, to keep the heat and pedestrian activities of food preparation from offending the eye, nose, and sensitivity of honored guests. Where a kitchen was inside the house—no kidding!—there was sometimes a small double-door window in the wall between it and the dining room so the ladies of the house (if there weren't servants) could set the food dishes from the kitchen, close the kitchen side, take off the aprons, straighten the hair and mop the brow, and then elegantly enter the dining room, open *that* door, and serve the dishes without the senator, railroad president, or bishop so much as getting a glimpse of such untidy horrors as cooking dishes or steaming ovens.

I don't imagine it took long for even the most hopeful Plains homesteader to realize that, well, this wasn't the way it was going to be out here. And as times changed, the family wanted less to be respected and more to be liked. The farmstead and function of the house reflected such wishes. While these changes were easier in the rural countryside than in cities because farms offered the flexibility of more room to modify things like roads, parking, paths, and porches, even in the cities entry to houses was soon made by way of the kitchen. Indeed, to this day new houses are built so that you enter the kitchen at the *front* of houses; when you are invited to a meal or just an afternoon cake and coffee, you sit at the kitchen table, not in a formal dining room. On farms the front porch was abandoned, piled with old furniture, a piano or sofa pushed against the front door from the inside. The front gate rusted shut, the old drive grew up in weeds, lilacs covered the porch entry, and the front steps eventually collapsed in disuse. All commerce and traffic moves today by way of the back door and the add-on "mud porch," even in the cities. No more porte cochere where carriages could discharge passengers out of the rain or sun and directly on the front porch. Now it's a garage out back or a carport clearly showing the entry of choice: the back door, and into the kitchen. Nowhere have these socio-architectural changes been more obvious or pervasive than in Nebraska.

Lawn . . . Yawn . . .

On the other hand, Nebraska residents have fallen prey to the religion second only to football: the monoculture, monotonous, bluegrass lawn. Even where the soil is utterly inappropriate and the water supply totally inadequate for the maintenance of a bluegrass lawn, and a nineteenth-century-style meadow lawn would be not only more attractive but also less expensive and more attractive, you will find . . . nothing but bluegrass. As with so many things, Nebraskans don't know anything other than golf-course, bluegrass lawns and therefore can't imagine anything else but golf-course, bluegrass lawns.

Where there is color and variation in Nebraska lawnery (I just made that word up), it takes two forms. The first is Go Big Red booster trash on the porch and yard—flags, statuettes, lighted displays,

all manner of signs of reverence to the Great God Foot-Baal; chance
are, inside the house an entire room is dedicated to the same divinity.
Strangers to Nebraska may think I'm joking. I'm not. Nebraska newspapers actually do weekly stories covering these Husker or Big Red
rooms as *news*, having contests to determine who has thrown away
the most money on this junk, who has the nuttiest notions . . . swimming pools shaped like footballs, couches made in the image of
favorite coaches (yes, that's right—coach couches!), quarterback
lamps, racks of old tattered team uniforms, unwashed and still reeking
of the Big Game. Okay, I'm exaggerating a little. But not much.

Much more interesting, imaginative, and evocative, to my mind,
is old iron in the yard that was once antique farm machinery or a
part thereof. Even in the city it's not unusual to see rusted old hay
rakes, milk cans, or cream separators holding up mailboxes, and in
the countryside much larger pieces up to and including balers, combines, and entire vintage tractors appear on groomed gravel beds with
plantings around them, as if with a kind of reverence for the old
days. In ranch country road gates and signs similarly recycle old tools
and equipment: iron wheels, branding irons, entire wagons or hay
stackers. Like me, I guess, the owners just don't have the heart to
throw away the old stuff no matter how much of an agony it was to
use it "back when."

A singular Nebraska practice in the rural countryside has
attracted its share of attention, even occasionally on network TV—
boots inverted on fence posts. Not just any boots, but *cowboy* boots.
West of the 98th Meridian—that is, roughly Grand Island on westward, especially in rural and ranching areas—it is not at all unusual
to find ten, fifty, maybe a hundred fence posts in a row sporting
upended cowboys boots. Many reasons are given for the practice.
Paul Harvey, so often so wrong about so much, once cited my work
with this folk practice and said that my conclusion was that there is
no reason for it. Well, that's not what I said. I said that the people
who do it give many reasons—to keep horses from chewing on the
posts, to protect them from the rain, to keep away coyotes, to boast

about the number of sons in the family, or because "cowboys' souls/soles go to heaven"—but they don't know the real reasons.

The rationales given are obviously all spurious and specious. Putting boots on a couple of dozen posts doesn't deter horses from chewing on the other thousand posts around the pasture, for example. And on the rare occasions when it does rain, the boots keep the posts wet, accelerating the deterioration of the wood. Coyotes don't really care about cowboys boots and again, can avoid them simply by crossing the fence at any of the rest of the mile or so that it stretches. Daughters and wives wear cowboy boots.

The keys to the practice lie in the fact that the boots are always placed along traveled roads and highways. And that boots are the one item of clothing we never wash. And that marking our territory is a practice so buried in antiquity that we do it without even knowing what we are up to. Ask your dog why he pees on every post, pole, tire, and fire hydrant in his path. He doesn't know. But he knows it's important and he does it.

Out here we put our old boots upside down on our fence posts. And pee around the edges of our yard just to be sure.

Speaking Nebraskan

Nebraska language is not only ordinary, it is the perfect example of ordinary. The Plains could just as easily be known as "the Land of News Anchors." From Paula Zahn to Tom Brokaw, Dick Cavett to Johnny Carson, the mainstream nature of Plains English and its enunciation reflects an inoffensive linguistic middle ground that the networks seek out. Sure, we have our peculiarities. If you're of Italian descent, you probably grump and growl at *EYE-talian*, and linguistic pitfalls lie in the path of newcomers to the TV news screen when it comes to pronouncing what might seem uncomplicated names— what's so tough about *Beatrice*, or *Chadron*, or *Norfolk*? Well, the problem is, *we* don't say them here like *you* said them there. In rural areas travel time is sometimes measured in six-packs, there's that thing about rain coming in hundredths, dinner, aka supper, is in the evening not at noon (which is when we eat lunch, by the way). (Yes, there was a time when dinner was at noon, and was the big meal of the day, complete with a nap before you went back out to the fields to work; that's now by and large a relic of the long-ago pioneer past.)

While we're on the subject, eight thirty or nine in the evening may be a good time for a bedtime snack of leftovers from supper or a dish of ice cream, but it is definitely *not* time for supper. How can you reasonably eat a heavy meal at nine in the evening, probably missing the evening weather report by the way, and then expect to get any sleep? No wonder people from the East Coast are so puny, grumpy, and tired all the time. You eat supper/dinner at 5:00 PM. That's in the Bible somewhere. And if you are from somewhere else and decide to entertain Nebraskans, you may want to take a note: To a Nebraskan, when you say "Come to our home for dinner . . . five o'clock would be fine," the presumption is, you *mean* five, and not five thirty or six. Definitely not seven or eight! If you are one of those East Coast bone-heads who eat supper at nine and invite guests to come by at seven and about six fifty-five you step out of the shower and start to get ready because in Ballltimmoooore the stylish time for dining is nine, you are really in for a surprise because your Nebraska guests are not going to want to inconvenience you by showing up late, so you are likely to come downstairs wrapped in a towel to find your new neighbors already ensconced in your front room watching the *evening* news at five thirty on your TV, eager to dig into those mashed pota-toes and slabs of beef because they'll want to be back home by ten to watch the *nightly* news and weather. Or maybe in the kitchen where they prefer to eat anyway, adding a bit of ketchup to the fishbait you call "horse doves" in order to make them palatable.

And sooner or later, if you are going to be here for any stretch of time, you need to get some idea of how big an acre is. And a sec-tion. When someone asks you how the university is doing, they aren't talking about the library budget or academic ranking. Many Nebraskans would be surprised to hear that there are such things as classes at that institution.

There is man-talk, and sometimes even women can be heard using it, but my impression is definitely that the coarseness of language that has become de rigueur elsewhere is still considered out of bounds in Nebraska. To this day my mother thinks "the f-word" refers to *fart*, and even that is not a word she abides in her presence, much less in her home. There are still fairly rowdy and open country taverns in Nebraska where you can be "barred," or thrown out, for using language that strong. In thirteen years I never could train my very urban, very eastern CBS News crew to watch their language while in Nebraska, not because of any prudery on my part but because it could cause real distress for people around us and bring down substantial disapproval from others and problems for us.

Communications

The same jokes and stories that are in fashion at any particular time across the rest of American culture are found in Nebraska, too, putting the lie to such unfortunate mislabels as *urban legend*, since they are as much at home, adapted to rural settings, in Nebraska as in New York City. But the sledgehammer crudeness of modern urban humor does not prosper here on the Plains. Jokes, even the most ribald Nebraska humor, is in fact sometimes so subtle, it can be told in front of children and delicate maidens—even my mother—without bringing any wrath down on the wag. I refer to the most common humor I have encountered in rural Nebraska as "civil ribaldry" to differentiate it from "dirty joke" because it clearly is not in the same class. An example will make my point clear:

> An old widowed farmer got himself a new hired girl—quite a cute little number—and eventually married her, to boot. As he headed out to the fields for the harvest that autumn, he told her, "Now, honey, if you get to feeling like you'd like a little loving, just step out of the back door and fire the shotgun and I'll come running." Poor old fellow died three weeks into hunting season.

The moral is, you can pretty much use regulation English in Nebraska, but you may want to watch your "French."

Another linguistic characteristic of Plains humor and even Plains talk in general is laconic delivery. You aren't going to be able to tell if someone is telling you a joke, delivering a tall tale, or simply giving you a bad time by looking at his or her face or listening for a sardonic tone of voice. Add this in with the fact that a good deal of Plains humor is subtle to the extreme and you can figure that if you're not paying attention, you may be missing about half of what's going on in any conversation. "I know that guy. He's the kind who would argue with a compass." "What do we do for excitement in this town? We don't get excited in this town." "We don't have a stoplight in our town. For a while we had a four-way stop. Had to take it out, though, because everyone got tired of sitting there waiting for three other cars to show up." "The crop this year wasn't as good as everyone expected. But then no one thought it would be." It took me close to three weeks to catch on to that last one.

An important expression of nonverbal communication in Nebraska is the finger wave. That one really baffles a lot of people not familiar with rural Nebraska. Say you're driving down a country road somewhere well outside of Lincoln or Omaha, especially west of Grand Island, probably on a county road—gravel more than likely, but it can happen even if you are moving along at 60 miles an hour on a state highway and there's not a lot of traffic. A battered old pickup truck is coming down the same road in the other lane. With perfect, elegant timing, the other driver will lift a finger or two from the steering wheel, or maybe a thumb. If he has one hand on the wheel and a cup of coffee in the other, he may just nod or jerk his head back just a bit. He's saying hello. A friend of mine from Chicago was puzzled by this and when I explained it to him, he said, "Waving? Why, in Chicago you could get shot for that!"

Later on the same city boy said to me, "What kind of place is this where people wave at people they've never seen before and may never see again?" The thing is, that driver might not see more than a handful of other drivers all day. That doesn't happen in Chicago. And folks here feel that waving at everyone on the road is a kind of connection with general humanity—an affirmation that we human beings are still hanging on out here and sharing whatever the heck is going on. A simple greeting seems in order. Moreover, Nebraskans are just like that. If you are walking down the main street of Dannebrog, even if you've never so much as been in Howard County before in your life, it doesn't matter. You're here now, and that's what counts, so people are going to at the least acknowledge this with a greeting, maybe a comment about the weather, also delivered laconically: "Pretty hot for being so cold, huh?" "Think the wind's going to blow [said while you are leaning into a 50-mile-per-hour gale and in danger of losing your underwear to the zephyrs]?" Or, while walking your tiny Chihuahua in the town park, "That little fella looks like a sheep killer to me."

Nebraska Socioeconomics

Class distinctions in Nebraska are all from the top down and are largely illusion. In every community, even a tiny village like Dannebrog, there are those who consider themselves to be the community elite, by virtue of wealth, genetic purity, power, religion, or value of the vehicle they happen to be driving at the moment (with no apparent consideration of the size of loan outstanding on that vehicle). But for whatever airs of superiority these people might presume, no one else pays much attention, which must really be frustrating. True honor and respect in Nebraska are generally reserved for those who merit them. Which must be even more frustrating for those who don't.

Huge, ostentatious, obscenely kitschy houses surround and infest cities like Omaha and are spreading, too, into the rural countryside; I am pretty sure that the intent of the builders and residents is to demonstrate their wealth and distinction. The result, of course, is that everyone snickers at the nonsense of it all—precisely the opposite of what was intended. Moreover, for those who want to seek out and gain favor with the truly rich and powerful, the task is made all the more complicated because Nebraska wealth and power are often very hard to identify. For example, a friend of mine wanted desperately to buy a business here in town and scrambled to arrange financing for it. He was at the threshold of pulling the business deal together when he went into a local bank and requested a mortgage, having put all the other details of the business to rest. He came out of the bank crushed . . . his application for the loan to purchase the business had been turned down.

When I heard this story, I could understand it to this point. My friend is a thoroughly good guy, scrupulously honest, thoroughly decent, but in the past he had made some mistakes—okay, a *lot* of mistakes—had had financial difficulties, and is to this day a bit cavalier about responsibilities. Still, there wasn't much doubt in my mind that he would have done well with this business if he'd had a chance. But the bank didn't think so, so . . . there you are.

But as my friend came out of the bank, his face etched with disappointment, he ran into an old friend of ours, a quiet little guy, an older farmer, always in overalls, always in good spirits, gentle, kind, another sweetheart with not an enemy in the world, a guy who would never put any muscle on anyone for anything. Just a plain old farmer. Another ordinary Nebraskan. At least that's what we thought. This gentle fellow saw the pain on our mutual friend's face, and so he stopped on the main street of town and asked him what the problem was. My friend who wanted the loan was reluctant to open up—he didn't want to air his financial problems, but mostly he didn't want to inflict personal difficulties of any kind on anyone else. But finally, reluctantly, he told our older farmer friend what had happened in the bank. Our older friend listened patiently, quietly, and then said, "Just a minute. Wait here. I'll be right back." He stepped into the bank and was gone for only a couple of minutes, coming back out and saying to our downcast friend, "They want to talk with you in there again." My friend went back into the bank and to his astonishment was told that, well, uh, there'd been a little mistake. His loan had been approved. What denominations did he want his money in?

We probably knew in the back of our minds that our farm friend is stinking rich, but it was never an issue. That's not why we love him. When he dresses up, he wears newish overalls, after all. He drives a relatively newish pickup but nothing flashy. He plays pitch in the tavern and exults when he wins a fifty-cent pot, laments the loss of a dime, so . . . It wouldn't have occurred to us that he was probably one of the largest depositors in that bank, perhaps worth millions. All he had to do was suggest that he was thinking of withdrawing his accounts if our friend didn't get his business loan—besides which, he would guarantee that same business loan—and, well, suddenly it seemed prudent to the bank officials to approve the loan. And right now. And they did. On the spot.

A truly notable contemporary example of this Nebraska notion of wealth and power is Warren Buffett, one of the richest men in the entire world. And a man who is thoroughly Nebraskan. The first time I met Buffett was at a very fancy dinner in the State Capitol rotunda, hosted by our governor and attended by an astonishing cast of some of the most powerful people in the state and for that matter the nation: the head of Union Pacific, the publisher of the *Washington Post*, Ann Landers of advice-column fame, heads of a dozen Nebraska state agencies, corporate executives, educators, rich people, powerful people . . . even, for God's sake, the coach of the University of Nebraska football team! The man seated next to me, president of a major national corporation, said that he had heard Warren Buffett would be there, and I said that I wouldn't recognize him since I'd never met him. My dinner companion said, "Well, just look for someone who looks like a slightly eccentric shoe salesman." And when Buffett arrived, there he was, as described. He drives ordinary vehicles, lives in a relatively modest house, dresses modestly, speaks softly, is self-deprecating, and rarely uses his immense power ostentatiously or frivolously. That is to say, Warren Buffett is a climax Nebraskan.

Hyannis, Nebraska, was once famous for having the highest concentration of millionaires of any community in the United States. You sure couldn't tell from driving through it. There are some nice houses in Hyannis, fairly big, fronting on a rail line, in what is otherwise a fairly seedy Sandhills town of no particular distinction, beauty, or impact. The thing is, ranchers who held tens of thousands of acres of ranchland, thousands of head of cattle, and perhaps their own air-plane(s), also had a house in Hyannis, perhaps so the children had a place to stay when they were at a boarding school (this arrangement of having a house in town for the children and women of the ranch is sometimes necessary because travel from ranch to school can become impossible during Nebraska's hard winters), or for a wife to stay when ranch life becomes impossible, or perhaps just as a place to break the monotony and isolation of Sandhills life, or a landing place after retirement. But just as you might not recognize Hyannis as a center of enormous wealth, or find the houses of the wealthy partic-ularly noteworthy, you might sit down at the town cafe and tavern at the Hyannis Hotel and not for a moment suspect that the battered old goats wearing filthy cowboy hats and cowboy boots reeking of corral dirt, eating roast beef and mashed potatoes at the next table, are multimillionaires who could buy and sell you a hundred times over.

I am not mentioning names here because that would be a viola-tion of the very virtue of modesty I am praising, but believe me, these stories I am telling you are the truth. I was once at an elegant cul-tural event in Omaha, staged on a scale I had a hard time grasping. There was about to be an enormous concert, produced as profession-ally as such a thing can be: full stage, full lights, full sound, for an audience of ten thousand. The Omaha Symphony was featured, and Opera Omaha, with guest performers of international achievement. All of which was free and open to the public. Before the huge con-cert, there was an elegant reception for the performers and other notables at the hosts' home, and then a lavish banquet honoring arts educators, served in the most opulent possible setting for hundreds of people. I can't even imagine what all this must have cost—certainly hundreds of thousands of dollars—but it was all being paid for by one husband and wife, unassuming arts supporters.

That evening I had the good fortune of sitting at the same table with this man and his wife for dinner. We were not on a stage where they could wallow in glory and honor for their generosity . . . no, we were in fact, toward the back of the room, behind some pillars, rather out of the center of things. I didn't know much about this man and his wife because, well, they'd never made much of a fuss about anything else they'd done, either. They proved to be wonderful people—as common as me—congenial, friendly, plainspoken, modest . . . that same attitude that seems to prevail with the truly rich and powerful in Nebraska. At some point I mentioned that I for one wanted to thank them for all they did to support the arts, well beyond this one evening of explosive splendor and public generosity. I said that they must, for example, really love the opera to support it so generously.

The modest nabob's response stunned me. He said that, well, uh, actually he didn't care much for opera. "But . . . but . . . but . . . !" I sputtered. As he explained, he knew that a lot of people *did* appreciate opera, and opera is a characteristic of a cultured city, and he wanted Omaha to be seen as a cultured city—in fact, he wanted it to *be* a cultured city—so he supported opera. He just wasn't particularly fond of it himself. When I later tried to get him to come on camera at an interview show I was doing for Nebraska Educational Television at the time to talk about this marvelously enlightened and generous point of view, he demurred, saying that he really didn't want to make that much of a fuss about it. Of course not every rich or powerful Nebraskan is like that, but there are more of those here than elsewhere, I believe, and I consider that kind of dignity with power and wealth to be one of the finest of Nebraska's contributions to civilization and civility.

Since the top of the Nebraska social scale has been knocked down so that the rich and powerful are reduced to a style not far removed from that of the peasantry, the lowest levels are also hoisted closer to the center. If you can't tell the difference between the stinking rich and the merely stinking, then the distance from the middle to the bottom doesn't amount to much, either. My family performed migrant stoop labor in the sugar beet fields in the west and manual labor in the factories of Lincoln just one generation ago. I can't imagine anything much more peasant than that. My parents worked their way up to being domestics, doing lawn work and housecleaning, working in Lincoln laundries, that kind of thing. My father was proud that he worked his way up to being a janitor in the university powerhouse from the truly menial job of shoveling coal from railcars outside the powerhouse . . . worked his way *up* to janitor. Because of my upbringing but also because I am a Nebraskan, I have never felt any compunction to apologize for coming from and being to this day within the peasant class. If anyone has a reason to apologize, in my opinion, it would be the aristocracy. And I imagine that's why so few Nebraskans like to claim membership within any kind of elite.

Nebraska politicians show the same tendencies. Of course in politics this is more of a result than a trait because anyone can become rich, almost by accident, but to be a successful politician you have to gain the favor of the masses. And to gain the favor of the Nebraska electorate you damned well better not get too big for your britches. If you should spot our governor, a member of the Senate or Congress, and most assuredly a mayor of any town from Omaha to Arthur, sitting down to lunch or just jaywalking across the street headed for a meeting, you can be absolutely certain that you can yell, "Hey, you . . . Senator Smith! I need to talk with you about something for a second," and he or she will stop in mid-traffic or mid-soup-slurp and take the time to talk with you, or he or she won't be in office after the next election. Nebraskans do expect their politicians to be from, of, and by the people, and as a result they most assuredly are.

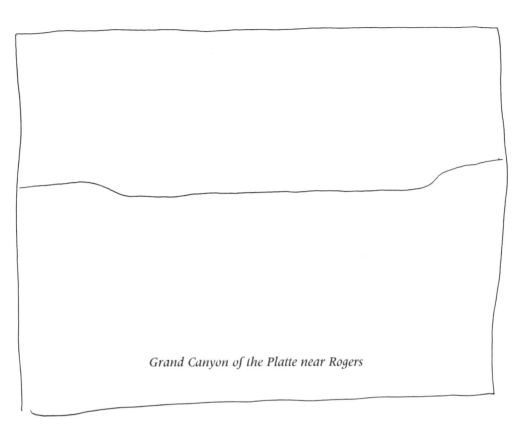

Grand Canyon of the Platte near Rogers

CHAPTER EIGHT

Ag and Econ

When I was doing my "Postcards from Nebraska" essays for CBS News *Sunday Morning*, the most common viewer complaint I got, almost inevitably from someone in Omaha or Lincoln, was that I was embarrassing Nebraska by wearing overalls as my standard on-camera garb. A schoolteacher in Omaha—where else?—wrote and said that she had been to a meeting where colleagues from other parts of the country poked fun at her because of my essays, asking her mockingly if her neighbors were cows. All I could say was that, well, uh . . . my neighbors *are* cows. And mighty good neighbors they are. As one old-timer responded when a detractor noted that there are more cows in Nebraska than people, "We prefer 'em."

Not only is Nebraska rural and agricultural, we are all, like it or not, farmers. I don't care what it appears that your job is—cabdriver, factory worker, clerk in a Gap outlet, railroad engineer, poet, computer programmer, state trooper. Doesn't matter: You're in agriculture and rural living up to your eyeballs. And one of the reasons Nebraska is at the bottom of the economic ladder in America (McPherson County is nominally the poorest county in the nation) is that way too few people recognize their own self-interest in the continuing viability—better yet, prosperity—of farming. For that matter, I wonder what percentage of Nebraskans knows the difference between soybeans and grain sorghum, let alone milo and grain sorghum. Several times in these pages, I make a point of noting things I think should be a requirement for full Nebraska citizenship, and this is one of them: If you can't tell what is growing in a field even as you drive by it at 65 miles an hour, I don't care what kind of Husker football booster you are, you are one damned poor example of the true Nebraskan.

Tell me, what kind of sense does it make that the people who produce our food have to pursue that most noble of man's occupations as a veritable *hobby,* more often than not having to hold down a full-time job in town, or at least have a spouse earning a regular wage somewhere, to continue farming? It's nuts, a kind of political-economic-social-cultural suicide. As with so many other neglected and abused segments of our government and society in America, we are headed for real trouble in agriculture, and since in Nebraska we are all in agriculture, prospects for our state's future aren't promising. The age of the average farmer keeps creeping up until now it is mostly geezers on those tractors you see in the fields. These days the average Nebraska farmer is well over sixty years old, and is almost an endangered species. Young people simply don't want to take the enormous financial risk and work like dogs. Even if young people want to become farmers, who can afford the monstrous outlay for land and equipment needed for even the most modest farming operation, running into the multi-millions of dollars? There are some small efforts to avoid the impending and apparently inevitable crunch and crash when impossible economics and an aging farming population come together. Nebraska's Center for Rural Affairs has a notable program to create apprenticeships within which young aspirants can work their way into ownership of land and equipment from farmers who want to pass along their skills and tools. Still, it's going to take a lot more than that to turn things around.

The Geezer State

There is a narrow spine of our population running all the way from Canada almost to the Mexican border in which the oldest segment of the American public is most concentrated. It's really a startling sight. You can get an idea of it at these Web sites:

> www.raconline.org/maps/mapfiles/elderly.jpg
> www.agingstats.gov/chartbook2000/population.html

Or try the very best one, showing the senior population by county right down the nation through Nebraska:

> http://nationalatlas.gov/articles/people/a_age65pop.html

Another good site for this perspective in a small but very clear image is:

> http://nationalatlas.gov/Natlasstart.asp

The best one I've found has the longest Web site address I've ever seen, which makes it almost worth the effort to visit:

> http://factfinder.census.gov/servlet/ThematicMapFramesetServlet?_
> bm=y&-_MapEvent=displayBy&-errMsg=&-_dBy=050&-redoLog=
> false&-_zoomLevel=&-tm_name=DEC_2000_SF1_U_M00073&-
> tm_config=|b=50||=en|t=400|zf=0.0|ms=thm_def|dw=1.955769704
> 8764706E7|dh=1.4455689123E7|dt=gov.census.aff.domain.map.LS
> RMapExtent|if=gif|cx=-1159354.4733499996|cy=7122022.5|zl=
> 10|pz=10|bo=|bl=|ft=350:349:335:389:388:332:331|fl=381:403:204:3
> 80:369:379:368|g=01000US|ds=DEC_2000_SF1_U|sb=50|tud=false|d
> b=040|mn=5.7|mx=17.6|cc=1|cm=1|cn=5|cb=|um=Percent|pr=1|th=
> DEC_2000_SF1_U_M00073&-PANEL_ID=tm_result&-_pageY=&-
> _lang=en&-geo_id=01000US&-_pageX=&-_mapY=&-_mapX=&-
> _latitude=&-_pan=&-ds_name=DEC_2000_SF1_U&-_longitude=&-
> %20_changeMap=Identify

In Nebraska this corridor of geriatrics runs roughly from the area of Cambridge and Arapahoe north toward Bassett and Ainsworth. But that's only folks over sixty-five. Hell, I'm over sixty-five. I can't find a map showing the distributions of seventies, eighties, nineties, or centenarians, and I'll bet those population distributions are even more dramatic. The top states for percentage of the population that is centenarians, in order, are South Dakota, Washington, DC (don't ask me to explain that one), then Nebraska . . . go Big Old Red! Other states clustered around this national spine of us seniors are Iowa, Missouri, Arkansas, Oklahoma, and Montana . . . right down the center, but Nebraska is once again the heart of it all.

On one hand, I suppose we have this geriatric concentration because living is so healthy out here, but sadly it's also because young people are getting the hell out, heading for greener pastures, going somewhere more exciting, getting to towns with better prospects. On the bright side, the good news is that this concentration has also occurred because a lot of people come back to this geriatric corridor once they get old enough (and smart enough) to relax and take it easy, to appreciate the peace, calm, and stability of the western Plains. And yes, even the weather. For many of us, one good Nebraska sunset is easily worth the trouble of a blizzard.

Proud to Be a Farmer?

There are also efforts to get out of the grinding problem of a one-grain (corn) economy in which the more successful farmers are at growing the stuff, the less it's worth, so they never get ahead. Experiments spring up in organic farming, vineyards, exotic crops like chicory or milkweed, and various government programs that always seem to fall short and waste the money on precisely those who don't need it— absentee landowners, corporations, and the already stinking rich. All in all right now, things agricultural look pretty bleak to me. I wince every time I see or hear a farmer revealing some embarrassment about his line of work. There are lots of problems with agriculture, and mistakes have been made, and continue to be made—squandering of resources like water, abuse of the land in an effort to squeeze one more bushel of corn out of tired ground, that kind of thing—but by and large I can't imagine a more noble pursuit in this world than producing food. We should all be proud of American agriculture, but that pride has to start with the farmer himself.

And it has to be admitted that Nebraska farmers haven't done much to help themselves economically or politically. There are ever fewer farms and farmers, which means they have ever less political clout, which means times get ever harder on the farm, which means there are ever fewer farms and farmers. In the nineteenth century 95 percent of Americans were on the farm and 5 percent in the cities; that proportion is now precisely the reverse. Moreover, rural residents—that would be Nebraskans—have systematically reduced their political and economic influence by squandering their votes on irrelevancies, a self-destructive trend that political exploiters have been more than eager to take advantage of. There are three congressional districts in Nebraska; the first is made up mostly of Omaha and its adjuncts, the second is Lincoln and some eastern counties, and the gigantic third district is the entire rest of the state and is almost entirely agricultural. So, guess which district threw away its one puny vote in the House to honor the University of Nebraska football coach? Yep . . . you got it. He admitted he knew nothing about agriculture, but was willing to learn. Terrific. Is the House really a training camp for amateurs? And guess where the loudest howling originates when it comes to political helplessness? I don't need to tell you . . .

A best-selling book currently theorizes that Kansans have frittered away whatever small influence they might have on the national level by ignoring their own, mostly agricultural interests while voting instead to assert goofy and irrelevant positions like prayer in school, creationism, rights for gun nuts, abortion prohibition, and showing the rest of the world who's boss. That may be true for the political scene in Kansas but I don't think it's that simple a case in Nebraska. Here voters elect people they like. Never mind what they say or how competent they are. "I like his looks, or the way he won a football championship, or how she talks about cutting taxes. Yeah, I want taxes cut [never mind that it will be for the already stinking rich and has nothing whatsoever to do with the voter him- or herself, or agriculture, or Nebraska] and the flag saluted but what's really important to me is that the person I'm voting for doesn't act too smart for his or her britches."

Investing in Education . . . or Not, as the Case May Be

Nebraska was once a major enthusiast for education. Immigrants saw it as their opportunity, or at least as the opportunity for their children and grandchildren. My parents hadn't graduated from high school, but they were determined that I go to college . . . even if they had only a faint notion of what that was about. Now Nebraskans vote against school bonds and wonder why no one wants to live in their towns, squander their university's resources on a game for boys, and sniff at the notion of competence, education, and brains as qualifications for office or employment. One of the reasons we moved from Lincoln to Dannebrog was to get away from huge schools and back to classrooms where students like our daughter could get closer attention—but by the time we got here, the move was already on to consolidate small schools into the impersonal school-factories we had hoped to escape. When I was teaching at the university, it was still easily possible to see the difference. With just a glance at their assigned journals, I could quickly determine the size school the individual students in my classes had come from: The more conscientious the effort, the more polished the writing, the better the spelling—the smaller the school. It was that predictable.

Higher education in Nebraska has suffered, too, from economic shortsightedness. Faculty, programs, plant, and staff are continually shorted, which means that students, the very future of Nebraska, are also shorted, an embarrassment and disappointment that is compounded by the fact that while on a back page of any state newspaper there are reports of slashed salaries and budgets at state universities and colleges, on the front page you will find blaring self-congratulations about multimillion-dollar new scoreboards at Memorial Stadium or obscene offers being thrown around for new coaches and staff in the Athletic Department. The bottom line has become that if you have a child who weighs 300 pounds and sets records in running the 100-meter dash, or if you simply want access to a few years of student gridiron tickets, you send your baby to the University in Lincoln; if you want instead for your darling to get a first-rate education, you consider one of the state colleges—especially the University of Nebraska at Kearney—or even better, one of the many premium private colleges here.

It's a damned shame, but that's the way it is. It's still possible to get a really great education at the University of Nebraska by virtue of dedicated faculty and staff and with some serious research into programs and individual classes and teachers; on the other hand, it is increasingly difficult to get a *bad* education at schools like Nebraska Wesleyan, Dana College, or Doane. There was a time when a major consideration in deciding a direction for higher education in Nebraska would have been the expense of private schooling, but as state support for its state universities falters and resources are instead pumped into Saturday-afternoon entertainments, the difference between costs for schools like Wesleyan and the university grow ever less important.

At one time not so long ago, Nebraska had the most school districts of any state in the Union, and the most—and last—one-room schools. That situation has almost disappeared now as small schools have been discontinued and joined to form larger, consolidated schools. To some extent that made sense: Ever lower pay and worsening conditions for teachers in small schools meant fewer qualified faculty, it was easier to bus kids to a central school than have them ride their ponies down the road to a nearby smaller school, and the only way around the problems seemed to be the unthinkable: higher taxes, money that could be spent by unthinking citizens on snowmobiles, plasma TVs, and trips to Husker bowl games. How could a one-room school possibly match the demands for advanced technological resources—encyclopedias, scientific equipment, advanced media tools—that required the big resources of big school districts? But things have changed. Now one relatively inexpensive computer terminal brings the resources of the world into every student's home, not to mention classroom. Transportation has become so outrageously expensive that school activities are increasingly curtailed because of the expenses involved for fuel, maintenance, and staffing of buses. Another good reason to have smaller schools closer to the students' homes.

No, faculty pay and employment conditions haven't improved in Nebraska—but then some people like me keep thinking that just one political leader with vision and courage could change that. Now the small schools have been almost completely eradicated, however, and—like our lost opportunities for a national rail system—the dream of quality education seems ever more fanciful.

Raising Less Corn and More Hell

There was a time when Nebraska farmers and ranchers were a lot smarter than that. They may not have made any more of a dent on the national scene, but they sure got heard. George Norris was probably the best example and the best of what Nebraska has produced, to my mind, giving us, for one thing, a unique system of public power in Nebraska. Some things are too important to the public good to be a matter of profit and private ownership—our highways, for example, or our National Guard. To my mind, and George Norris's, that would include electricity, the very thing that makes life possible out here on the Plains. I would also add mass transit like our railroads and health system, but that opinion (among others) puts me well outside the Nebraska norm, I realize.

That wasn't always the case. There was a time when agitators were the rule rather than the exception in Nebraska. Nebraska farmers and ranchers were then tigers instead of sheep. For example, for all the grief William Jennings Bryan has taken for his stand for creationism in the Scopes Monkey Trial, through most of his political and social history Bryan was remarkably progressive, establishing a reputation for being pro–women's rights, a spokesman for minorities, and anti-war. The Farmers Alliance was strong in the state and sought to organize agriculture to give it the strong voice it deserved and needed, a sense of cooperation that has totally died now; most people in ag struggle alone in a sea of enormous, overpowering, and well-organized counterforces.

My own maternal grandfather, Johann Flach, newly arrived from a virtually medieval society in tsarist Russia, nonetheless worked to organize migrant German-Russian sugar beet fieldworkers in the western part of the state in 1916 and 1917. He worked hard at a contest selling newspaper subscriptions to win an automobile! Can you imagine this guy coming from the steppes—where he had almost no freedoms and had probably never seen a vehicle that wasn't horse-drawn—now in Nebraska trying to round up his compatriots into a workers' union and get himself behind the wheel of an automobile? I am proud of him even though I never met him. He was an agitator and hell-raiser. We could use more like him today.

Equally remarkable to me about early Nebraska was the presence, if not dominance, of women in a society where they had little power but lots of leverage and a very loud, sometimes strident voice. The name *Carry Nation* is familiar to most Nebraskans who have any interest in history. I don't know if she ever worked her anti-saloon violence in Nebraska, but while I disagree with her philosophy I certainly admire her, uh, activism. There are a lot of misunderstandings about Ms. Nation that are relevant to this discussion. That famous image of her little round, scowling, thin-lipped face somehow suggests that she was a petite thing, so the understanding is that when she came into a saloon with her little hatchet, men probably stood gallantly aside and tolerated her prohibitionist fury. Well, think again. Carry Nation was close to 6 feet tall, and when she started swinging that ax of hers at the back bar, anyone with any sense at all dived out the back door or cowered under the pool table.

The frontier years of the Plains were a time of eccentrics. After all, you had to be a nut to come out here in the first place, or at least to stay more than a week or so. Besides, eccentrics were like the

weather. Averages, moderation, middle of the road . . . all concepts
contrary to Nebraska and the Plains. This should be—and was—a garden of bizarros. Old Jules, Willa Cather . . . an anti-vivisectionist les-
bian! Bill Cody. Luther North. Louise and Roscoe Pound. William
Jennings Bryan. All nut cases. Mother Bloor, an outspoken
Communist, raged in Loup City, and ax-handle-wielding opponents
cleared out the town park where she spoke. Okay, that doesn't
adhere quite properly to Robert's Rules, but by God you can't for a
moment accuse the participants at that event of being indifferent.

At Farmers Alliance meetings thousands of voices rose to sing
songs like this one, to the tune of "Nellie Gray":

When first I took my prairie home, my heart was free and light,
And I sang as I turned the prairie sod;
My hair that then was thick and brown today is thin and white,
And I've lost all faith in man or God.
[Chorus]

Chorus:
Oh, my dear prairie home! Never more in years to come
Can I call what I made by toil my own;
The railroads and banks combined, the lawyers paid to find
Out a way to rob me of my home.

It was many years ago that I first saw through this scheme,
And I struggled from their meshes to be free;
But my neighbors all around me then were in a party dream,
And they voted to rob my home from me.
[Chorus]

Now their homes are gone as well as mine, and they're awake at last,
And they see now the great injustice done;
While some few their homes may save, yet the greater part, alas!
Must be homeless for all time to come.
[Chorus]

We must now the robbers pay for a chance to till the soil,
And when God calls us over the great range,
All Heaven will be owned, I s'pose, by men who never toil
So I doubt if we notice the exchange.
[Chorus]

The author of that popular song in the 1890s was a prolific songwriter by the name of Mrs. J. T. Kellie. She obviously took the advice of another female agricultural activist on the Plains, Mary Elizabeth Lease, who urged farmers to "raise less corn . . . and more hell" and boasted that the reason she could rouse crowds of farmers to a fury was that her "tongue was hung on a swivel . . . and was loose at both ends." Sadly, now Nebraska farmers take what is offered them, pay what is demanded, eat the difference, and are as a result ever fewer. What can they do? Well, for one thing, they could raise less corn and more hell. And not elect football coaches to Congress.

I often wonder when an American Legion honor guard salutes our long-standing, venerated State Poet Laureate John Neihardt if they have ever read any of Neihardt's early poetry. Not just his erotic verses from *A Bundle of Myrrh* like "If This Be Sin" or "Let Down Your Hair" (gulp!)—rhymes in fact that I used to win my fair companion, Lovely Linda—but the raging political rants of his youth like these lines from his "The Red Wind Comes!" (from his collection *The Poet's Town*, 1908–1912):

The Country of the Free? -- O wretched lie!
The Country of the Brave? -- Yea, let it be!
One more good fight, O Brothers, ere we die,
And this shall be the Country of the Free!

What! Are we cowards? Are we doting fools?
Who built the cities, fructified the lands?
We make and use, but do we own the tools?
Who robbed us of the product of our lands?

My disappointment in Nebraska's loss of agricultural passion is to some degree mitigated by a remarkable reality: Nebraskans are,

despite what appears to be docility or even surrender, largely unpredictable when it comes to politics. At this writing we have a Democrat
and a Republican in the Senate, which is already something of a
curiosity. I mean, jeez, these two guys were elected by the very same
people! But what's more, the Democrat is a nominal Republican, and
our Republican couldn't be more of a pain in the rear of a totally
Republican administration if he were a raving liberal. Any Democrat
worth his salt is contemptuous of "Bend-Over" Ben, and letters to the
editor attacking the Republican are inevitably from the right. We
have sent outright liberals like Bob Kerrey to Washington, and radical
right-wing zeros like Roman Hruska (who once famously argued that
mediocrity deserves a voice on the Supreme Court) and Carl Curtis,
whom one national political observer finally had to admit was not
selling his vote out to the insurance industry . . . he was simply too
dumb to know any better.

Nebraska is distinguished with the only state legislature that is
unicameral—that is, has only one house and is nonpartisan—
although anyone who knows up from down knows that it is as parti-
san a club of political hacks as can be found anywhere in the nation.
It's just that the political labels are kept politely quiet in the hope that
the voters won't notice.

I have been asked repeatedly to run for Congress, the governor's
mansion, the legislature, and the university's board of regents (never,
however, for Howard County sheriff). There was that one time I ran
for the Lancaster County Weed Control Authority . . . on a pro-weed
ticket, a stance that won me that eccentric vote to the degree that I
became known for a while as "Landslide Welsch." The first time I was
approached by a group of Democrats and asked to run for Congress, I
was obviously flattered and called my mother to tell her about the
contact. Without hesitation she said, "Roger, I raised you better than
that." So I had to report to my would-be supporters that I couldn't
run for Congress, because my mother still thought I might amount to
something. Besides, my father always said we are judged by the company we keep, and there aren't many reputations that could hold up

for long being surrounded by that pack of scoundrels in Congress.

There was a time when Nebraska was a fertile ground for rebels. People came here, as I have said, not just to find freedom for their religion but to find freedom *from* religion. Now the grandchildren and great-grandchildren of those freethinkers work to impose the very theocracy on others that their ancestors came here to escape. Others came to the Plains to escape the endless wars of Europe, only to find themselves embroiled in the same damned mess all over again as American citizens. There were protests in Nebraska against war. William Jennings Bryan was a notable opponent of sending Nebraska immigrants' sons to fight in the Germany they had left for that very reason. Even in my little town of Dannebrog there was violence protesting the public recruiting of soldiers. Here there were crops to be harvested, families to be raised, and freedom to be enjoyed. The notion of returning to the same bloody ground in Europe to fight the same weary wars seemed an absurdity beyond possibility. Now my own Howard County, Nebraska, has the twentieth highest recruitment rate in the nation—the nation!—even during these times of wars based on frauds and halfway around the world. An even 10 people per 1,000 in the age group eighteen through twenty-four from my 25-mile-by-25-mile county enlist in the military and are regularly welcomed home maimed or dead as heroes. Military service is seen in Nebraska, especially rural Nebraska, as a demonstration of love of country, and it therefore is. Even I, a passionate liberal, have to admit that there is something to be said for people who vote so solidly for right-wing politicians and war and at the same time are willing to put themselves and their children where their political opinions are, right on the front line.

Table Rock on the Nemaha

CHAPTER   NINE

Communities

As you can probably tell by now, my opinion is that Nebraska's character lies more in rural fields and pastures than in cities and towns.
But cities and towns being fairly unavoidable anywhere in America—
though rarer in Nebraska than in most places—they deserve a look, I
guess. Nonetheless, and in fair warning, I should note that the
smaller the community, the more I like it. I find that as I get older
and ever more settled in my life in Dannebrog, population 354, I am
ever less enchanted by Omaha. And Lincoln. And Grand Island. And
St. Paul. I suppose the time will come when I wind up grumping and
moaning about the traffic in Dannebrog, and how sometimes now I
have to park as much as fifteen steps away from wherever I'm going

and sometimes there are as many as two people ahead of me in the line at the post office. None of that has happened as yet, but the way things are going . . .

Once Again . . . Omaha

As cities go, I do like Omaha. I joke about that most city-ish of Nebraska cities being only marginally Nebraskan because one minor shift of the Missouri River and *zing!* it's back in Iowa, but whatever separation from Greater Nebraska that Omaha has is mostly a matter of its own manufacture. That is, Omaha far too often elects to reject its Nebraskan-ness . . . mostly because it is embarrassed about being in Nebraska. Omaha wants soooo desperately to be sophisticated, urbane, cultured, and eastern. Nothing annoys Omaha more than to be labeled "the Paris of the Pig Belt." But as of this writing and without misjudging next spring's thaw, Omaha is still on the western bank of the Missouri, on what the pioneers called "the *Nebraska* shore."

Don't get me wrong, now: I like culture. I have performed with both the Omaha Symphony and Opera Omaha, leaving only Ballet Omaha to be conquered. (I once mentioned this gap in my résumé to the director of Opera Omaha, who told me what the problem was: If I were to make an appearance with the ballet, they would have to dress me not in a tutu but a "four-four.") What I dislike about Omaha is not so much what is Omaha as what is unavoidably urban . . . that is, sprawl and traffic.

I admire New York cabdrivers; yes, they drive like madmen, but I have never been in a New York cab when it was in an accident, nor have I even seen a New York cab in an accident. New York traffic seems chaotic and even anarchical to outsiders, but the fact that there are so few catastrophic collisions speaks to a hidden order that we outsiders simply don't see, but which nonetheless is there. Not so in Omaha. There is no such détente or skill in Omaha when it comes to driving. The chaos and anarchy are real. People in Omaha simply drive like idiots and way too fast, not out of necessity or plan but because they feel it is a sophisticated, *city* thing to do.

It doesn't help that I have an ugly habit of forgetting that. I get accustomed to the slow and casual pace of rural Nebraska and then unthinkingly plunge one afternoon about five o'clock into the Omaha snarl, not realizing what I am in for until it is too late. I recall once making my way along Interstate 80 at about 72nd Street and, fool that I am, I had the utter temerity of going only 10 miles an hour above the speed limit, an unforgivable sin in Omaha. What's more, as has been the case for almost fifty years now, I–80 as intended but never achieved through Omaha was under construction. Traffic was three or four lanes wide. I was moving as quickly as I could considering that ahead of me was nothing but solid traffic, all lanes, well into Iowa and probably all the way to Des Moines. But a guy behind me with Omaha plates was so close on my bumper that my Ford Taurus was flashing a light on the dash warning me that it had intentions of filing charges of sodomy. Glances in my rearview mirror showed me that the driver behind was growing ever more agitated. His face was now visibly red. He pounded on his steering wheel, bobbing one way and then the other to see if he could swerve around me and thus gain 20 feet in the traffic. Finally he got his chance, veered into the lane beside me, maneuvered to my side, and shook his fist at me in rage. Six miles later he was still there, of course, because there was no way he could go any faster than I had been going, so I smiled and waved, which curiously didn't make him any friendlier at all. Finally he pulled far enough ahead of me that I could see the reason for his fury: In the bed of his clearly urban pickup truck he didn't have fence posts, seed corn, or irrigation equipment. No, he had his golf clubs. You see, the reason he was so furious with the traffic—and me—was that he was in a hurry to relax. To me, that is Omaha.

Where Omaha shines is where it is not a city, not urban, not sophisticated but still neighborhood and small community, which is to say Nebraska. Nebraska, and for that matter America, is not, and should not be a melting pot where all the various textures, flavors, and colors are melted into one homogeneous mess. No, if we need a metaphor, it should be that of the crazy quilt, the distinctions of the components remaining vivid and separate. So for me the best part of Omaha are things like the Bohemian Café in the historically Czech part of town, by the Prague Hotel, where Linda's grandfather John Kresse wandered as a homeless orphan until he became one of the first boys rescued by Father Flanagan—yes, John Kresse is one of those waifs in the famous statue—where to this day I have never gotten past the sweetbreads, liver dumplings, sweet cabbage, Urquell beer, and slivovitz, because they are just so damned good I can't bring myself to make a departure and try anything else on the menu. There are the Old Country sausage makers, Italian social group luncheons, Vietnamese grocery stores, African American soul food joints smaller than your living room, Mexican bodegas where no one speaks English, tiny Lithuanian bakeries where bread is sold by the pound and outsiders make the mistake of ordering one pound and thereby wind up with less than one slice, and Hindu temples where everyone is welcome but few find the courage to go. This is where Omaha is really a city, and yet it tends to be the part least celebrated or enjoyed by the average Omahog or Omahen. Far more likely to be promoted as examples of Omaha's civic pride are the artificial ethnic festivals where Boy Scouts do Indian dances and bored housewives demonstrate belly dancing learned at the YWCA.

Omaha is still a frontier town, which to my mind is not an insult at all because it means that fresh and lively experiences are still there for the taking if only you make a small effort to take advantage of them. Its pretensions to sophistication add nothing to the city's appeal but in fact detract from them. That is, I love Omaha . . . but not for the reasons the Omaha Chamber of Commerce wants me to love Omaha.

Star City

Lincoln is only now emerging from being a small town to being a city and is taking precisely the same idiotic approach to a nouveau kitsch level. The thing is, I've never lived in Omaha. Omaha has always been "the city" in my bumpkin mind. But Lincoln is the town where I grew up. I remember scissors grinders driving streets slowly, working from the trunks of their battered cars. I remember a fruit vendor coming by our home at 2665 South 12th Street in a wagon pulled by horses. I grew up walking the streets of Lincoln as a solitary little boy, even exploring the subterranean storm sewers, without fear or danger. My classmates where people like Dick Cavett, and Sandy Dennis, and, well, okay, sure, there was Charles Starkweather, but hey . . .

Now Lincoln drivers are almost as loony as those in Omaha, in a desperate hurry to get nowhere for no particular reason. There is the constant howl of sirens. The news of the day starts with the day's crimes. Other drivers give us country folks the finger. Nobody gives a shit. And if you really want a fight, suggest to a Lincoln booster that the town is still small-time, small-town, backwoods, and pretentious. Lincoln *wants* to be like Omaha. Or Chicago. People there *want* to divorce themselves from the best of Nebraska's virtues, from our proud intellectual heritage, from our solid grounding in agriculture, peasantry, and plain speech.

One of the saddest events of my advancing Geezerdom has been that I have had to abandon a project I found one of the most exciting of my long career in folklore, that of city folklorist for Lincoln. We— the Lincoln Arts Council and I—had the funding and opportunity to research, focus on, and present to the public the rich traditions of our New Americans, and New Nebraskans. For reasons I don't know and don't particularly care about, Lincoln has become a major terminal for immigrants to America—Bosnians, Somalis, Iraqis, Guatemalans, Lao-Hmong—all with incredibly rich traditions, all relatively unfamiliar to the larger population of my hometown. You simply cannot imagine the lust I felt in attacking this project.

I got a good start at it before some bad turns in my health—most notably a realization of approaching geriatritude—brought me to my knees and reality and I had to abandon it with, no kidding, tears in my eyes. But I did spend enough time at the job to make all the more clear to me what I had already considered evident: The very best

201

Americans are our New Americans. So much so that I consider them
a potential salvation for the miserable decline in our civility, democracy, and sense of decency. The situation is that drastic, in my opinion. Even in Nebraska, where civility, democracy, and decency
survive in Lincoln's New American communities while they are in
obvious decline elsewhere. As I started my initial explorations, I
encountered the kindest, gentlest, most generous, most genuinely
patriotic, most genuinely religious Nebraskans I had met in a long,
long time . . . but they were newly arrived from Afghanistan,
Vietnam, Uzbekistan, Nigeria, and Ecuador rather than Chadron,
McCook, or Norfolk. That is, what was jarringly evident to me was
that this new infusion of fresh blood into our gene pool was the very
best thing that could happen to Nebraska.

Not the least of which by a long shot was—my favorite cultural
expression—food. In my most bland of all hometowns, Lincoln,
Nebraska, where Jell-O with mandarin orange slices had always been
considered an adventure in ethnic foodways, there were now truly
wondrous markets where I could find fifty kinds of dried peppers,
thirty varieties of green tea, cheeses from around the world, soups
made of things I couldn't even mention to my children, blood
sausage, smoked eel, pickled pig skin, dried pig skin, pickled dried pig
skin . . . I slowed down in my shopping so I could listen longer to the
Mexican polka being played by the market owner at La Mexicana, or
the singing of the Koran at the Homeland Market, or whatever it was
I was hearing at the Vina Vietnamese grocery. Wow. This was my
Lincoln! Finally truly in the world, and in a big way. And what's
more, in the right, positive way.

Then I was jarred back into reality by the word that Lincoln
boosters, when showing the place to potential new residents, businesses, or visitors, were avoiding precisely the kinds of things I found
so dynamic and attractive about the new Lincoln. Scouts for new
businesses, professionals from major urban areas thinking of moving
to Lincoln were purposely being steered away from North 27th
Street, the genuine ethnic restaurants embedded within their home

communities, because . . . because, well, they are . . . what? Unseemly, I guess. You know—these people don't speak English all that well. And what the hell is that they are eating? Baba ghanoush? What in the name of God is baba ghanoush? Eggplant! Who eats egg-plant?

So the boneheads in charge were showing off the new McDonald's locations and a chichi fern bar specializing in salads, and a lounge where you can actually find exotic things like Fuzzy Navels served in scooped-out grapefruit halves. Yikes. Why wouldn't some-one from San Francisco want to enjoy cutting-edge culture like that? I did what I could to make the point that the very most attractive ele-ment of Lincoln to outsiders interested in the genuine sophisticated and urbane are the tiny Greek, Iraqi, and Thai markets and cafes springing up around town. I think I started to make a dent, but then my health went all to hell and the project died, to my intense pain and regret.

So what happens to Lincoln now? I have no idea. All I can do, all I have is hope.

Bland Island

My litany of pain shall continue. Even close to home I find disap-pointment and worry. Grand Island, where Linda is at this very moment shopping while I sit here in my study writing, is dealing with a dilemma. As the newspaper sometimes describes it, we have this Hispanic . . . uh . . . "problem." You know, there are all these darker-skinned people, speaking another language, eating weird stuff, dancing to strange music that sounds for all the world like a polka but is much more lively, that kind of thing . . . What the hell can we do about this? It has to stop!

Well, I have a solution. Stop calling it a problem and consider it instead an incredible opportunity, a gift dropped into our laps just when we need it. This new influx of Spanish-speaking workers is our opportunity to shed the painful impression of "Bland Island" and become truly grand. The entire area from Kearney through Lexington to Grand Island has become heavily Hispanic, immigrants drawn to work in the meat industry—turkeys, hogs, chickens, and beef—doing work no one else wants to do. The complaints from established residents are the standards: Since these are obviously the lowest economic classes and have come to a new cultural setting, the names on the police blotter have tended to be distinctly Spanish . . . sort of like they were German when Germans were the new immigrants, and Scandinavian when they were the newcomers, et cetera, et cetera. The most common complaint I have heard, no kidding, is that Hispanics put an undue burden on local laborers by doing their jobs way too well, way too fast, and way too cheerfully, thus making more "American" workers who work slower, and less, and with less skill look *really* bad in comparison. We had a solid American from here in town put a roof on our house when we first moved it and renovated it, for example; it took many weeks for him to do the job and it leaked at the first rain. He resented our complaining and never fixed the problem. We had another roof put on by a Mexican team; it took a day, they did a beautiful job, and it was less expensive. In fact, the only complaint I had was that they opened their lunch boxes within my sight and didn't ask me to join them for the wonderful foods I saw they had brought with them from home.

So here's my plan for Grand Island and its Hispanic "problems": Make them an asset. Grand Island is now something like 30 percent Hispanic, so revel in that reality. Begin to call Grand Island "the Plains Guadalajara." Promote our new, imported heritage. Have one movie screen showing nothing but Spanish-language films. Invite Mexican, Puerto Rican, or Colombian industries to locate here. Require Spanish for every student in every public school at every grade. Install Spanish street signs and encourage businesses to speak Spanish and promote Spanish products. Make Grand Island the place to go if you are interested in Spanish culture, or want to hear the language, or want to eat Spanish food or buy Spanish goods.

Grand Island was once German. Okay, that's fine. There's the Liederkranz, Krug's, and the Plattdeutsch, vestigial cultural fragments from those times. But times have changed and now we can move on. Now the times in Grand Island, Nebraska, and America for that matter, are Hispanic, and to our good fortune we have it right here, and we are at the cutting edge. Can you imagine the prospects for students of Grand Island high schools graduating with twelve years of Spanish language, culture, history, and geography behind them? College or corporate recruiters would be lined up at the end of the diploma presentation line hoping to grab at least one of these prizes. Even bilingual plumbers, welders, and nurses are in enormous demand and would be snapped up by employers from all around America. Grand Island would become an economic and cultural mecca.

Yeah, that's some kind of problem all right. So, what are we going to do with all this opportunity? Nothing to do but throw it away, I guess.

Small Towns = Big Times

The neglect and subsequent failure of our local schools has had its impact on Nebraska's smaller towns. Towns like Dannebrog lose their school and they lose vitality. It's not just athletic teams, although that is part of it. It's also the life of the economy. As the school goes, soon also goes the town tavern, then the grocery store, then the post office. And the town dies. And Nebraska suffers.

Nebraska abounds in ghost towns. You don't even have to go out of your way to go through one. The next time you are zinging along on Interstate 80 and go through the Exit 348 interchange, take a quick look around. Dead in the center of that overpass you are also in the middle of Charleston, a town now long gone. Within a short drive of Dannebrog there is Dannevirke with its one residence, or Nysted with its half dozen, all towns in their last throes. I suspect that the only things that have brought Dannebrog back from the brink of extinction is that it is close enough to Grand Island to have become a bedroom community, a couple of community sparkplugs refused to say "Uncle" and let the town die, and it had a decade of attention on national television as the usual setting for my "Postcards from Nebraska." The railroad has been taken out, we lost one of our two service stations, the school is gone, we have lost our bank now and then, fortunately not permanently, our drive-in is now dead . . . We're hanging on, but it isn't easy. Our population has grown by 10 percent since the last census, and if you counted new houses just outside the village limits I'd bet the percentage would be more like 25 or maybe even 35. Farmers are growing ever fewer, local businesses are struggling, and young people are headed off for greener pastures, but acreages, hobby farmers, people who've seen the town on television and come to retire here, and commuters to Grand Island are moving in and building, which doesn't much help community spirit or local businesses—these transients still bank and buy their groceries, repairs, and fuel in Grand Island—but it means the town probably won't die quite yet.

Another rule for anyone claiming Nebraska citizenship: You have to spend at least one week every, oh, five years in a Nebraska town with a population of less than 5,000. Any town. I used to do a lot of travel in Europe, some for pleasure, mostly for my academic work or as a representative of some federal agency or another. I developed what I still consider a really good system for getting to know a country and its people well. I'd go first to a big city, usually wherever airplanes land— London, Frankfurt, Oslo . . . I'd spend three or four days there doing the usual tourist stuff, sort of getting steady on my feet, retuning my ears to the language, figuring out my next steps, that kind of thing. Then I would set out into the countryside for two medium-size towns or cities, about the size of Lincoln at the time, perhaps a with a population of 100,000 or so, where I would spend again three or four days in each. Mixed in with those larger communities, I would seek out two or three very small communities pretty much at random, with a population of perhaps 1,000 but sometimes consisting of not much more than a dozen houses and farms clustered around a crossroads with an inn, pub, or tavern, again for three or four days each. Without exception my best experiences, the ones I still talk about, were in the smallest of the communities. That's where I got to know people, their food, ideas, and ways. That's where I had fun and tucked away memories.

The first time I came back from a summer of bicycling all over Europe, I was filled with the Continent and contemptuous of the United States; everything there was so much better, more beautiful, more interesting, more cultured, more fun. And then one day I did some cross-country cycling just outside Lincoln and I discovered that it wasn't the scenery that was different. It was the way I was seeing it! I think we would all have more of an appreciation for where we are if we took the time to see it the way we so often see Europe. So that's what I am suggesting you consider for improving your appreciation for Nebraska: Spend a few days in Omaha or Lincoln, especially if that's not where you already live anyway. Then do the same in Blair, Chadron, Scottsbluff, McCook, or Nebraska City. And finally, with no particular agenda in mind, travel to and spend a few days in Henderson, Peru, Arthur, Ord, Dwight, Ong, or Fairbury. Or . . . how about Dannebrog? Just hang around the tavern an evening or two and get to know some of the regulars. Hit the cafe for breakfast in the morning. Take in a ball game or church service. Sit and read on a bench outside the grocery store or at a picnic table in the town park. Read up on the local history. Talk with some geezers. Buy a couple of tickets to the American Legion pancake feed or the Knights of Columbus duck and kraut dinner. Drop into the local storefront "museum." Stay at the bed-and-breakfast. I'm betting you will come to consider the place to be your second hometown. It's almost like visiting another country.

Some of my favorite towns in Nebraska to visit are the reservation towns of Winnebago, Macy, and Walthill. Yes, that can be a bit on the depressing side because in these cases that "other country" is a third-world nation, but I have also found some of the finest people I have ever known in these very communities. Now, you may be uneasy about jumping headfirst into a culture so different from your own—I mean, yes, it's one thing to enjoy the Czechs in Clarkson, Swedes in Stromsburg, Germans in Henderson, and Italians in South Omaha, but quite another to step in Plains Indian culture on a reservation. So if you want to take it a little easier, even with those Czechs or Italians, plan your visit around one of the inevitable community festivals when special provisions are made precisely for outsiders like you.

Festivals Legit and Otherwise

Caveat emptor! Do consider the purpose of those "ethnic" festivals! Some are designed *completely* for outsiders. Anyone who lives in the town on a day-to-day basis gets the heck out of there for the occasion, which may have absolutely nothing to do with honest tradition but be nothing but fabricated showbiz for outsiders. What you want is a genuinely community celebration that is primarily for the people of that community but to which outsiders are invited and welcome. It won't take you long to figure it out: Do you think people normally dress in those hokey outfits, say at a wedding, or is this just for the tourists in town? And how about the food? Who's peddling it? If it's the ladies over at the Lutheran or Catholic church, you can pretty much figure this is legitimate stuff, the kind of food they might actually fix for their own families now and then during the year and not just at festival time!

An old friend and colleague of mine has observed from her view as a professional folklorist that we can't just dismiss local festivals or storefront museums simply because they don't reflect an accurate picture of the past. Her point is well taken: These events and constructs tell us how people and communities see themselves and their past, whether that is the way things actually happened or not. I suppose we might have an argument with whether the food we are eating is the way kolaches taste in Moravia or if a tractor pull is legitimately a part of Danish tradition, but we do know that this is the way things are done among the Czechs and Danes in Nebraska. So sit back, relax, and pass the kolaches.

Frankly, I'm not sure if the old definitions of villages, towns, and cities, neighborhoods, townships, that kind of thing, make any sense anymore. For one thing, transportation by auto is now so rapid and easy, especially in places like Nebraska where the roads are good, level, and straight, that it often takes a lot less time to go from one rural village to another than to cross even a small city like Lincoln from one shopping mall to another. Moreover, cities are growing ever closer to each other as borders grow and blur, and Omaha, Lincoln, and even Grand Island and Hastings are gobbling up smaller communities that lie in their path. I think that if someone were to look at our population patterns with an objective eye unbound by those old and outdated definitions, he might see Nebraska as one large urban city in the East—that is, Lincoln-Omaha, probably known by a very old name still emblazoned on the old lighthouse at the swimming hole I remember from my youth, Linoma. Sure, there are green, open areas between, but they are traversed in minutes now, they are anything but permanent, and already at this writing large populations from both "cities," Omaha and Lincoln, commute regularly to the other for work or entertainment.

I'm not sure what our outside observer would make of a cluster like Haskegra, previously known as Hastings-Kearney-Grand-Island. If someone had the common sense—it seems doubtful at this writing—to build one large state airport amid these three towns (or one midway between Lincoln and Omaha, for that matter), current boundaries would be gone and the cities would be one. But the fly in the ointment of my grand plan for community consolidation of Lincoln and Omaha is that I believe there is another configuration that is even more definitive and which is developing so fast that it may wind up with Haskegra only as a kind of central node: Platte City, the 200- or 300-mile-long main street right down the transportation spine of Nebraska, mostly along the Platte, from Omaha to Fremont to Columbus, on to Central City, Grand Island, Kearney, North Platte, Ogallala, maybe even as far west as the Wyoming border near Scoger (né Scottsbluff-Gering).

I'd love to call this New Braska City "Nebraska City," but I suppose the folks in Nebraska's Big Apple, the southeastern town already called Nebraska City, would be stuffy about that. So maybe we could just start calling that town Omaha since that city will no longer be using the name. Okay, if the notion of a Pearls-on-a-String City across Nebraska along the Platte hasn't sent you off for a cold shower, how about this? The City of Lariat! A real tribute to the West! The long rope starts out west by Scoger and runs east to Grand Island, where it forms the loop of the lasso, following the Platte up to Omaha, then down I–80 to Lincoln, and then back through Seward, York, and Aurora to close the loop at Grand Island.

Or maybe a more mysterious and international air could be obtained with Ankh City, the great, eternal, mystic symbol that can be seen from alien ships far in space as they observe earth through their super-hydrex-proton telescopes . . . the aforementioned Lasso City but with a vertical north–south bar a la the Egyptian symbol, crossing the alternative lasso form at the "knot," running from Hastings north on Highway 280 to St. Paul?

Have you seen one of those satellite images of the earth at night? The one with all the lights where towns and cities are? Take another look the next time one of those pops up. (Check the Web site http://antwrp.gsfc.nasa.gov/apod/ao040822.html or, better yet, http://antwrp.gsfc.nasa.gov/apod/image/0011/earthlights2_dmsp_big .jpg. Another good site for this image—there are quite a few, I sus-pect, because it is such a stunning idea and shows how painfully puny we human beings are—is http://nationalatlas.gov/natlas /Natlasstart.asp.) Gazing at these images, where the lights of towns at night clearly define our population patterns, you will see and under-stand better the point I am trying to make here. In the lights of all the towns strung out along the Platte River, in the "lariat loop," or the crossbar that transforms the rope and loop into an ankh, you will see where we Nebraskans truly live.

While you're looking at this remarkable composite image, note the huge and wonderful black hole that tells you precisely where the Nebraska Sandhills are! If you have trouble orienting in this image, find the black holes that are the Great Lakes, spot the splashes of light that are Chicago, then find Des Moines, Kansas City, or Minneapolis, which should lead you to Omaha and Lincoln . . . and then you can see the distinctive, much dimmer string of pearls that are our towns along the Platte. You'll see exactly what I am trying to get at with this wild mind-rummaging.

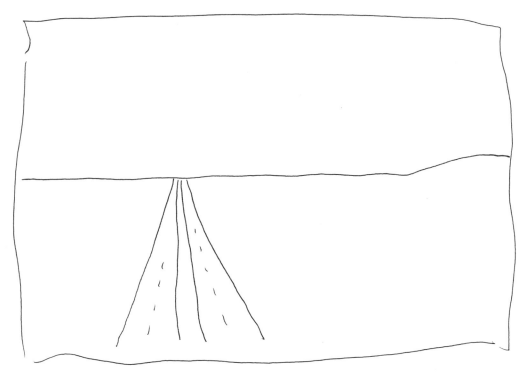

Interstate 80 near Cozad

History

The field of history—or more precisely, its practitioners—has always baffled me. Historians start with what has to be the most fascinating subject in the world, the story of ourselves, and still they manage to screw it up enough to make it boring and irrelevant and, what's more, get the punch lines wrong. Part of the problem has been the idiotic effort of historians over the past fifty years or so to put themselves into a position of greater respect—read: more generous funding—by removing their studies from the humanities and jamming them incongruously instead into science . . . that is to say (ugh!), the *social* sciences. And how have historians accomplished this? In large part by devising a language that sounds impressively scientific, mostly by being impossible to understand. Voilà! you got yourself a science.

In the main, however, the study of history has left Academe and moved instead into the realm of popular writing, fiction, movies, and television. This would be fine with me, except the surrender has meant that along with history becoming a good deal more interesting, it has also occasionally become less accurate.

Not that historical scholars have always done all that well. One of the reasons I love folklore and folk history is that it tends to be far more reliable than scholarly historical research. I know that the popular opinion is exactly the opposite—that oral history is less reliable because it isn't written down—but that simply isn't true. Historical accounts written by one person are subject to that one person's whims, opinions, and errors; a history that is recited within the reinforcing fabric of an audience that has heard the same story many times before, insists on accuracy, does instant critique and stern editing that permits no variation—well, *that* is reliability! And that is called *folklore*, sadly a word often misused to mean precisely the opposite of reliable truth.

Moreover, the conventional understanding of academic, scholarly historical study is economic-political history, which is—again—one of the most boring possible ways to look at the past. Nothing is less interesting than important, powerful, rich people. Moreover, they aren't nearly as important, powerful, or rich as you (or they) might think. The really important people in the forces of history, the real movers and shakers, are the masses, ordinary people, the nameless, the truly heroic, and their stories are represented not in dates and recognizable names but in everyday activities that sweep along the "important, powerful, and rich" in the force of their inevitable, irresistible social current. And once again, another name for that is *folklore*.

History Is Bunk, Saith Henry Ford

Within the stories of the ordinary, you can also find an honesty that isn't always present in the approved versions. I once raised some major industrial-grade hell about a Nebraska history that had been written by a professor whose loyalty was not to the truth, or to his readers, but to his immediate profit and a misguided hope for acceptance. His work was riddled with accommodations to popular opinion and social taste not so much by distorting the truth as by omitting what didn't fit the desired effect. For example, this Nebraska "historian" was once commissioned to write an "official" history for the state. He referred in several places to the wit and accomplishment of a man by the name of John M. Chivington.

Reading this "official" account, you would think Chivington was a fellow you might enjoy sitting next to at a banquet head table—bishop of the Nebraska Methodist Church, a pioneer, something of an adventurer, and quick with the clever phrase. What the "historian" had omitted, however, was Chivington's involvement in one of the most appalling atrocities of American history, the inexcusable butchery of peaceful, sleeping old men, women, and children at a place called Sand Creek. Chivington was a commander of the troops who cut off their victims' private parts, using the male members for tobacco pouches, and female parts for hatbands. Even the nineteenth-century American military, scarcely noted for civility or mercy toward Native populations at the time, was compelled to condemn the actions of Chivington and his men—actions that this very visible "Christian" never felt inclined to deny or excuse.

Not only was the historian who so blithely misrepresented Chivington in this case indignant about being held to some standard of accuracy rather than rampant boosterism in his writing, but Nebraska's principal newspaper jumped right into the issue and had the gall to accuse *me* of bowing to "political correctness," even publishing an editorial cartoon to that effect, for suggesting that accuracy should perhaps trump popular fantasy when it comes to official histories! Real history is more interesting, but let's face it, it can also be less amenable to what we wish were true. That's something we simply have to deal with.

Or conversely, to enjoy. Because something else historians miss in their plunge into irrelevance and obscurity is that we don't really like rich, powerful, important—and boring—ancestors. Give a hundred people a choice: Who would you rather find perched in the branches of your family tree? (1) Percival Pickle, a Methodist bishop of celebrated virtue, or (2) a woman named Marybel Teddy, who was successful in her millinery business and became famous as the namesake for a fancy lady's undergarment? How about this choice: (1) Clarence Birkenbeck, a solid citizen who never once in his life missed voting in an election, or (2) Wilber Klinkhammer, who rode with Jesse James? Even more than we like our heroes, we cherish our villains. We love the seamy and untidy. We like the whiff of scandal. And take it from me, that's what we want to know about our history.

Of course toes will be stepped on with this approach of telling honest history from the point of view of real people who lived it. There are notions we cherish and are not at all amused to be told are pure hogwash. Take our own courageous, stalwart, self-reliant, resourceful pioneer Nebraska forebears, those who brought civilization and agriculture to the Plains. Well, uh, okay . . . there were already substantial cities here with rich culture, complicated religion and mythology, remarkable civility and ingenious survival methods among the various tribes who had been here centuries before the first white man crossed the Missouri. And what's more, we could profit from the wisdom of Native peoples to this very day if we would simply stop, sit down, and listen for a change. And, of course, a remarkable number of the pioneers on the trails and among homesteaders failed and went running back east with their tails between their legs, or died ignominious and totally unnecessary deaths because they were too stubborn or stupid to learn from the Indians around them who were doing just fine on the very same ground. And well, yes, they were the beneficiaries of the robbery of these tribal people by standing in line for the most enormous welfare dole in the history of the world, the Homesteading Act, in which they were virtually given . . . *given* a farm, having only to survive on it for a relatively brief period of time . . . which an astonishing number of them couldn't accomplish.

True History

Which is to say, the pioneers were for all the world just like us. Just as brave, just as resourceful, just as independent, just as hardworking—or not. Just as flawed, just as lazy, just as incompetent, just as mean-spirited, just as larcenous, just as stupid. Most of the frontiersmen had no idea what they were getting into when they came onto the Plains, whether it was for them simply a matter of getting across to somewhere else or with the actual intention of staying. Even today Americans traveling in Europe are caught by surprise to find that other countries tend to be on a much smaller scale than America, that what we consider usual behavior, normal activities, common foods, and so forth, are only our own regional practices and may be seen elsewhere as peculiar. Or disgusting.

The reverse is also true. Europeans coming to America even in this day of universal education, instant communications, and international broadcasts, Germans, Danes, and Bosnians, are simply not prepared for the enormity of America, the ferocity of our commerce and conversation, the violence of our weather, the scope of our horizons. For example, American students have told me that they intend to travel Europe for a month, going to Hamburg and renting a car to tour Germany. I ask them what they're going to do that afternoon when they get to Holland. Germany is the size of Nebraska and Kansas in a lump. Germans tell me they are coming to see America by bicycle, spending their month here in America cycling from New York City to Chicago (to see gangsters), then to Dannebrog to visit us, on to Yellowstone Park, maybe the Grand Canyon, San Francisco, New Orleans, Florida, and perhaps spending their final week in Washington, DC. It does no good to tell Nebraskans about the size of Denmark in kilometers or Danes the size of Nebraska in miles. It just doesn't register. Europeans know Europe and its dimensions; Americans know America.

And that's now. Imagine what it was like for the travelers on the Oregon Trail in 1848 or prospective homesteaders in 1867. They had not a clue. Worse yet, in many cases they were not only ignorant, but also misled. People wanting to sell land or lure wives told outright lies. "Should be able to get from Nebraska City to the California gold fields in, oh, four weeks or so . . . "—when the truth they would discover was that in four weeks they would have gotten to Fort Kearney, scarcely even a good start on the long journey they were making. "No problems with crops here . . . plenty of rain, balmy temperatures, easy winters, no such things as grasshoppers. Or cows piling up and freezing to death in canyons. Or tornadoes leveling towns and cities. Or heat that'll bake potatoes right in the ground . . ."

Some of the jarring realities faced by newcomers to the Plains and what is now Nebraska are beyond our modern minds to conjure up. Just can't do it. They are too extreme. Just for fun, though, try to imagine growing up on an eight-acre farm, mostly vertical, mostly rock, largely treed with towering spruce trees, deep in a Norwegian fjord where your family has toiled since Viking times. You can't possibly imagine such a thing, but *try*. The sun doesn't shine into your steep-sided valley until shortly before noon, then settles along the horizon high above you on the other side of the valley early in the afternoon. And that's in deep summer, because as far north as you are, there isn't much sunlight during the winter months even when you go out onto the sea fishing and can actually see horizons far off into the distance. You eat cod in various forms, grow barley and rye enough to feed your family, milk a cow that feeds on the sparse grass at the edges of your "farm," a plot you can easily walk completely around in a matter of a quarter hour. Your bread is baked in a stone fireplace over a pinewood fire. Your neighbors are within easy shouting distance; you can see the church towers of three villages from your front door. Of course they are all Lutheran. That's the official national religion, after all, but it is also the only true religion, and since there are no churches of any other denomination—and certainly of no other faith than Christianity!—within a year's travel, you have no idea what they might be about. You once met a Spaniard who was in the city at the end of your fjord buying salt the same day you were there; an uncle who was a professional soldier for the king killed Germans during a war you heard about. He once brought home a bit of dry sausage he had taken from a German prisoner and let you taste it. It snows a lot where you live. You home is a solid log house built by an ancestor a little over four centuries ago. You have seen seals in your fjord.

And now somehow you have wound up in this place called America. In a state with the peculiar, almost unpronounceable name *Nebraska*. An Indian word. An *Indian* word! You know, like the wild savages you had only heard rumors of in your native fjord. There are no rocks, no trees. The land that has been offered to you—virtually free!—is the size of twenty average farms back home. Like your neighbors you have built your house out of sod blocks piled up like a mud hut. There are no fish because there is no water, so you eat buffalo, and deer, moldy bacon and wormy hams; during bad times you once even resorted to cooking up a badger. Your bread is made of a coarse grain called maize. You know there are neighbors—Poles, you've heard—to the west, and some Irish to the south . . . but they are so far away and the winter has been so hard, you can only hope to meet some of them in a few months when the weather clears. When you filed your claim, you had to walk 20 miles to the courthouse in the county seat, but that's not such a big deal because after you got off the steamboat at Omaha you arrived here at your new homestead by walking for seven days . . . and pushing a wheelbarrow with all your earthly effects in it, and when you send the kids to town to exchange a dozen eggs for thread and needles for the wife, they have to walk 6 miles each way. But what the heck, the last time you went to the county seat to do some legal work at the courthouse you actually saw a Chinaman, who is running the new laundry in town, and not far away and just across the river a claim has been taken out by a family of Negroes, which might turn out to be darned handy because this guy has a reputation as one heck of a blacksmith. You understand there is a Lutheran church a few hours away at a Swedish settlement, but the closest other church is one of those accursed Papist blasphemies run by some Bavarian Germans, in

constant conflict with a settlement of Czech Freethinkers who insist
that they came here to escape religious oppression and damned if it
didn't go ahead and follow them all this way, they complain, right to
their very back door. The sun is up long before you are, even though
you sleep only a few hours, and it is still up when you fall into bed.

By the way, if you think I have stretched things with the long
paragraph above, I haven't. Nor have I resorted to empty stereotypes.
Each and every detail of the previous paragraph would have been the
exact, true case for any settler in the area of Dannebrog, Nebraska, in
the late nineteenth century.

The very best literary (and historical) depiction I know of these
things is Ole Rolvaag's stunning masterpiece *Giants in the Earth*.
Rolvaag conducted extensive interviews with Norwegian immigrants
who settled in the area of his own interest, not in Nebraska but not
all that far away either, just north of our own northeast corner near
Sioux Falls, South Dakota. There is no better ethnography for the settlers on the Plains. I like Cather's *My Ántonia* and Sandoz's *Old Jules*,
but even these giant works don't come close to the truth of Rolvaag's
Giants in the Earth. In fact, you should read the entire series of his
books if you want to understand the story of the Plains.

In the sequel to his *Giants in the Earth*, *Peter Victorious*, Rolvaag
writes of the first American-born generation of his Norwegian family
and again nails down the truth in his fiction. To some degree the irony
he explores in the second book is telegraphed by the frightening
hubris of the name he gives his son, *Victorious*. What could be a more
certain way to ensure a miserable destiny? And Peter Victorious, the
son of the original Norwegian immigrants, does indeed bring disgrace
to his family. Now, think about it. What could a son of an immigrant
Norwegian family do that would be the very worst sort of insult to his
legacy? What would be the very worst disappointment he could throw
into the face of not just his family but his entire heritage?

That's right: Peter Victorious married . . . gulp! . . . a *Catholic!*
And what's worse, an *Irish* Catholic! But Rolvaag's genius is that he
understands and depicts not only what this would have meant to the

Norwegian parents, but also what the inevitable problems are for the cultural mixing that would have been unthinkable if not impossible in the homeland, and was inevitable and unavoidable on the pioneer Plains. Peter Victorious and his Irish bride manage to deal with their linguistic and cultural differences, and even their religious conflicts. But where they finally slam up against a personal and social wall is . . . God, Rolvaag is such a genius! Only a truly learned anthropological scholar would be aware of this . . . Where this new family finally meets the barrier impossible to deal with intellectually is . . . the supper table! You can compromise the religion, and the language, and the culture, and the—well, everything. But you cannot wish away or reason away the fact that those other people simply don't know how to cook or what to eat. In Norway (read: Germany, Ireland, China, Italy, Ukraine, Russia, what have you) no such issue was ever considered, and yet now, here in this Nebraska, you are suddenly in immediate contact with ten other cultures. And ten other ways of cooking and eating.

Nebraska, a Mere Child

Another feature of Nebraska's history that all too often escapes both historians and the common Nebraskan is the incredible youth of our past. For all our centennial celebrations and proud ownership of things that are inevitably and famously "one hundred years old!" we are green newcomers at best. Our history is recent. Not only was the frontier not all that long ago; I firmly believe we still are on the frontier, still trying to figure out what this landscape is capable of—and not capable of. We are still sorting out who can make it here and who cannot.

To begin with, a century is no time at all—easily a period within one modern lifetime—but even beyond this there isn't all that much here yet that has reached even that puny level of antiquity. My entire family has not yet been here a full century. I am the second generation born in America, and even at that some of my aunts and uncles were born abroad. We are, in short, still on the frontier. We still have no idea what this geography is like. We can't really consider ourselves permanent as long as farms and villages are still dying and the population is in constant flux. Our communities still show strong reflections of their origins and have not come to grips with the cultures around them . . . including those other peculiar foodways. (Czech duck blood soup, anyone?)

This past spring I received the remarkable honor and privilege of being adopted by a Lakota brother in the ancient Hunkapi or "kin-making ceremony" on the Pine Ridge Reservation near Wounded Knee. As I learned what I could about it, I found in my research that not many white men are honored with a Hunkapi because Lakota elders "still consider the white man to be a passing phenomenon." I love that! Even though some white people may think they have become a permanent fixture of the Plains landscape, for many Native peoples the issue is still open.

Solomon Butcher set out with his camera and interview notepads in the mid-1880s to put together his book, *A History of Custer County, Nebraska,* a concept I have always admired: Why wait until there is so much history you don't know where to start or how to sort it all out, after all? Write up a region's history before it gets too complicated. That is, write the history precisely while it is happening. If not before. And that's pretty much where we are today in Nebraska. Centennial celebrations or not, frankly, we don't have much history under our belts yet to draw a lot of conclusions. We seem to be writing the history of the day before yesterday. I have sat down and talked with homesteaders, builders of sod houses, farmers who grew up tilling the soil with horses and whose homes didn't have electricity until I was a grown man myself.

Nothing brought the reality of the brevity of Nebraska's history to me more than an occasion when I was talking with a Lakota holy man by the name of Richard Fool Bull. I was cutting some cedar heartwood for him—he was a traditional maker of Lakota love flutes—and we got to talking about the troubles in the 1970s when young Lakota occupied the church and a good part of the town of

Wounded Knee to protest a century of neglect and abuse. They were surrounded by U.S. marshals and military troops with heavy weaponry in an unheard-of and unconscionable demonstration of force and coercion. Mr. Fool Bull told me that he was proud that even at his advanced age (he was then well into his nineties) to have been asked by the young people staging the protest to be the spiritual leader of the occupation. We talked and talked, covering several subjects, and somehow got back to the topic of Wounded Knee. Mr. Fool Bull said, "You could hear them guns going, like this"—and he clapped his hands rapidly together.

"Were those the automatic weapons the U.S. Marshals had, or were those the AK-47s some of the veterans had brought back from Vietnam?" I asked, horrified at the notion of this elder caught in the middle of a firefight between American citizens on his own reservation land.

There was a moment of confusion in our conversation. It was obvious that Mr. Fool Bull was struggling to understand my question. "Nooo," he said. "Those were the Hotchkiss guns." My God! Then it occurred to me—he wasn't talking about the events at Wounded Knee recently. He was talking about the only slightly less recent events for him—although still well within his memory—the slaughter of Big Foot's Band at Wounded Knee in 1892 by the Iowa Seventh Cavalry! History had suddenly collapsed before me, happenings of ancient Plains history I had only known about from books folding into the events of recent months in the eyes and words of a single man. Mr. Fool Bull's family was within hearing distance of that first clash at Wounded Knee. Yes, he had heard the marshal's guns and the AK-47s at the *second* Wounded Knee encounter in 1973, but the explosions of the Hotchkiss guns murdering hundreds of innocents in one of this nation's worst atrocities also echoed in his ears.

Suddenly I understood the real nature of Plains history. It's not book history at all. It's rumors and anecdotes from the people who were there. Some people may be embarrassed that we don't have colonial or Revolutionary War period sites (although of course we

actually do—in Native tribal history) or that our "antiques" are adver-
tised as "at least a hundred years old!" while in Florida or
Pennsylvania they see things from centuries that aren't even mentioned in a history of Nebraska, but I find it all the more exciting. Our
history here is not something dead and gone. We are smack in the
middle of Nebraska's history, actually at the doorway into our history.
We may no longer be able to talk with homesteaders and Lakota hos-
tiles as I have had the opportunity to do, but we can still find plenty
of people to tell us about what it was like to put up hay with horses,
or light a home with kerosene, or milk cows by hand twice a day. As,
in fact, I can tell my own children from my own personal experience.
Still today we can attend celebrations, prayer meetings, games, and
funerals on Native reservations and hear songs that might have been
heard by Lewis and Clark in 1804, as well as new songs that are still
being born within that living, dynamic culture. Our history here on
the Great Plains is not as long ago as we might think. Nor is it even
yesterday. Our history is with us today. We are in fact our history.
That is, in Nebraska we don't so much remember our history as live
with it.

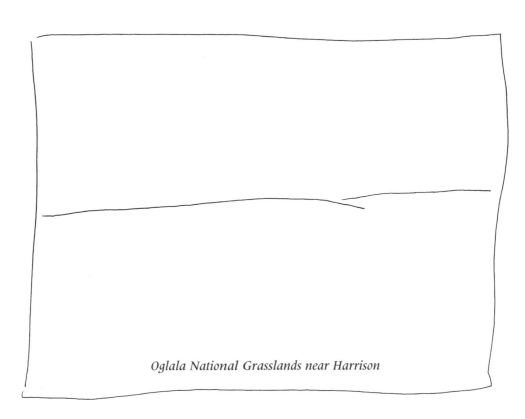

Oglala National Grasslands near Harrison

CHAPTER ELEVEN

Culture and Art

Just as Nebraskans are lucky because we can and do rub shoulders on a regular basis with our rich, famous, powerful, and elected, we also gain through sparse population and refined natural selection a remarkable proximity and familiarity with our artists and poets. Unfortunately I didn't realize that until late in life, presuming like way too many other Nebraskans that there was nothing unusual about seeing an internationally celebrated poet, novelist, or artist hoeing weeds in the garden, slopping down a beer in a neighborhood tavern, or waiting for his dog to poop in a local park. I never had the opportunity to meet or even see Willa Cather, but I did once get a glimpse of Mari Sandoz signing books at the Miller and Paine

Bookstore near 13th and O Streets in Lincoln as I was strolling by. Of course at the time I didn't know enough to go in and bask in her prickly presence. I saw the equally irascible Louise Pound walking across the university campus once . . . again not having the sense or courage to approach her. In 1977 I was on an errand for the University of Nebraska to assess the library of Ben Botkin, famous American folklorist and student of Miss Pound's, and was scheduled to stop by Haverford, Pennsylvania, on the way back to visit with Loren Eiseley about the possible acquisition of his papers for the university. I can't tell you how excited I was about that prospect, being absolutely gaga about Eiseley. I was in Croton-on-Hudson surveying the Botkin papers when I got word that Eiseley had died while I was en route. I was crushed.

I also learned a lesson about carpe-ing the diem, as it were, and I didn't miss a chance from then on to make the acquaintance of Nebraska's creative souls whenever and wherever I could. I have had my disappointments, but on the other hand I am absolutely delighted to say that I knew John Neihardt well and profited immensely from every exchange I had with him. I didn't imagine I would ever meet another favorite of mine, Wright Morris, who was born and raised at least in his earliest years just down Ormsby Road from our place in Dannebrog, in Central City, Nebraska, so you can imagine my delight when he came to the university as a visiting faculty member in 1975. I made a point of attending every lecture he gave while he was there—and they were brilliant—and approaching him reverently. To my enormous pride, he knew my work, was willing to talk with me and answer some questions I had about his work, and autographed some of his books for me with personal messages I consider to be among my dearest treasures.

Among Nebraska's contemporary literary giants I can say I know Bill Kloefkorn, our state poet, as a dear friend and former colleague; Ted Kooser, our nation's poet laureate, also as a good friend; John Janovy, nationally famous nature writer; Don Welch, an accomplished poet; and several dozen other writers and poets. In large part this is because the sparse population density of Nebraska, combined with a higher-than-usual concentration of literary talent, makes it almost impossible to go anywhere or do much around the state without running into a major Nebraska literary figure sooner or later. And as if there weren't enough native sons and daughters of literary merit, nationally renowned figures seem drawn to Nebraska whether they had the good fortune to be born here or not. Jim Harrison, one of America's most accomplished novelists and screen-writers, makes a habit of wandering around the Sandhills and incorporating this landscape into his novels and movies, occasionally even dropping by our place here in Dannebrog to walk our river bottoms and refresh his spirit. If you read Jim's *The Road Home* carefully, you'll find me in its pages.

The same is true of Nebraska's artists. I have already mentioned cartoonist Saul Steinberg, and once again it is my impression that we have had a richer than expected or usual history of artists within our relatively thin population . . . world-famous artists like Robert Henri from Cozad, or Augustus Dunbier from Shelby. (I never go through that town without wondering why in the name of all that makes sense it doesn't have huge signs up celebrating its great contribution to world art in the person of Dunbier!) And contemporaries like Harold Holoun, now in Bellevue but originally from Ord, Keith Jacobshagen in Lincoln at the university, world-famous photographers like Joel Sartori and Mike Forsberg, on and on. And of course, the artist in my life, currently out of her studio buying groceries for our supper, my own wife Linda, whose thoughts about art are as stunning to me as is her staggering talent.

Competitive Creativity

I am often asked to rate Nebraska's writers and artists on some kind of scale, but I am reluctant to do that because, for one thing, art and literature are not entries in some kind of contest (although for some reason the art world insists on doing precisely that, organizing contests where there are no rules but one or two judges' personal and utterly unpredictable taste, a thoroughly nutty idea if there ever was one). In the case of literature, how can you compare Sandoz, Neihardt, Cather, Eiseley, and Morris? It's not even like comparing apples with oranges; more like contrasting dill pickles with tractors.

Our writers—and our artists—are for one thing distributed over a wide geography and deal with different times and different people. And they speak to different tastes. I've never been all that drawn to Bess Streeter Aldrich's work . . . it seems too scattergun to me, but she is my mother's favorite. I know that some people love Sandoz, hate Cather—or love Cather, hate Sandoz. And they don't even know who Wright Morris is. I do like that Sandoz writes about the Sandhills in the early twentieth century and Native tales while Cather focuses more on the late nineteenth century and looks to small-town and city views. But even that isn't precisely accurate, because there are Cather's novels from the Southwest, and Sandoz did after all write *Capital City*.

Rather than contrast Nebraska's writers as if to judge their relative importance, I prefer to consider what they all seem to me to have in common, especially as they look at Nebraska and Nebraskans. That is, I tend to see even our fiction writers, poets, and artists as geographers and anthropologists, offering us yet another perspective on who and what we are. This is not simply a matter of my own inclinations toward geography and anthropology: In order to capture authenticity, for one thing, good writers and artists research their topics carefully, sometimes conducting firsthand interviews precisely as a good historian, folklorist, or anthropologist would. Second, Nebraska writers and artists have, to their credit and our benefit, selected subjects and characters from their own Nebraska experience or even their own families, so they are not so much inventing detail as reporting it.

The main point I would insist on making here is that while some names in both art and literature are widely known to Nebraskans, what is amazing to me is not so much that we have a few brilliant luminaries known around the world as that Nebraska has a remarkable population of creative people scarcely known and little appreciated even by their neighbors. Cather said that Nebraskans judge art by the degree to which it is useless, and you know, that is pretty much the truth. If you look at what Nebraskans read, hang on their walls, or buy for museums and galleries, it does tend toward the mindless. I suppose that is inevitable among the masses, but even within the circles that pretend to sophistication—you know, the artsy-fartsies—art and literature are matters not so much of taste as of fashion trends and politics. Linda's work was once rejected by an "art cooperative" because she had included some paintings of nudes; the "artist" who complained loudest is a sculptor who also does nudes but gives them biblical labels: *Ruth at the Well*; *Lot's Daughters*; *Eve Cast from the Garden*. That makes it all okay.

Prophets in Their Own Land

It's not as if Nebraska's greatest have enjoyed universal acceptance even among our hometown arbiters of taste—at least not until they've been safely dead for a period of time. It is one thing to make a living writing or painting while in Nebraska; it is quite another to try to make a living as a writer or artist in Nebraska. That is, you can do creative work here, but you'd better have a "real job," a major inheritance, or a market well removed from Nebraska or there are almost certainly some hungry days ahead. I'll bet there aren't five houses in Dannebrog where there is a book on the shelf by that village's best-known author.

There was Neihardt's radical political poetry and those racy verses of *A Bundle of Myrrh* that sure weren't the stuff of Bancroft, Nebraska. Cather's questionable sexuality is a topic of suspicion and even antagonism in Nebraska and Red Cloud to this day. Wright Morris used naughty words way too freely in his work in the opinion of many. Sandoz was an agitator who clearly didn't understand her place as a woman. The whole family of Cozads, Henris, whatever they called themselves, were about as disreputable a crowd as has embarrassed proper, upstanding citizens of any Nebraska town. And as for Eiseley . . . what the heck is his fancy talk all about anyway?

But once these grand figures have been dead long enough that they offer some commercial opportunities, well then—then!—they can be celebrated. We at least have that. The true and loyal admirers of these artists and writers have been wise to seize the opportunity to promote them as native sons and daughters whatever the motivations of the community as a whole, and I think that's just fine. Celebrating our artists and writers when they are safely dead is better than never recognizing their accomplishments at all.

Part of the reason our most famous Nebraska writers haven't always enjoyed community approval is that while they have written about Nebraskans, and Nebraska, they have tended to focus on the kinds of characters and those features of Nebraska and Nebraskans that aren't generally popular in fact. Sandoz didn't win herself any favor with her father when she wrote about him in *Old Jules,* nor around Gordon with her scandalous *Slogum House,* a book still mentioned in some proper circles with hushed tones. *Capital City,* in which she lampoons the Aksarben Society and Nebraska football insanity, brought her enough negative attention in Lincoln that she retreated to the safety of New York. Cather? The title character of *My Ántonia* is a disgraced outcast from her community. Other of Cather's books also deal with impropriety, disgrace, infidelity, suicide . . . not the sort of feel-good stuff the hometown folks might prefer. As outcasts themselves, our writers have written about other outcasts. They found their most interesting characters among the common people—or more precisely, the uncommon people among the common people. Cather, Sandoz, Neihardt, Morris, Eiseley . . . they all knew well that the most boring people in the world are the rich and powerful whom less imaginative Nebraskans might have preferred to have celebrated in literature.

Nor have Nebraska's best writers sugarcoated their opinions of our home state. They are in fact painfully honest about the brutality of the weather, landscape, frontier, and even our citizens—again, not the stuff of chamber-of-commerce brochures. Our writers speak of the loneliness and isolation of the Plains, the mistreatment of Native peoples, the failures and foolishness of the frontier. It's not that they don't love the Plains; no, the thing is, they love the Plains for precisely what our region is, not for what it might be, or should be, or could be. And they know their stuff. Even Nebraskans who have not exercised the keen observation of Cather are puzzled when she speaks of the wine-red grass—which is a precisely accurate description of Nebraska's autumn grasses. Sandoz mentions coyotes stealing watermelons—which they do. Neihardt knew the Missouri River, because he canoed it. Food and foodways play a very important role in Cather's works not because she was a cook but because she carefully observed and reported the ethnogastronomy of her times and region.

Of all the themes and motifs in Plains literature—and art—the single most common one is the most obvious and honest, the Plains as a sea. A sea of grass, a sea of windblown soils and sand. Again and again, in metaphor and simile, from the migrants' wagons—prairie *schooners,* after all!—to the sod house frontier, the allusion of choice is the Great Plains as the Great Inland Sea. It makes a lot of sense: The sea and the Plains are formed by the same force, wind, and have therefore taken on the same shapes and feel.

Nebraska's True Arts—the Folk Arts

I don't think it's just a matter of my field of choice being folklore—no, I believe I am absolutely right in saying that for all the achievement of Nebraskans in the fields of the sophisticated *fine* arts, our real strength lies within our traditional arts, our *folk* arts. My interest in folklore began with the "folk music" craze of the 1950s: the Kingston Trio and Harry Belafonte, then Burl Ives and Pete Seeger, then on to real folk songs as sung by people for whom they were a regular part of life rather than performance materials, then Nebraska folk songs, and then all manner of traditional materials from folk medicine to folk architecture, folk art to folk foods. There's not much left in our day-to-day lives now by way of folk songs. Some small pockets of traditional music persist—on Indian reservations, within New American communities like Iraqis or Colombians, some children's activities like skip rope rhymes, that kind of thing—but by and large we don't put a lot of energy into musical or song traditions. Our music is popular music composed by individuals, performed on recordings and the radio.

But other forms of folklore thrive—the joke, for example, the rumor or modern legend mistakenly labeled the "urban" legend by my old folklorist friend Jan Brunvand—and what is most important to me is that even within our short past, our history, the folk arts and folklore in general have been much more important as channels of expression and culture than have our formal mechanisms. Quilting, traditional housing forms like sod or baled-hay construction, square dances, the polka, or powwow dancing, the tall tale, auctioneers' chants, proverbs . . . in those traditional forms we have shone. Even our authors and poets have found a lot of their local color in what they have found in our folklore. The next time you read Cather, Kloefkorn, Kooser, Neihardt, Sandoz, or Morris, look for the folklore—traditional speech, metaphor, custom, belief—in their words. You will see what I mean. Nebraska's true artistic strength is where we notice it and appreciate it least—in our folk arts.

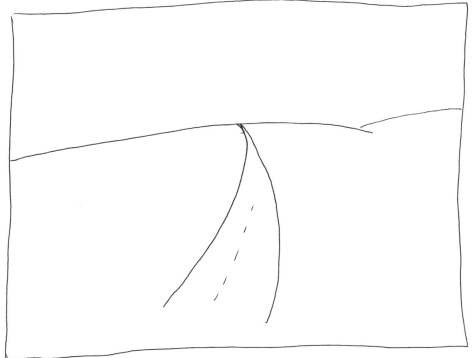

Highway 92 near Arthur

CHAPTER TWELVE

Ways and Byways

Now I'm going to pull a reverse play on you—one of those backfield deceptions where you think the play is going one way, then all of a sudden everything turns around and the ball is headed the other way. Remember how I snarled and sneered at the dumb boobs who insult our beloved Nebraska by saying it's just an impediment on their way to where they really want to go? You know, the ones who call us "fly-over country"? And say things like, "One day I spent a week crossing Nebraska . . . ," or "Nebraska . . . ~~Possibilities~~ Endless," or "the Great American Desert," or "The only good thing coming out of Nebraska is Interstate 80"?

Well, now that we know each other a lot better, maybe we can talk, huh? You know, in all honesty, those bad things the bozos say about Nebraska . . . well, they all have one thing in common: They are all to some degree true. Nebraska is huge, and . . . well . . . it's kind of in the way of getting anywhere. That is, if your only intention is arriving and not getting, if you catch my drift. It's a new and wacky notion that travel is only a matter of leaving one place and arriving at another with everything in between being nothing but a waste of time and space. Maybe that wacky notion comes from air travel, which now is mostly a matter of sitting, waiting, being insulted, being abused, being canceled or delayed, being overcharged, and having your belongs lost or stolen. But there was a time when arriving somewhere was okay but the real fun was what lay in between. Nebraska is Lay-In-Between Country.

So What's the Hurry Anyway?

Not to mention that one of the things that makes America great is its expanse—which is to say, expansive places like Nebraska. Napoleon and Hitler both faltered and failed on the Russian steppes. No one has even given a second thought to taking on the American steppes. Which is to say, Nebraska. This is the place where we built bombs and airplanes during World War II because we knew for damned sure no Luftwaffe or kamikaze planes were going to get this far inland. This is where the most dangerous of the German prisoners of war were brought and interned because, what the hell, even if they escaped, where were they going to go? One of those German prisoners told me that when he was interned in south-central Nebraska during World War II, the word was that no one was going to get very excited about escape attempts because a runaway prisoner escapee could be gone for two days and still be in sight of the guard towers.

Look, the miles are there. That's not going to change. The complaints about Nebraska seem to run to what it is that you see in getting across those miles. So you'd maybe prefer something more mountainous or perhaps wooded? All the corn and cows bore you? Maybe if you gave up eating, we could do away with Nebraska.

I am reminded of a story Charles Kuralt liked to tell about a time when he was chatting with an old-timer high up an Appalachian hollow. Kuralt kicked at a rock in the tiny, tilted field the old man was plowing with a mule and said, "My friend, I just don't see how you can make a living on ground like this." The old man looked at Kuralt and said, "You know, Charles, I was once in New York City standing on a street corner and I thought exactly that same thing."

Yeah, that would serve those Nebraska clods right, wouldn't it? Just give up eating and run us out of business! Then we can bring in the 'dozers and gouge out canyons, pile up mountains, dig lakes, deepen rivers, plant trees, wind the roads in picturesque sweeps and swoops—and then it'll take you a week to cover the same 400 miles like it does in Vermont or Utah. You'd like that, would you? I don't think so. I think the whiners and wieners who complain about what Nebraska is are going to complain no matter what.

The truth of the matter is, Nebraska's wonderfully far horizons and long vistas are precisely what lets America cross the Plains from the Missouri to the Rockies in a day or two at the most instead of a week. Your automobile, your fuel gauge, and your schedule like that flat, straight highway on the banks of the Platte if you give even a moment's thought to the alternatives.

It's been that way for a long time, too. Interstate 80 didn't take a whole lot of surveying. The route had already been pretty much laid out by the Union Pacific and Burlington Railroads many years earlier. And by the Oregon and Mormon Trail crossers half a century before the railroads. And the explorers, trappers and traders, bison herds and Native nomadic wanderers before that. And the waters of the Platte even before that. Nebraska offers good and easy ground for travel, and so people funnel through here on their way to somewhere else. And then a few complain because they decided to go from Chicago to Denver, but they didn't really want to go . . . they just wanted to get. People like that should take a plane and watch a movie, but for Pete's sake don't bore the rest of us with your puling and mewling about how long it takes to get across Nebraska and how boring the trip is.

Certainly one of the reasons for the complaints and complainers is that they take, to a soul, I–80 across Nebraska, without question the most boring, least scenic, brain-numbing way to cross the state. Whenever possible I avoid I–80, and so should you unless you enjoy staring straight ahead, communing with idiots, eating garbage, and toying with death. I don't care how long it is between my venturing into the chaos of I–80, it is always boring; I don't care how many times I take any of the many less traveled highways paralleling I–80, they are always interesting. Between Lincoln and Grand Island, for me it's always Highway 34, and even then at every trip—and I've made a lot of trips on that road over the years—I revel in the scenery, even if it's nothing more than a great blue heron in a roadside pond, a combine at work in a milo field, or a coyote bounding through a soybean field. Moreover, when it is at all possible—that is, when it isn't so wet that the gravel would be soggy—I get off even that modest highway at Aurora, go north on Highway 14 to Central City, and then head across to Dannebrog on county roads. When I go even the short distance from Dannebrog to St. Paul to visit my mother there, I take one of the five or six graveled country roads rather than paved highways. Yes, the gravel offers a shorter trip, to be sure, but I also know the drive will take me longer, not only because the gravel pretty much requires slower travel but also because there is so darned much to see that I find myself not even going as fast as conditions allow because I drive so much more slowly. I don't want to miss anything I might see along the way, after all.

The Grand Wilderness

West of Grand Island—and the farther west, the better—I hope you'll consider getting off the Slab, as the interstate highway is called by CBers, and take a spin on Highway 30. I'm not crazy about 30—it tends to be crowded and dangerous, and it goes through the dreariest parts of towns made dreary by that highway, but the farther west you go, the better it gets. As a child, and even today, I feel a sudden exhilaration and breath of freedom when I am headed west on Highway

30 and somewhere just east of North Platte notice the Platte Valley walls closing in from both sides. Sioux Lookout, the obvious clay prominence just southeast of North Platte, is the sentinel signaling to me that I am no longer in the East. I am out of farming ground and into ranch country. The air is clearer and smells better. I am now truly on the frontier and have shed the oppressive effeteness of the Degenerate East. And every day spent west of here is a day that doesn't come off those allotted to your life. That's what I think anyway.

The moral is, if you are even the slightest bit bored by travel in Nebraska, if you would really like to see things that amaze and amuse you, if you want to meet interesting people, see stunning historical sites, eat good food . . . get the hell off I–80. Or for that matter, get the hell off pavement! Those who won't make this small effort, to my mind, have no complaint coming about how boring Nebraska is. They may want to look closer to home to find out exactly where the basis of their ennui might be found.

See my tale above about the county road from Dunning to Arnold. There are hundreds of roads like that in Nebraska. And dozens of lesser-known highways that will leave you stunned, not only by the scenery and wildlife, but also through wonderful little towns you've never even heard of. Ever been to Worms? You'll find there a true gem of a country tavern. And Worms likes to boast that it is the only town in Nebraska in which all the streets are paved. Well, uh, yeah, of course there is that little detail . . . that there is only *one* street in Worms. And it does happen to be a paved county road, but well, you have to admit, they aren't exactly lying!

There is also the benefit (for many of us at least) that many of these obscure, unnumbered roads carry almost no traffic. Linda always worries what would happen if her pickup broke down on one of these remote, untraveled roads. Well, another driver will come along before long, you can be sure, and you can also bet on that driver stopping to help you, so you're probably closer to help where there seems to be no one at all than you might be on a crowded eight-lane interstate in the bowels of Omaha.

Not long ago my buddy Mick and I were returning to Dannebrog from the Pine Ridge Reservation north of Rushville, Nebraska. Early on a Sunday morning in April, we headed east on Highway 20 to Merriman (follow us on your map, kids!), and then south on State Highway 61 to Hyannis. Two things—at least two things—struck us on this drive like two-by-fours planted firmly and squarely between our eyes. First, in the entire trip of almost 100 miles and almost three hours from Gordon to Hyannis, we saw not a single other moving vehicle. Second, we could have made the trip in half the time if we hadn't had to stop again and again to admire the incredible variety of waterbirds on the Sandhills lakes we passed, the antelope running up a hillside, a coyote running across the road right in front of us and then visible for another half mile as he dashed across the grasslands, eagles, buzzards, a family of skunks demanding the right-of-way, on and on and on . . . Our only regret was that it didn't take six hours to make the short trip. Not long ago there was an area the size of Delaware in the Nebraska Sandhills through which not a single paved road passed; now there are several paved passages through that grand wilderness, but believe me, they are modest as roads go, often one lane, thinly paved, grandly lonely and stark. Which is to say, you are not going to fight traffic on these roads, you are clearly passing through wilderness and frontier areas, and when you are in this region, you are witnessing one of the most unusual and unspoiled environments in the world.

Yeah, right, Nebraska is really boring.

So, which road would I recommend? It doesn't matter. Just avoid I–80. The less "important" the highway, the better it will be. Yes, north–south Highways 250, 27, 61, and even 97 way over at the eastern edge of the Sandhills are particularly dear to me because I love the Sandhills, but it truly doesn't matter where you are in Nebraska or which minor road you take. That's part of the adventure. Highway 47 from near Eustis to Cozad is beautiful. I love 23 from Holdrege west to the Nebraska–Colorado border—not to mention that you pass through Dickens, the only Nebraska town bombed during

World War II. The county spur from Silver Creek to Genoa is a great shortcut, but it's also beautiful. The drive up 75 from Omaha to South Sioux City is a favorite of mine, and then you can stop for a powwow in Macy or Winnebago and maybe stay overnight at my favorite hotel in this world, the Marina in South Sioux City . . . be sure to ask for a riverside room. I like Highways 136 and 8 along the Kansas–Nebraska border, and 20 on the north just south of our border with South Dakota. Highway 29 from Harrison to Mitchell shouldn't be missed. Highway 91 through Bohemian Country, 50 south through what passes for Nebraska's woodlands . . .

Nebraska has always been primarily an east–west state: The Oregon, Mormon, Overland, Pony Express, and Oxbow Trails all went east and west, following the course of the Plains rivers. As did the railroads and the interstates. As I lie in my backyard hammock trying to find clouds that look like Cindy Crawford, I can't help but notice the high-altitude condensation trails from airplanes so far above me, I can just barely hear their engines . . . and they are all east and west.

But the low-altitude fliers—the geese, pelicans, cranes, herons, and butterflies—know this landscape is also good for transverse travel, that is, north and south. Surprisingly, while the interstate highway system has never done much about anyone doing anything but following the sun, there are nonetheless some very interesting highways that have. Frankly, highways like 2 and 92 are pikers compared with some of the long and interesting north–south byways like 283, 281, and especially 81. For one thing, because there is less north–south traffic, on these routes you will find far less congestion and far less spoiled countryside. Yes, they're probably a bit slower, maybe narrower and less straight, but we're talking about interesting routes here, not arrows-for-idiots. Where do Highways 83 (crossing I–80 at North Platte), 81 (at York), and 281 (at Grand Island) go? All the way, baby, all the way! From Canada right on down to Mexico . . . and beyond. So do Highways 75 and 77. There's a good chance your patience and maybe even your automobile will wear out long before you finish these Nebraska highways from one end to the other.

Before you travel in Nebraska, get a good map and look at it. See if there isn't an alternative way to get where you're going *on something less than a major highway*. Take some chances. Be a pioneer! Be a poet! Take the path less traveled!

Now, having said that, I want to tell you about my favorite highways in Nebraska. To my eternal joy and pride, Highway 2 from Grand Island to Crawford was not only my favorite, but was once touted by Charles Kuralt, who at one time or another saw pretty much every highway in America, as one of the ten most beautiful in the country. Between Lincoln and Grand Island it tends to clutter up pretty badly, but even that stretch is lovely when the traffic or the weather isn't bad. It goes through the heart of the Sandhills, and I get a thrill every time I see the sign—I think it's in Anselmo—that says something like WARNING! SANDHILLS NEXT 166 MILES! I love a landscape that carries warning signs!

I hope I don't make any enemies along Highway 2, but I have to confess that my heart has been stolen away. By another highway: Highway 92 from St Paul to the Wyoming boundary, especially the section between Merna and the north shore of Lake McConaughy. I can figure that a trip on this highway will take me twice as long as it should because it is simply too painful to rush through such a stunning landscape. Another rule for the Compleat Nebraskan: You are required to drive both Highways 2 and 92 from one extreme to the other or you simply cannot credibly maintain that you know diddly-squat about the state. In fact, if your windshield isn't blasted with gravel from your endless hours on gravel roads . . . you don't have my respect.

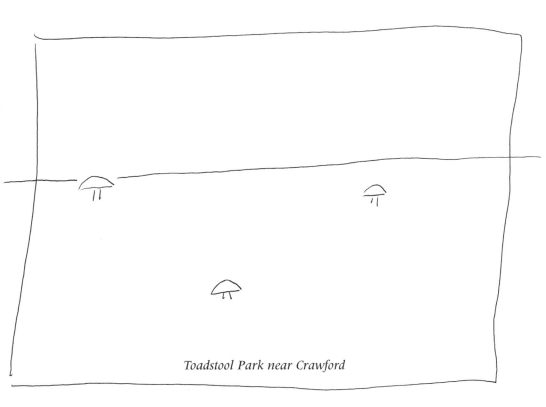

Toadstool Park near Crawford

An Afterword

I am asked about once a week how I write a book, or how long it takes to write a book. I have an immediate answer for the second question: According to my most recent calculations, it takes seventy years to write a book. Linda keeps insisting that I write an autobiography but the truth of the matter is, each of my books—thirty-four at this writing—is a chapter of my autobiography. My smart-aleck response to the first question is usually "The most important thing about writing a book is to sit down." To a large degree, that's true: Way too many people want to write a book but never take that first step. The bottom line is that to write a book, you simply have to write a book. There is some kind of inner drive that won't let you alone until you write that book. It can get downright creepy how a book will take over the writer, go beyond the writer, carry the writer away on the power of its own life. All real writers will tell you this same thing. I'm sure it's that mystic possession that the classical metaphor of a "Muse" was meant to depict.

That demon possession of an author is, I suspect, more prevalent in fiction than nonfiction, but it certainly was the case with this book. This is not the book I wanted to write or started to write. I had another book in mind, believe me. And I started it perhaps five times. A couple of times I got the introduction and maybe a few chapters put together before I lost interest and the inspiration trickled away. Another couple of times I got outlines finished . . . and then forgot about the idea. But in this case the real key was finding a format I was comfortable with. Initially I wanted to steal an idea from my old friend and colleague Charles Kuralt. (Man, is that ever presumptuous—calling Charles Kuralt a "colleague"!)

I can remember the exact moment Charles Kuralt told me about his plans to write a book in which through an entire year, week by week, he would tell his readers where in America he would choose to be that week . . . precisely the right place, at precisely the right time. It was a great idea. After all, who knew America better than Charles Kuralt? I can also remember the twinge of envy I felt at that moment: *Damn. Why didn't I think of that? Except instead of my perfect* American *year, I'd write about my perfect* Nebraska *year!*

Charles never did do precisely the book he had in mind. That turned out to be a much bigger project than he thought or wanted. So, instead, he wrote the very successful *Charles Kuralt's America* (Putnam, 1995), telling us where he would spend each *month* of his perfect year. (While Charles was working on the manuscript, we were once talking on the phone and I asked him how he was coming along. He said that he had every chapter done but the twelfth, and he was wrestling with whether he would rather spend his perfect January in Dannebrog, Nebraska, or Hilo, Hawaii. While I was recovering from this remarkable pair of options, he said, ". . . But does the word *aloha* mean anything to you?")

Charles is now gone, far too soon, and so I thought that taking his idea and adapting it to a book about Nebraska wouldn't be so much a matter of borrowing or stealing as a tribute to his genius. And to Nebraska. Well, this book obviously didn't turn out to be quite that. I had a hard time pinning down only twelve places to visit in the perfect Nebraska year, so I returned to Charles's original idea: Where I would spend each of fifty-two consecutive weeks in our state for my own personal perfect Nebraska year?

Even that proved too hard for me. There were too many places I wanted to be, and I wasn't comfortable with nailing things down so firmly. I knew that there would be plenty of complaints about my choices and timing in putting together my perfect Nebraska year. That's okay. I figured I would try to inspire everyone to put together his or her own perfect Nebraska year. And yet specific places and times aren't what I love about Nebraska, or what I wanted to say. Besides, I'm not a facts-and-structure kind of guy. Or writer. I am a storyteller. I like to write as if I were talking with some friends. And so that's what I finally decided I wanted to do with this book: talk with a bunch of friends about Nebraska and what I love about it and what drives me nuts about it and what I know that I don't think my friends know.

When I first sat down to write this book, I figured I'd be telling you about Roger Welsch's perfect Nebraska year, *a* perfect Nebraska year, one of thousands of perfect Nebraska years. If anything, I wouldn't so much try to convince you to like what I like as to nudge you toward thinking about where you would go, given the time and opportunity. And then hopefully to do it. I hope there is still some of that spirit, some of Kuralt's original idea, in these pages.

The first time I met Charles Kuralt, back in the summer of 1973, he was shooting one of his "On the Road" segments for the *CBS Evening News*. We were leaning across my backyard fence, me in utter awe, he handling everything with his usual grand dignity. The cameraman was Isadore Bleckman, who fifteen years later would be my cameraman for "Postcards from Nebraska"; the soundman was Larry Gianneschi, who would also become my soundman, eventually being replaced by his son and our dear family friend Danny.

During a lull in the action, I told Charles that a lot of my friends who knew he was going to be visiting us had asked me to tell him how much they enjoy his work. In fact, they asked me, almost to a soul, to tell him that he had the best job in the world—traveling, seeing America, visiting interesting people, hearing and passing along stories . . .

Without a moment's hesitation (it was obviously something he had thought about before) he said, "No, Roger. *You* have the best job in the world. Tomorrow I'll be down the road, in another state, spending a couple of hours here or there, chatting briefly with someone, then moving on. You . . . ah, *you*, my friend . . . you will still be here. You will be learning more and more about this place, discovering the real secrets, the genuine treasures. You will get to know the people I only meet for a few moments. Roger, I'm the one who envies you."

As usual, Charles was right. Over the years the truth of his words has become increasingly evident. I have been lucky. I live in Nebraska. And I have lived here all my life. And I will die here. I have lived in the city (Lincoln), and town (Blair), and rural countryside (Dannebrog and Howard County). I have had the chance to travel Nebraska: with my parents Chris and Bertha, on my own, with my families, on the job. I was educated here, and studied this place. I have worked and taught here, and met thousands of good, interesting people (a few miscreants and bores too, but . . .). Even as I sat down and got ready to write this book, I was surprised to find that I've felt this way about Nebraska for a long time—much longer than I would have guessed. The first clippings in my files of thoughts and research leading to this book were from March 1962. I was just a kid, and yet I was already fascinated by Nebraska and for some reason felt it was a good idea to start saving interesting facts about it.

I love this place, and I love its people. More, perhaps, than I sometimes realize myself. After I had finished laughing at Charles's line about December in Dannebrog and *aloha* being a key word in his decision, he asked me casually where I would spend my perfect year, given the same twelve months. I had never considered such a thing. I've traveled the world, but I like being at home. I thought about his question a few moments and then had to admit, "Charles, you know, about the best I can come up with is that I would spend January here in Dannebrog, enjoying the cold and snow and beauty of the Loup River, and probably February, too. And March and April I would like . . . to be here, watching spring arrive and the river come to life, and the cranes and geese flying north. And May and June, here, fishing with my buddies Dan and Bondo. And July . . . well, here for Danish Festival and the Fourth of July. And . . . well, jeez, Charles . . . I guess Roger Welsch's perfect year would be spent in Nebraska. Every day."

He laughed. A calendar like that would have driven him and his itchy feet crazy. But I sensed in his laugh an understanding, too. And maybe a longing.

Of course I am not stupid enough not to turn down a few hours on a white sand beach on the sky-blue waters of the Bahamas for a cold February day or, worse yet, a cold April day staring at a gray Nebraska sky. And neither did Kuralt. I have spent glorious winter days in Jamaica, on the Yucatán, in the Bahamas. And wonderfully chilly summer days in Glacier Bay, Alaska, and Odense, Denmark, thinking of friends and family suffering through a steamy, miserable Nebraska broiler. No, Nebraska is *not* a paradise.

But besides considerations of money and time, there is inclination. Given a choice of being just about anywhere, I'd just as soon stay home, thank you. I cherish hours spent in my shop, working on old tractors. A moment's respite from the fury of our schedule in the hot tub on a wintry day with my Lovely Linda. A book, and a quiet fire in the fireplace, snow piling up outside, a snifter of good single-malt Scotch. Now, that's good times in my opinion, and Charles Kuralt understood that.

Nonetheless, I urge you to take a hint from Charles, and at least from my good intentions in the matter, and think about that Perfect Nebraska Year for yourself. Make the list that I tried to make. It's more fun than winter shopping in a seed catalog! Where would you like to go if you had a week to spend in Nebraska in May? Or in October? How about if you could go to five different places, one a week, in the Nebraska Panhandle in August? I hope your journeys in Nebraska (or anywhere else, for that matter) go well. In fact, I hope your Nebraska year is . . . well . . . perfect. As for me, most days in my Perfect Year won't involve straying much farther than up to town on a tractor to get our mail. As my friend Albert Fahlbusch once said so wonderfully for us all, "Why would I want to go anywhere? I'm *in* Nebraska!"

As Wright Morris said, even if we leave this place, love it or hate it, we'll never get over it. Cather, Sandoz, Henry Fonda, Cavett, Carson . . . they all left, and not a single one ever got over it. Nebraska continued to haunt their work and their hearts. Well, those of us who haven't left can't get over it, either. This "hulking giant," as it turns out, is also a giant that defies being forgotten. I've never left it, and have no intentions of doing so. Not a morning goes by that I don't step out my door, look into whatever sky the wonderful place is dealing up at the moment, and repeat the thought of Albert Fahlbusch: Why would I want to go anywhere? I'm in Nebraska! In *my* Nebraska.

(The three Nebraska counties named for animals? Antelope, Buffalo, and . . . groan! . . . Garfield.)

About the Author

Roger Welsch is a popular folklorist, humorist, and essayist who has written dozens of books and hundreds of articles about history, culture, and folklore. He is the best-selling author of *Old Tractors and The Men Who Love Them* and more than thirty other titles. Welsch was a regular guest who presented his "Postcards from Nebraska" on the CBS *Sunday Morning* show with Charles Kuralt. Kuralt called Welsch "America's premier storyteller" and wrote: "From his lips, small-town life takes on the dignity of history."

Welsch hosted *Roger Welsch &* on Nebraska Educational Television, and in 2005 he received the Henry Fonda Award, Nebraska's highest award for leadership, vision, and dedication to state tourism. Welsch, an adopted member of the Omaha Tribe, lives with his wife Linda near Dannebrog, where he continues to write and restore old tractors.

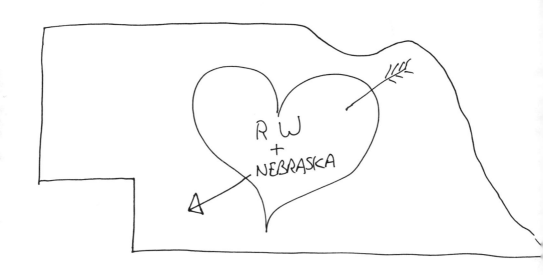